8.95

A Guide to Psychotherapy with Gay and Lesbian Clients

A Guide to
Psychotherapy
with
Gay and Lesbian
Clients

Edited by

John C. Gonsiorek

A Guide to Psychotherapy with Gay and Lesbian Clients was originally published in 1982 by The Haworth Press, Inc., under the title *Homosexuality and Psychotherapy: A Practitioner's Handbook of Affirmative Models.* It has also been published as *Journal of Homosexuality,* Volume 7, Numbers 2/3, Winter/Spring 1981/1982.

Harrington Park Press
New York • Binghamton

ISBN 0-918393-03-5

Published by

Harrington Park Press, Inc.
28 East 22 Street
New York, New York 10010

Harrington Park Press, Inc., is a subsidiary of The Haworth Press, Inc., 28 East 22 Street, New York, New York 10010.

A Guide to Psychotherapy with Gay and Lesbian Clients was originally published in 1982 by The Haworth Press, Inc., under the title *Homosexuality and Psychotherapy: A Practitioner's Handbook of Affirmative Models.* It has also been published as *Journal of Homosexuality*, Volume 7, Numbers 2/3, Winter/Spring 1981/1982.

Library of Congress Cataloging in Publication Data

Homosexuality & psychotherapy.
 A Guide to psychotherapy with gay and lesbian clients.

 Reprint. Originally published: Homosexuality & psychotherapy. New York: Haworth Press, c1982. (Research on homosexuality; v. 4)
 Includes bibliographies and index.
 1. Homosexuality. 2. Homosexuals—Mental health—Case studies. 3. Homosexuals—Mental health services.
I. Gonsiorek, John C. II. Title.
RC558.H65   1984   616.89 '00880664   84-19275
ISBN 0-918393-03-5 (pbk.)

To Michael and Walter, whose love and support gave me
the strength to complete this undertaking.

JCG

ABOUT THE EDITOR

John C. Gonsiorek is a Clinical Assistant Professor in the Department of Psychology and in the Program in Health Care Psychology (School of Public Health) at the University of Minnesota. He is currently in private practice as a Licensed Consulting Psychologist in Minneapolis. Previously he has served as Clinic Director at Walk-In Counseling Center in Minneapolis, Clinical Director of Gay Community Services in Minneapolis, and a staff psychologist in the Department of Physical Medicine and Rehabilitation at the University of Minnesota Medical School. He received his Ph.D. in Clinical Psychology from the University of Minnesota in 1978. He has authored a number of works on homosexuality and other topics. He has served as a Review Editor for the *Journal of Homosexuality* since 1977, and served as Associate Editor of the Society for the Psychological Study of Social Issues Task Force on Sexual Orientation. He recently edited *Homosexuality: The End of a Mental Illness, a special issue of American Behavioral Scientist* (Vol. 25(4), Sage Publications).

CONTENTS

The *Journal of Homosexuality* is devoted to theoretical, empirical, and historical research on homosexuality, heterosexuality, sexual identity, social sex roles, and the sexual relationships of both men and women. It was created so serve the allied disciplinary and professional groups represented by psychology, sociology, history, anthropology, biology, medicine, the humanities, and law. Its purposes are:

a) to bring together, within one contemporary scholarly journal, theoretical, empirical, and historical research on human sexuality, particularly sexual identity;

b) to serve as a forum for scholarly research of heuristic value for the understanding of human sexuality, based not only in the more traditional social or biological sciences, but also in literature, history, and philosophy;

c) to explore the political, social, and moral implications of research on human sexuality for professionals, clinicians, social scientists, and scholars in a wide variety of disciplines and settings.

A Guide to Psychotherapy with Gay and Lesbian Clients

FOREWORD

The historical struggle to detoxify relationships between individuals of the same biological sex, and to remove from them the taint of sinfulness, criminality, and sexual perversion with which they were bridled in the nineteenth century, is now almost 150 years old. During that period the institutional guardianship of sexuality was surrendered by the Church and handed over to law, medicine, and forensic psychiatry where it still rather anxiously resides. Above all, psychiatry and its historic offshoot clinical psychology have been the arbiters of what is normal in human sexuality and what should be exposed to the cornucopia of treatment and cure.

In 1973 and 1974, the psychiatric hegemony over homosexuality was challenged by leaders in the Gay Liberation movement and their supporters, some of whom were prominent, fully accredited psychiatrists and clinical psychologists. They succeeded in getting the American Psychiatric Association, somewhat timidly but nonetheless officially, to depathologize homosexuality.

While that conflict raged and following its resolution, mental health workers belonging to several professions throughout Europe, North America, and Australia were setting up clinical practices that were specifically devoted to treating individuals who wanted to make relationships with persons of their own sex a pivotal part of their lives. It is indeed no easy matter for two men or two women, encumbered as we all are by the ideology of innate sex differences, to build and succor relationships. Nor is it an easy matter for psychotherapists to provide appropriate counsel. Many therapists, then, have leaned heavily and openly on their own personal experience.

Dr. Gonsiorek has been remarkably successful in assembling a cadre of psychiatrists, psychologists, and clinical social workers who are among the leaders in this effort and who have contributed to this volume out of their rich professional training and experience. He, along with his co-authors, deserves enormous credit for providing what I believe is the first practitioners' handbook in the art of scrupulously respecting clients' sexual perceptions, beliefs, and intentions while providing them the help they need in getting on with their relationships and with their lives.

Homosexuality and Psychotherapy, besides appearing as a special double issue of the *Journal of Homosexuality*, joins a growing list of volumes published in the series, *Research on Homosexuality*, under my general editorship and the auspices of The Haworth Press.

San Francisco, 1981
John P. De Cecco, PhD
Editor

PREFACE

Even a glance at the bibliographies in the chapters of this excellent volume will show the reader that almost all serious scholarly work on the subject of homosexuality has been done in the past ten years; in fact, most of the scientific literature was written in just the past five years. It is not that the authors of this volume are restricted to a contemporary focus or are lacking in historical perspective, it is simply that credible theory and empirical studies of merit did not exist before about 1970. Some of the authors do note Freud's early speculations and some do refer to the pioneering research of such investigators as Alfred Kinsey and Evelyn Hooker, but for the most part they tell us recent history—research of their own and that of contemporary scholars. They might have mentioned, but did not, the fact that artists (e.g., Walt Whitman, Radclyffe Hall and Mary Renault), rather than scholars, first wrote with sensitivity and insight about this subject. It was not until 1977 when Gonsiorek published his rigorous review, that a competent critical analysis of published work in the field was available.

That attitudes and behavior manifested by millions of people in every society and each generation should virtually be ignored by the scientific community is a remarkable commentary on how social values shape and, in fact, impede academic freedom of inquiry. I wonder if a brawl in 1969 in an ugly bar in Greenwich Village, the Stonewall Riots, not only brought homosexual behavior out of the closet and into the spotlight of public attention, but also to the attention of the scientific community.

The collection published here is a most valuable contribution. It covers a broad range of subjects concerning gay men and lesbians. And it covers the subjects in depth as well. The editor has achieved a feat rarely realized in edited volumes. While broadly conceived, it succeeds in having a unity of high scholarship and should be a standard reference on homosexuality for many years. It includes chapters of enormous concern to social policy as well as basic research on homosexual behavior. There is a consideration of topics not only of interest to social scientists and mental health professionals, but also to ministers, physicians, legislators, families and to persons who are themselves homosexual. While of high scholarship, it is not written in excessively technical language that would restrict its usefulness to a small array of readers. Nor does it offend by taking a militant stance on important issues, though it does correct many widely held misperceptions with convincing data. It is neither polemical nor soft in facing difficult issues.

The time for a thorough survey of the field had surely come, and these papers are a fine collection of the first effort to fill that need. I am pleased to have had the opportunity to read these manuscripts from which I learned a great deal. I am sure many other readers will find them of equal value.

Robert D. Wirt, PhD
New York City
May 1, 1981

Robert Wirt received his PhD in clinical psychology from Stanford University in 1952. Currently, he is Professor and Director of Graduate Education in Clinical Psychology at the New School for Social Research in New York City. Formerly, he was Professor and Director of Health Care Psychology at the Health Sciences Center, University of Minnesota, and before that, Director of Graduate Education in Clinical Psychology at the University of Minnesota. He has published widely on a variety of topics in clinical psychology and has served in numerous professional organizations. He has been a member of the American Psychological Association's Council of Representatives.

INTRODUCTION:
PRESENT AND FUTURE DIRECTIONS
IN GAY/LESBIAN MENTAL HEALTH

John C. Gonsiorek, PhD

Mental health practice with gay and lesbian populations has undergone enormous change in the past 20 years. Until recently, the prevailing and almost exclusive view was that homosexuality was a psychiatric illness. The efforts of mental health practitioners were geared toward diagnosing and curing homosexuality.

Research in the 1960s and continuing into the 1970s, however, profoundly altered these beliefs. Homosexuality began to be understood as more complex and harder to define and measure than ever previously imagined (see Gonsiorek, 1982a). Results of psychological testing on heterosexual and homosexual populations did not support the belief that homosexuality *per se* was a psychiatric illness (see Gonsiorek, 1977; 1982b for a review of this literature). Social psychological models began to provide increasingly more powerful and useful explanations of some aspects of homosexual behavior than the illness model had (see Gonsiorek, 1982(c). Serious questions began to be asked about treatment outcomes in attempts to cure homosexuality. Generally, long-term results are very disappointing (see Coleman, 1978, for a review of this literature). Finally, the ethics of attempts to change sexual orientation have been highly controversial (see *Symposium on Homosexuality and the Ethics of Behavioral Intervention*, 1977).

The old illness model of homosexuality has all but disintegrated under the weight of empirical research; yet new gay/lesbian affirmative models have been slow to emerge. This volume is an attempt to forge the beginnings of such models. It is imperative that they do emerge. Clinicians who want to work affirmatively with gay and lesbian clients more often know what not to do that what to do in therapy. This creates a vacuum in which psychotherapists, as most people, dislike working. If new affirmative models do not fill the vacuum, the old beliefs will gradually re-establish themselves because practitioners must have something to guide them in their work.

Happily, such models are emerging. At least one relatively comprehensive

5

volume on affirmative counseling techniques with gay men and lesbians has been published (Woodman & Lenna, 1980) and the *Journal of Homosexuality* has been for some years publishing articles of high scholarship, many of them on mental health issues or relevant to mental health. Gay and lesbian affirmative views are beginning to show up in health care textbooks (e.g., Gonsiorek, 1980). Other major works are nearing completion and will soon be published. There have also been some false starts, such as Masters' and Johnson's (1979) extremely disappointing volume on homosexuality (for a review, see Gonsiorek, 1981). The balance suggests, however, that the next decade will be a creative and productive one in terms of the development of new gay and lesbian affirmative models of mental health practice.

Any worthwhile gay/lesbian affirmative models must from the start meet a number of requirements. They must be relevant to the life experience of gay men and lesbians in a society that to varying degrees is unsympathetic, uninterested or hostile. The models must enhance the mental health of gay men and lesbians and assist them in meeting the challenge of the primary task confronting them: the creation of an equal, healthy, ethical and useful place in society. The models must be clinically useful and must creatively assimilate those ideas from the mainstream of traditional mental health practice that have something to offer gay men and lesbians. Finally, the new models must function over a full range of psychological adjustment and must be able to speak to the concerns and clinical issues of well through poorly functioning gay men and lesbians.

A necessary, but later task of viable new models must be the accumulation of strong empirical support. The new models must be able to generate testable hypotheses, generate new theory, and survive the tests of empirical validation. But that is not the main issue for the present. The task at hand, and the purpose of this volume, is the creation of new models; that is, this volume operates in a context of discovery, as opposed to a context of justification (Meehl, 1973).

The papers in this volume are derived from a variety of theoretical orientations—psychodynamic, humanistic, behavioral, systems and others. They address a variety of therapeutic modalities: individual, couples, family and group psychotherapy. Different client types and different problem types are addressed. Diagnostic and organizational issues are addressed, as are various aspects of the client-therapist relationship. The volume is diverse, and deliberately so, as it is intended to be a basic reference and handbook for the practicing clinician. All of the contributors hope it will positively affect your clinical practice and will stimulate your thinking toward the further creation of gay/lesbian affirmative models of mental health practice.

REFERENCES

Coleman, E. Toward a new treatment model of homosexuality: A review. *Journal of Homosexuality*, 1978, *3*, 4, 345-359.

Gonsiorek, J. Psychological adjustment and homosexuality. JSAS *Catalog of Selected Documents in Psychology*, 1977, *7*, 45. (Ms. No. 1478)

Gonsiorek, J. What health care professionals need to know about lesbians and gay men. In M. Jospe, M. Nieberding & B. Cohen (eds.), *Psychological factors in health care*. Lexington, MA: Lexington Books, 1980.

Gonsiorek, J. Review of *Homosexuality in perspective* by W. Masters and V. Johnson. *Journal of Homosexuality*, 1981, *6*, 3.

Gonsiorek, J. Introduction to mental health issues and homosexuality. In J. Gonsiorek (Ed.), *Homosexuality: The end of a mental illness*, special issue of *American Behavioral Scientist*, March/April 1982, *25*, 4. (a)

Gonsiorek, J. Results of psychological testing on homosexual populations. In J. Gonsiorek (Ed.), *Homosexuality: The end of a mental illness*, special issue of *American Behavioral Scientist*, March/April 1982, *25*, 4. (b)

Gonsiorek, J. Social psychological concepts in the understanding of homosexuality. In J. Gonsiorek (Ed.), *Homosexuality: The end of a mental illness*, special issue of *American Behavioral Scientist*, March/April 1982, *25*, 4. (c)

Masters, W., & Johnson, V. *Homosexuality in perspective*. Boston: Little, Brown, Co., 1979.

Meehl, P. *Psychodiagnosis: Selected papers*. Minneapolis: University of Minnesota Press, 1973.

Symposium on Homosexuality and the Ethics of Behavioral Intervention. *Journal of Homosexual*, 1977, *2*, 3, 195-259.

Woodman, N., & Lenna, H. *Counseling with gay men and women*. San Francisco: Jossey-Bass, 1980.

THE USE OF DIAGNOSTIC CONCEPTS IN WORKING WITH GAY AND LESBIAN POPULATIONS

John C. Gonsiorek, PhD

Many paradigm shifts in mental health are characterized by a phase of reaction against the previous orthodoxy and a negation of what has been associated with it. The newer, non-disease models of homosexuality have often done this and have been to varying degrees impoverished as a result. Fortunately, a phase of synthesis often follows, in which the more useful of the new ideas, tempered by exposure to clinical realities and stripped of green dogmatism, are integrated with selected core ideas of the previous orthodoxy.

Many chapters in this volume are such attempts. This chapter will attempt a synthesis in the area of clinical diagnosis. No comprehensive conceptual sweep of this topic will be offered. Rather, a few preliminary efforts to synthesize diagnostic nomenclature and gay/lesbian affirmative viewpoints will be made. The areas covered will be the importance of differential diagnosis in sexual identity crises, and the notion of environmental impetus for certain characterological-appearing overlays to the personality structure. Although traditional nomenclature and gay/lesbian affirmative concepts will both be drawn upon in this discussion, the impetus for these ideas is rooted in the author's years of clinical practice, much of it on sexuality issues, and a good portion of it with gay men.

Clinical diagnosis has often suffered guilt by association among gay/lesbian affirmative mental health practitioners. The empirical invalidity and logical inconsistencies of the disease model of homosexuality, as well as the human suffering and clinical malpractice arising out of practice within the disease model, have lent themselves to the logical error that if diagnosis of homosexuality as a disease entity is faulty and destructive, then diagnostic concepts applied to homosexual individuals, and perhaps diagnosis itself, is faulty and destructive. This erroneous view has been exacerbated by the historical linkage of the emergence of gay/lesbian affirmative models with the anti-diagnostic theorizing of the 1960s and early 1970s (e.g., Mischel, 1968; Rosenhan, 1973; Szasz, 1961), which was often rooted in an anti-trait, and social psychological view of human behavior.

Adherence to this strict anti-trait, anti-diagnostic stance ignores the interactionist synthesis, albeit partial, of the once polarized trait vs. situation controversy, and the research and theorizing that has led to such a synthesis (e.g., Bowers, 1973). It also ignores a variety of refinements of diagnostic procedure in the past decade (for example, as Straus & Gift, 1977, detail in regard to diagnosis of schizophrenia) and the impressive results that can be obtained when careful diagnostic practices are employed (e.g., Cooper, Kendell, Garland, Sharpe, Copeland, & Simon, 1972; World Health Organization, 1973). It is clear that diagnostic nomenclature is alive and flourishing, and approaching its task in an increasingly complex and richly descriptive manner, as the multi-axial structure of DSM-III (American Psychiatric Association, 1980) suggests.

In addition, the anti-diagnostic viewpoint is frequently not at all useful in many clinical situations. When a clinical practitioner in faced with a gay or lesbian client who may be giving indications of severe depression, thought disorder, persistent characterological problems, neuropsychological impairment, etc., in addition to or instead of issues related to societal oppression, coming out, etc. (which may at times fit reasonably well with the anti-diagnostic model), anti-diagnostic views are not only less than helpful, but their *sole* application may constitute incompetence or malpractice.

This is not to say that the ideas which have to date constituted gay/lesbian affirmative mental health are not useful or effective; rather, they are necessary but not sufficient conditions for competent practice with homosexual populations. Likewise, competencies in traditional diagnostic and psychotherapeutic skills are necessary but not sufficient conditions for such practice. It is the central thesis of this paper that the combination of traditional and gay/lesbian affirmative mental health concepts constitute the necessary and sufficient conditions for competent practice with homosexual populations.

Finally, this paper makes certain assumptions. The first is that homosexuality *per se* is unrelated to psychopathology and psychological adjustment. The evidence for this is strong and consistent (for reviews, see Gonsiorek, 1977; 1982b). It is important to keep in mind that this does not mean that there are no psychologically disturbed homosexual individuals, or even that some persons are not disturbed on account of their homosexuality. Rather, it means that base rates of psychological disturbance are roughly parallel in homosexual and heterosexual populations (see the above reviews for more detailed discussion of this). The second assumption is that diagnosis, if it is to be useful, must be done with care and precision by individuals who are professionally trained in its use, limitations and shortcomings.

Differential Diagnosis of Sexual Identity Crises and Psychopathology

There are a number of clinical conditions in which individuals at times manifest homosexual behavior or concerns, and the client may therefore appear to be coming out or having a sexual identity crisis when, in reality, these behaviors or concerns are part of serious psychopathology. On the other hand, the coming out process in itself can produce in some individuals considerable psychiatric symptomatology reminiscent of serious underlying psychopathology; but, in fact, such pathology does not exist and the individual is having a particularly difficult time coming to terms with his or her sexuality. Finally, the coming out process may serve as a precipitating event for some individuals who do have severe underlying problems; that is, both may be present. The term "homosexual panic" has sometimes been used to describe any or all of these three different possibilities, creating considerable confusion. Rather than attempt to sort out what has been meant by this term, this writer would like to suggest that the term "homosexual panic" be permanently assigned to the junkyard of obsolete psychiatric terminology.

The first differential diagnosis, and one of the most common, is with schizophrenia, especially paranoid varieties. This differentiation has been made especially difficult due to the unfortunate linkage, in traditional Freudian thinking, between paranoia and homosexuality. Briefly, Freud, based on his analysis of the Schreber case (Freud, 1911), suggested that paranoia was a defense against homosexual impulses. Strict adherence to this viewpoint has confused theorizing about both paranoia and homosexuality. Stoller's (1968) view, which suggests that *any* major threat to one's core sexual identity *may* elicit paranoid defenses, is probably a more useful statement of any linkage between paranoia and homosexuality.

Clinically, however, there is a need for clear differentiation. Some clients who are paranoid and thought-disordered will have delusions and ideas of reference about homosexuality, and may be in considerable distress about this. On the other hand, some clients having severe sexual identity crises about their homosexuality will be panicky and paranoid, and may appear thought-disordered.

Some ideas for effecting this differentiation are as follows. In those individuals for whom homosexual thoughts are delusional and have little or no basis in a developed homosexual object-choice, the thoughts will be just that: cerebral, ruminative ideas with little or no component of homosexual *desire*, either in the present or past, as determined by history. Likewise, those individuals who are in a sexual identity crisis and paranoid, but who do have a genuine homosexual object-choice, typically can verbalize some degree of homosexual desire (either in the present or recent past).

Another point is crucial here. Paranoia and other florid reactions of a sexual identity crisis in a genuinely homosexual person are more likely to be partially, or at times completely, reality-based, as a result of severe interpersonal rejection, physical or sexual assault, impending or actual loss of job or a host of other possible ways in which a person may be traumatized because he or she is homosexual. Delusional ideas about homosexuality tend not to have such a reality base, or the connections are far more tenuous and idiosyncratic. A thorough history, detailed current symptom picture and clear chronology of precipitating events, then, will be crucial in making this differential diagnosis.

As suggested above, it is possible that both may be present. These may occur simultaneously, as in the case where the emergence of homosexual behavior with genuine desire may precipitate a schizophrenic episode in a marginally functioning pre-schizophrenic individual. They may also occur over the history of an individual. This may be especially true of homosexual individuals with late-onset paranoid schizophrenia, who may experience a coming out crisis in late teens or early 20s (often with a paranoid flavor) with clear indications of homosexual desire and occasionally behavior. For example, these individuals can recall strong erotic longing for certain high school friends. Later, in their 20s and 30s, they may slowly develop classic paranoid schizophrenia, characterized by a decrease in sexual desires and behavior as anhedonia develops, and an increase in ruminative, intellectualized delusions about homosexuality. This author treated one such individual who was sexually interested and active in young adulthood, but became increasingly anhedonic and delusional during his 30s. When he was first seen in his early 50s by this author, he was completely anhedonic, had been so for some years and had an elaborate delusional system about homosexuality, complete with ideas of reference and occasional auditory hallucinations. The early material was discernible only through careful history taking and examination of past treatment records.

Some gay/lesbian affirmative therapists do an enormous disservice to their clients who are gay or lesbian and schizophrenic by minimizing or ignoring the client's schizophrenia. This usually takes the form of illogical sloganeering along the lines of "Diagnosis of homosexuality as an illness is wrong; therefore diagnosis is wrong; therefore my schizophrenic client is not schizophrenic but merely oppressed (misunderstood, stigmatized, etc.) because of his or her homosexuality." The client may be all of those things—and also schizophrenic.

Perhaps most cruel of all is when such clinicians, out of ignorance, inexperience or anti-intellectualism, interpret aspects of schizophrenia (such as interpersonal awkwardness; chronic lack of desire; pleasure deficit; disordered thought processes; pervasive ambivalence; etc.) as signs of "not really accepting one's gayness." They may then pressure or shame such clients into moving beyond their capabilities. This can be genuinely damaging, particularly if done in a group psychotherapy setting where group members mimic the therapist and provide considerable pressure. Some years ago, this author had to hospitalize one such individual who became psychotic and suicidal as a result of such pressure in a coming out group, encouraged by a paraprofessional group leader who didn't "believe in schizophrenia" because it was "medical model garbage." This group leader's disbelief was singularly ineffective in treating the client's schizophrenia.

However, certain group psychotherapy modalities can be very useful in treating gay or lesbian schizophrenics. In the mid 1970s, Gay Community Services of Minneapolis offered group therapy for chronic schizophrenic gay men. This group lasted over a year and utilized supportive, task and reality-oriented, non-exploratory techniques which were useful in helping some of the participants improve the quality of their lives and interpersonal relationships. However, change was slow and gradual, and most of the participants were also being administered anti-psychotic medications.

Similarly, differential diagnosis problems exist with the affective disorders. Some individuals who are having sexual identity crises may respond with mood swings, hyperactivity and impulsive behaviors which are reminiscent of hypomania. Likewise, some hypomanic individuals may engage in indiscriminate and atypical (for them) sexual behavior, and may offer a variety of explanations about these. This may at times resemble a coming out situation. Further, the extensive denial about their behavior which hypomanic individuals often maintain may appear similar to denial about homosexual feelings and behavior in individuals prior to or during a genuine coming out process.

Generally, this differential diagnosis is easier because although some individuals with a sexual identity crisis may exhibit hypomanic-like symptoms, few will exhibit the symptom pattern and intensity of full-blown hypomania. For those few, a careful history can be helpful in determining either earlier affective problems, or previous same-sex interests. Also, the denial in hypomania has a rigid, brittle quality, and when confronted, is usually met with irritability, hostility, or flight into euphoria. The quality of denial in a person with a sexual identity crisis is often more consciously painful, and perhaps panicky. When confronted, an increase in anxiety is more common. Finally, treatment with lithium compounds typically yields a dramatic reduction in symptoms (including impulsive behaviors such as indiscriminate and atypical sexual behavior) in a hypomanic individual, while it does not do so in individuals with sexual identity crises.

Again, there may be some individuals who are gay or lesbian and hypomanic, and who may engage in impulsive sexual behaviors that are atypical for them. These atypical sexual behaviors may be homosexual or heterosexual; the crucial point is that they are atypical for that individual. It would be fallacious to attempt any determination of sexual orientation based on these impulsive, atypical sexual behaviors during a hypomanic episode. For individuals who are clearly hypomanic and who may also be experiencing a sexual identity crisis, determination of the latter must await stabilization on medication for the affective disorder.

On the other end of the affective spectrum, gay men and lesbians who have experienced a major life stressor (such as death of a lover) and ensuing reactive depression with no opportunity to work through the issue, or who have a series of major life stressors, may erroneously appear to be chronically or perhaps endogenously depressed. This is more likely to occur when an individual is very closeted and so cannot discuss the event(s); when the individual has a minimal or non-existent support system in the gay/lesbian communities; where the individual is subject to overt and/or continuous pressure and harassment because of his or her sexual orientation; or in other situations where the social supports which help most individuals through such life crises are unavailable. Over time, these situations can be corrosive to self-concept and may give the individual a "depressive" quality. A careful history, with attention to stressors, is crucial before concluding that a severe depression in a gay or lesbian client is chronic or endogenous. When given the opportunity in therapy to work through these issues, and/or when a support system develops, these individuals will often improve dramatically, and the "depressive" quality to their character structure may prove ephemeral.

The final differential diagnostic question to be discussed is that of borderline personality disorders. Because a variety of very different clinical syndromes are at times subsumed under this label, the syndrome as discussed by Kernberg (1975) will be the point of reference in this discussion. The diagnostic difficulty with this group is that these individuals may appear to have coming out concerns, or problems in adjusting to being gay or lesbian. However, the real issue is a relatively severe, chronic and characterologically based lack of ego differentiation and boundaries, in that the individual may not be able to distinguish between acquaintanceship, friendship, affection, love and sexuality, and in fact has a chaotic and undifferentiated, not homosexual, object choice. On the other hand, an individual who is experiencing a genuine sexual identity crisis may go through a period where such differentiations are poorly made, and where splitting operations may temporarily occur in response to a stressful situation for which more typical coping styles are ineffective. The first instance requires longer-term therapy aimed at underlying characterological issues to effect resolution of the problems with ego boundaries and differentiation; whereas the latter may be situational, and may accomplish the same resolution in a more short-term, supportive and problem-oriented approach. The key to this differentiation is in a careful examination of ego functioning and object relations *prior* to the current crisis over same-sex feelings and behavior. The true borderline personality will exhibit a chronic pattern of "stable instability," poor ego differentiation, relatively primitive object relations, and splitting operations in a number of areas of conflict; whereas the individual in a sexual identity crisis will usually not display these in his or her history.

A few other aspects of this differentiation should be noted. At times, the person having a sexual identity crisis may appear more floridly disturbed and "borderline-ish" than a true borderline personality in crisis. When a person who typically operates with firm ego boundaries and more or less clear differentiations in object relations goes through a period of impaired functioning as part of coming out, it may be especially frightening and ego-alien precisely because he or she is used to a higher level of functioning. The perceived impaired functioning may then in itself add to the stress and panic. The true borderline in crisis, on the other hand, will have certain dysfunctional coping mechanisms, such as splitting operations, both easily available and relatively more ego-syntonic. The true borderline will be more accomplished in utilizing such defenses; the person who is coming out may utilize them, but in an ineffective manner.

This differentiation also raises the question of therapeutic goals. If a true borderline personality is working toward characterological change, coalescing a better differentiated ego structure, learning more reality-based coping skills in place of splitting, etc., it is much more important *that* these occur than *which* sexual orientation the improved functioning develops around. The client may have a belief that one sexual orientation is preferable for him or her. As long as this is based on a reality-oriented appraisal by the client of him or herself, a realistic appraisal of the challenges inherent in either choice, and the choice is ego-syntonic, it is probably more therapeutically efficacious to honor this choice. Therapists who have an axe to grind about sexual object-choice with these clients may put an additional roadblock in their already difficult task.

This discussion has so far presented an overly simplified, essentially dichotomous view of homosexuality and heterosexuality. This has been done in order to explain more easily the diagnostic issues in question. However, it is important to offer a caveat about the increasing complexity of the diagnostic endeavor when one begins working with individuals who are more in the mid-range of the Kinsey scale; i.e., bisexual individuals. Even this Kinsey concept of a homosexual-heterosexual continuum does not capture the complexity of the components of sexual orientation and sexual identity. Readers are referred to Shively and DeCecco (1977) and Gonsiorek (1982a) for thorough grounding in the complexities of these issues. However, this paper will continue to use a simplified notion of sexual orientation in order to illustrate more clearly the diagnostic concepts.

One final word about sexual identity crises. The processes of coming out are often profound and may shake an individual to his or her core. This alone may account for the production of florid symptoms. In addition, the coming out process may occur at an age chronologically removed from adolescence, a stage which it resembles in some ways (see Coleman's chapter on coming out in this volume). This disparity in developmental levels may be perceived as frightening and ego-alien by some, and so contribute to subjective distress. Finally, some individuals with obsessional or counterphobic personality features may experience a flooding when coming to terms with same-sex feelings. While equilibrium usually returns with time, the flooding may be dramatic when control is perceived as lost. Individuals with other personality styles may respond in temporarily dramatic ways, but consistent with their style.

Characterological-Appearing Overlays to Personality Structures

Another area where diagnostic concepts can be useful if applied well—and dangerously deceptive if applied improperly—is in characterological-appearing overlays to personality structure. What the writer means by this concept is that a group of individuals with diverse personality structures experience similar kinds of stressful situations and develop a similar range of adaptive, or not-so-adaptive, coping mechanisms. This similarity in coping mechanisms may then give the appearance of similarity in personality structures.

This concept is not unfamiliar to diagnostic nomenclature, although neither can it be said to be common. Other examples of this concept are combat neuroses; chronic stress reactions to situations such as concentration or prisoner-of-war camps, and acute stress reactions to cataclysmic events such as earth-quakes, plane crashes, floods, etc. (see Kolb, 1973, pp. 431-442 for a description of some of these). The basic concept is that a variety of personality structures, undergoing a similar stress, produce a similarity of reactions. The examples described below have appeared in the author's clinical practice frequently enough to warrant notice as patterns. More could certainly be described, and others may develop as groups of individuals share common stresses.

The primary example to be described is the development of borderline-appearing personality features in response to repeated anonymous sexual behavior. This is a behavior in which some gay men may engage because of their developmental stage (see Coleman's discussion of the Exploration Stage of coming out in this volume); because it represents, in its own right, the kind of intermittent reinforcement schedule that tends to produce stable behavior; or because it can meet any of a variety of needs, both sexual and non-sexual, that are idiosyncratic to the individual involved. These latter may range from relatively benign, such as occasional thrill-seeking, to psychopathological, such as a wish to be assaulted or arrested. Regardless of why the behavior becomes at least temporarily established, a similarity in its effects may develop in some of those who engage in it.

Consider the following scenario: A gay man begins to frequent back-room bars, baths, public restrooms, parks or other public places for anonymous sex. He, on occasion, does have anonymous sex, which may be reinforcing and perceived as a boost to self-esteem. On another level, it may elicit a variety of guilt and self-recrimination responses if the individual has beliefs that sexuality, or same-sex activity, or some forms of sexual activity in which he has been engaging, are wrong, immoral, improper, etc. If this behavior is danger-ous due to its location (e.g., likelihood of assault or arrest) or because of the status of the individual (e.g., closeted, married man, public figure, etc.) and the possible negative effects of disclosure, both the thrill of success at sexual conquest and the negative feelings may become even more highly charged.

Also, lack of success at sexual conquest may elicit feelings of poor body image, low self-esteem and others. Particularly if other social, intimate or sexual outlets are not available or perceived not to be available, these anonymous sexual outlets may be highly valued. For some closeted men, they may be the only perceived outlets; in more rural areas, they may be the only actual outlets.

The result may be a situation which generates simultaneously positive and negative affects, both highly charged, and both possibly profound in their ability to mobilize deeper psychological issues such as self-esteem, body image, feelings of physical and bodily safety, and others. If these powerful affects, especially the negative ones, were experienced directly, the result might be immobilization. One way of handling this situation is via splitting operations (see Kernberg, 1975). Intensely positive and negative affects, overcharged, and often poorly differentiated due to lack of reality-testing about them in a socially supportive framework, are simultaneously developed and walled off from each other and from emotional integration with the rest of the personality.

The splitting mechanism itself tends to be disruptive to healthy ego functioning, and may therefore increase the likelihood that in other situations (probably those that are generalizable either in a behavioral sense or in terms of unconscious meaning to the individual) splitting operations are performed. The result in these individuals is an overlay of borderline-appearing personality functions on a variety of pre-existing personality styles.

This concept may also provide an alternative to one of the more persistent myths about lesbian relationships; namely that they are characterized by intense jealousy, blurring of ego boundaries, absence of autonomy, possessiveness, symbiosis and a high degree of fusion between the two women involved (e.g., Bergler, 1962). In essence, such disease-oriented writers have described lesbian relationships as a pathological interaction between two individuals with borderline features, if not actual borderline personalities. In this volume, Anthony has provided some description of stresses on lesbian couples, and McCandlish has provided a detailed non-disease, affirmative model of working with these same issues in lesbian couples. Krestan and Bepko (1980) have offered a richly descriptive and comprehensive family systems model that illustrates how forces acting upon lesbian couples by the larger society, as well as from within the lesbian communities, can create "fusion" problems in the couples. The Krestan and Bepko model of how this occurs is in some ways very comparable to the concept of characterological-appearing overlays in this paper, but is grounded in a family systems approach.

A variety of other examples of characterological-appearing overlays have been noted. Individuals who are married and closeted; who are public figures; who work in a job where dismissal is likely should the person's sexual orientation be known; who perceive threat of physical or sexual assault; or who find themselves in other situations where severe repercussions to disclosure realistically exist may develop a paranoid-appearing overlay characterized by hypervigilance, ruminations, ideas of reference, hypersensitivity, etc. A variety of mechanisms may serve to strengthen this coping strategy. These include real, imagined or vicariously observed situations where hypervigilance prevented disclosure and/or lack of vigilance led to disclosure, the generally self-fulfilling prophecies which eventuate when people act noticeably paranoid and suspicious, chronic lack of reality-testing about ruminative ideas, and others.

Earlier in this paper, differential diagnosis between affective disorders and sexual identity crises was discussed. Much of that discussion is germane here in that an individual who has experienced a series of unresolved stressors, especially if this is coupled with a weak support system, may give the appearance of a depressive-appearing characterological overlay. This author worked with an older lesbian client who lived with her lover in an isolated rural area in the upper midwest. Both women were especially isolated from other lesbians. The death of her lover, resulting problems with with property inheritance and finances, geographical move, medical problems and a series of other stressors produced a serious depression. The referral source had concluded that the woman had suffered from a long-standing depressive neurosis, which was exacerbated by the current stressors—a conclusion supported by psychological testing. However, after treatment which focused on grieving, working through these painful events, and establishing a support system, the depression lifted. What was most interesting was that post-treatment testing offered no support for the existence of a depressive-neurosis. One explanation is that the chronic isolation and lack of a support system created a depressive-appearing characterological overlay in this client.

A final example is a narcissistic-appearing overlay. These individuals often come from environments which are noteworthy for extreme intolerance and harshness toward homosexuality, such as certain rural areas, the "Bible-belt," and ethnic working class neighborhoods in large cities. Often, such individuals literally have never knowingly interacted with another gay or lesbian person prior to coming out. After a protracted period of not acting on same-sex feelings after disclosure is made to the self, such individuals may suddenly and dramatically come out by informing people indiscriminately, moving to a gay or lesbian neighborhood in a large metropolitan area, or drastically changing career, clothing, non-verbal behavior, speech and a whole variety of attitudes to conform with what they perceive to be the standards in gay or lesbian "society." These individuals then cling to the most overt and public institutions in the gay and lesbian communities, such as bars, political organizations, etc., and to social networks which are maximally different from their previous pre-coming out milieu. This attempt to find an identity and a support system often involves mercurial shifts as the individuals attempt to conform to their chosen reference group. The appearance of these individuals may be one of extreme narcissism, shallowness and almost complete immersion of the personality in the changing whirlwinds of high fashion, the latest chic, or the "right" social circles.

The concept of an overlay to other personality structures raises issues about which is the chicken and which the egg. Of course, some people get involved in these situations precisely because they are borderline, depressive, paranoid, narcissistic or whatever. The concept of an overlay should not be construed to mean that such personality types do not "really" exist among homosexual populations. The rationale for this concept is that while those personality types do exist, there *also* exist other groups of individuals who, as a result of similarities in situations and stressors, develop similarities in coping mechanisms despite a variety of premorbid personality structures different from the overlay. And, of course, some individuals faced with the identical situations and stressors do not develop such an overlay.

In terms of psychotherapy, this concept suggests that diverse individuals with similar overlay may respond well in early phases of psychotherapy to an approach oriented toward working through that particular overlay and its issues. Once this has been accomplished, a variety of other issues consistent with the pre-existing personality dynamics may then emerge. The psychotherapy, then, may need to shift emphasis as appropriate.

It is also helpful to bear in mind that for the purposes of this discussion, the line between the overlay and the pre-existing personality structure is drawn artificially sharp. Any overlay, if it remains part of the person's functioning for a prolonged period of time, may begin to set down increasingly deep roots and begin to dwarf the pre-existing personality structure. Just as some effects of combat neurosis, concentration camp syndrome and stress reactions to catastrophes may be slow to diminish, and indeed may never be alleviated, so too these overlays may be tenacious or even become permanent aspects of the personality. Some victims may be scarred psychologically with the marks of social oppression of homosexuality as indelibly as some concentration camp victims retain their tatooed numbers.

It is hoped that the ideas presented in this paper will encourage a synthesis of those concepts that are most useful from the newer gay/lesbian affirmative viewpoints and from traditional diagnostic concepts.

REFERENCES

American Psychiatric Association. *Diagnostic and statistical manual of mental disorders* (3rd ed.). Washington, DC: Author, 1980.

Bergler, E. *Homosexuality*. New York: Collier Books, 1962.

Bowers, K. Situationism in psychology: An analysis and a critique. *Psychological Review*, 1973, *80*, 5, 307-337.

Cooper, J. E., Kendell, R. E. Garland, B. J., Sharpe, L., Copeland, J., & Simon, R. *Psychiatric diagnosis in New York and London*. London: Oxford University Press, 1972.

Freud, S. *Psychoanalytic notes upon an autobiographical account of a case of paranoia* (1911). In J. Strachey (Trans., Ed.), *The standard edition of the complete psychological works of Sigmund Freud*. London: Hogart Press, 1958.

Gonsiorek, J. Psychological adjustment and homosexuality. JSAS *Catalog of Selected Documents in Psychology*, 1977, *7*, 45. (Ms. No. 1478).

Gonsiorek, J. Introduction to mental health issues and homosexuality. In J. Gonsiorek (Ed.), *Homosexuality: The end of a mental illness*, special issue of *American Behavioral Scientist*, March/April 1982, *25*, 4. (a)

Gonsiorek, J. Results of psychological testing on homosexual populations. In J. Gonsiorek (Ed.), *Homosexuality: The end of a mental illness*, special issue of *American Behavioral Scientist*, March/April 1982, *25*, 4. (b)

Kernberg, D. *Borderline conditions and pathological narcissism*. New York: Jason Aronson, 1975.

Krestan, J., & Bepko, C. The problem of fusion in the lesbian relationship. *Family Process*, 1980, *19*, 3, 277-289.

Kolb, L. *Modern clinical psychiatry* (8th ed.). Philadelphia: W. B. Saunders, 1973.

Mischel, W. *Personality and assessment*. New York: Wiley and Sons, 1968.

Rosenhan, D. L. On being sane in insane places. *Science*, 1973, *179*, 250-258.

Shively, M. G., & DeCecco, J. P. Comonents of sexual identity. *Journal of Homosexuality*, 1977, *3*, 1, 41-48.

Stoller, R. *Sex and gender: On the development of masculinity and femininity*. New York: Science House, 1968.

Straus, J., & Gift, T. Choosing an approach for diagnosing schizophrenia. *Archives of General Psychiatry*, 1977, *34*, 1248-1253.

Szasz, T. *The myth of mental illness*. New York: Harper and Row, 1961.

World Health Organization. *The international pilot study of schizophrenia*. Geneva: Author, 1973.

SEXUAL ORIENTATION OF THE THERAPIST AND THERAPEUTIC EFFECTIVENESS WITH GAY CLIENTS

Martin Rochlin, PhD

ABSTRACT. The psychotherapeutic effects of client-therapist similarity and difference have been investigated and reported in the areas of social class, gender, race, religion, culture, politics, wealth, education, age, personality, and sexual mores, but very rarely with regard to sexual-affectional orientation. This paper examines the literature on relationship variables in psychotherapy, and on client-therapist similarity as one of those relationship variables. These broader issues are related to the more specific subject of similarity or difference of sexual orientation between client and therapist, and to the implications of that variable for psychotherapeutic process and outcome with lesbian and gay male clients.

The pros and cons of matching clients and therapists in terms of sexual-affectional orientation have been a topic of innuendo, private discussion, and sometimes heated debate in convention corridors and cocktail lounges, but rarely a focus of serious attention or systematic study. Issues of client-therapist similarity and difference have been investigated and reported in the areas of social class, gender, race, religion, culture, politics, wealth, education, age, personality, and sexual mores. Thus far, however, with the exception of an unpublished student project on lesbians' experiences in therapy (Wandrei, Note 1), only one study has been reported in which the variable of client-therapist similarity with regard to sexual orientation has been deliberately tested as a relevant factor in psychotherapeutic outcomes (Liljestrand, Gerling, & Saliba, 1978).

Until recently, the existence of homosexual therapists was virtually unknown.

Dr. Rochlin was the first openly gay clinical psychologist in Los Angeles. Formerly on the Executive Board of the Los Angeles Society of Clinical Psychologists and on the Steering Committee of the Association of Gay Psychologists, and a Director Emeritus of the Los Angeles Gay and Lesbian Community Services Center, he is a frequent lecturer and consultant to universities and mental health centers. He has recently been appointed by the California State Psychological Association to be their delegate to the Committee on Gay Concerns of the American Psychological Association's Board of Social and Ethical Responsibilities for Psychology. He practices gay-oriented psychotherapy in West Hollywood, California.

It was traditionally assumed that heterosexuality is the only suitable orientation for therapists (Bergin & Strupp, 1972). At the 1972 annual convention of the American Psychological Association, the chair of a symposium on homosexuality remarked that "the panel had no knowledge of gay psychologists within APA and/or were not willing to request that any psychologist jeopardize his/ her career by making an appearance as a homosexual on the panel" (Morin, 1973). At present, however, publicly self-identified gay male and lesbian mental health professionals are growing in number. Their increasing accessibility gives the issue of client-therapist matching on the dimension of sexual-affectional orientation practical as well as theoretical relevance.

Relationship Variables in Psychotherapy

Since 1952, with the beginning of the Eysenck-Strupp debates regarding the effectiveness or ineffectiveness of psychotherapy, there has been an increasing accumulation of evidence that the core conditions common to all effective psychotherapy are relationship variables (Herron, 1975). At this point, most theories of psychotherapy give the person of the therapist a central place, the primary question being whether relationship variables are necessary and sufficient conditions for effective counseling and psychotherapy (Rogers, 1957), or only necessary but not sufficient. (That relationship variables are necessary is consistently supported in the literature.)

Based on the work of Rogers (1957, 1962), Truax and Carkhuff (1967) boiled therapeutic effectiveness down to three "key characteristics" of the therapist: (a) empathic understanding, (b) positive regard, and (c) genuineness. In addition to these core dimensions, Carkhuff and Berenson (1967) identified seven other characteristics worthy of mention, though less empirically substantiated: (d) appropriate self-disclosure, (e) spontaneity, (f) confidence, (g) intensity, (h) openness, (e) flexibility, and (j) commitment. With regard to the latter, Swensen (1971) found the one common characteristic of successful therapists, regardless of method, was the "therapist's commitment to the client." Oden (1974) asserted that "it is the therapist and not the theory and/or method that will make or break the therapy." Herron (1975) concluded that although there is still no substantive evidence that one type of therapy is more effective than another, there is evidence that some types of therapists are more effective than others.

Client-Therapist Similarity

Among the relationship variables found necessary for effective counseling and psychotherapy is that of client-therapist similarity. Guntrip (1969), drawing largely from the object-relations theories of Fairbairn and Winnicott, wrote: "Psychotherapeutic success depends ultimately not on theory . . . but on the individual therapist's ability to understand intuitively and accurately this particular patient" (p. 316). The intuitive and accurate understanding of an individual characterized by a stigmatized minority status requires more than just a shared humanity. It requires considerable commonality of the cultural context in which the basic human feelings are experienced and expressed. Guntrip emphasized that the therapist "knows, not just theoretically but in his own experience, what the patient is passing through. . . . Only that enables the patient to feel no longer alone. Neither love nor insight alone cures" (p. 353).

Calia (1966) found perceived similarity between counselor and counselee to be positively correlated with "unconditional regard" and "empathy," the emotional ingredients emphasized by Rogers (1957, 1962)—along with "self-congruence" of the therapist—as requirements for effective growth-promoting relationships. Guntrip asserted that "patient and therapist need to be 'matched' to secure the best results" (p. 328).

More than twenty years ago, Hollingshead and Redlich (1958) found that counselors' feelings toward clients of their own class were more positive than toward those of different class status. The *Journal of Psychology and Judaism* is dedicated to the study of the "distinctly Jewish" problems of identity and dynamics in therapy with Jewish clients. With regard to race, Jones and Seagull (1977) referred to "the basic issue in therapy" as the question: "How do we treat with dignity and positive regard those who differ from us on some major dimension?" (p. 855). (This question is particularly critical in a dimension as emotionally loaded as sexual orientation.) In a review of research on the question of whether white therapists can effectively treat black clients, Jones (1978) found "the preponderance of these studies indicates that blacks respond more favorably to black counselors than to white counselors." His investigation revealed that "blacks prefer black counselors, achieve greater rapport and engage in greater self-exploration, and are better understood by black counselors than white," and concluded that "race rather than experience was of greater importance in working with black clients." In a study of psychotherapy with Chicanos, Roll, Millen, and Martinez (1980) found that "Chicanos are relatively comfortable with a number of situations and life-adjustments which make the Anglo (therapist) either anxious or envious," and recommended generally "increased recruitment efforts to attract minorities to the psychological professions."

The issue of client-therapist similarity has special significance for gay male and lesbian clients. Along with the feeling of being alone, the reality of difference and alienation even in the family of origin constitutes the distinctive pain of early gay experience, unparalleled in the family experiences of members of other oppressed groups. In the author's clinical experience, the perpetuation of that pain in therapy with a non-gay therapist is one of the commonly reported reasons for gay male and lesbian clients' dissatisfaction or failure in traditional psychotherapy.

Homophobia and Heterosexism in Psychotherapy

Homophobia may be defined as the irrational dread and loathing of homo-sexuality and homosexual people (Weinberg, 1972). Heterosexism, a more insidious form of anti-gay prejudice, refers to the culturally conditioned bias that heterosexuality is intrinsically superior to homosexuality. Just as Brover-man, Broverman, Clarkson, Rosenkrantz, and Vogel (1970) demonstrated that therapists' criteria of mental health and illness are biased by sex-role stereo-types, Morin (1977) described how heterosexist bias in psychological research perpetuates stereotypical beliefs among mental health professionals regarding the purported psychopathology of lesbianism and male homosexuality.

A racist white therapist is clearly disqualified to treat black clients (Jones & Seagull, 1977); correspondingly, a homophobic or heterosexist therapist, regardless of sexual orientation, cannot be helpful to lesbian and gay clients. In a study of gender-matching versus cross-gender pairing of client and thera-pist, Lerman (1978) pointed out the "possible harmful effects" of sexism in cross-gender therapy. The danger of heterosexism in cross-sexual-orientation therapy might likewise be considered.

Both sexism and heterosexism, unlike racism, are built into the very foun-dation of traditional psychiatric theory, training, and practice. Even racist therapists are unlikely to view dark skin pigmentation as either an arrest in normal development or a sociopathic, narcissistic, paranoid, or masochistic mental disorder. In contrast, despite the 1973 decision of the American Psychi-atric Association that homosexuality per se does not constitute a psychiatric disorder, a 1977 survey by the journal *Medical Aspects of Human Sexuality* revealed that 69% of members of the American Psychiatric Association still held the personal belief that homosexuality is a pathological adaptation (as opposed to a normal variation), with only 18% in disagreement and 13% uncertain. In addition, 70% of the respondents said the problems of homo-sexual men and women have more to do with their own inner conflicts than with stigmatization by society.

Just as being black or female by no means precludes holding racist or sexist prejudices, being homosexual does not guarantee freedom from homo-phobic and heterosexist bias. The consciousness of the therapist is only indi-rectly related to the therapist's fortuitous membership in a category. Even with equivalent degrees of gay consciousness in gay and non-gay therapists, how-ever, additional factors may favor the matching of gay clients with gay thera-pists when that choice is available.

Gay Consciousness

The concept of gay consciousness, sometimes termed gay sensibility (Moss, 1979), refers to the degree of awareness of and sensibility to the personal and social complexities of gay experience. The well-known "conspiracy of silence" associated with homosexuality has precluded such awareness for the bulk of society, and most lesbians and gay men repress or conceal the pain unique to gay experience. Consciousness-raising (CR) involves getting in touch with one's hidden feelings and sharing them with others. From the notes of a CR group (A Gay Male Group, 1972): "In seeing the common roots of our experiences, we break down our isolation from other gay people and begin to recognize our condition in society as an oppressed class" (p. 295). In the notes of the same group, the following comparison was made between CR and traditional therapy:

> Consciousness-raising is unlike therapy or encounter groups. Those of us who have been in therapy have seen it as a straight man pressuring us to think in a certain way about experiences he has never had. Therapy doesn't make clear that the relationships which cause us to have difficulties are determined by the anti-homosexual atmosphere that surrounds us.
>
> We have been defined by the churches, by psychiatrists, by sociologists and, generally, by our sector in society which is not homosexual. Through the process of consciousness-raising, we have begun to define ourselves. (pp. 295-296)

Consciousness-raising is an integral part of the self-actualization of gay male and lesbian clients and is also essential for therapists who would foster their clients' growth. The importance of the personal sexual-affectional orientation of the therapist is a more controversial and delicate issue.

Client-Therapist Similarity of Sexual Orientation

At present, research data on the effects of sexual orientation in client-therapist dyads are sparse but suggest that, when the therapist is openly gay, sexual-orientation congruence in such pairings facilitates effective counseling and psychotherapy for lesbian and gay male clients. Riddle and Sang (1978) noted that "the discretionary use of self-disclosure can have profound healing effects since the sharing of the therapist's experience validates the client's struggles. . . . Not having to explain the nuances and stresses of one's life can be enormously helpful in accelerating therapeutic process" (p. 97). The quality of empathy expressed when a gay therapist tells a gay client, "I know how it feels," is of a different order than when a heterosexual therapist says, "I know how it must feel."

In a survey of 124 therapists regarding the effects of their values on clinical work with patients (Roman, Charles, & Karasu, 1978), 67% considered homosexual experience acceptable for others, while only 4% considered such experience acceptable for themselves. The counselors who could generally accept changing mores or sexually diverse life-styles were found to be more liberal in attitudes toward clients' choices, more accepting, and more professionally supportive.

Wandrei (Note 1) found that lesbian clients with lesbian or gay male therapists, when compared to those with heterosexual therapists, felt more favorably toward their therapy. They believed their therapists held more positive attitudes toward the clients' homosexual feelings and were more effective as therapists. Liljestrand et al. (1978) found that client-therapist similarity of sexual orientation is related to positive therapeutic outcomes when client and therapist are mutually disclosive. This supports the earlier findings of Carkhuff and Berenson (1967) regarding the value of "appropriate self-disclosure" by the therapist. The similarity of sexual orientation, mutually disclosed, facilitated trust and enhanced the qualities of *both* therapist and client that have been found to be related to therapeutic success. For clients, those qualities mainly concern motivation and confidence in the therapist. For therapists they are understanding, empathy, warmth, interest, attentiveness, recognition that the problems are genuine rather than imaginary, respect, and being a good listener. Sharing personal experiences of "being different" and of "coming out" particularly enhanced confidence and risk-taking. The willingness of therapists to disclose their homosexuality possibly minimizes homophobia and indicates a significant degree of gay consciousness, in contrast to homosexual colleagues who feel the need to remain closeted.

Therapist as Role Model

It is widely recognized that lesbians and gay men are generally deprived of positive gay role models in their natural development, that such role models are growth-enhancing, and that role-modeling is a frequent ingredient of effective psychotherapy. Voeller (1980) asked "By what logic are young gays less needful of gay role-models than heterosexuals are of heterosexual models?" (p. 241). Warren (1980) noted that "role-models of homosexuals are absent in early childhood . . . the child lives in a world where heterosexuality is taken for granted" (pp. 131-132). Without the availability of gay adults who are decent, accomplished, and fulfilled human beings as role models, "it is not possible to escape . . . oppressive self-hatred and impoverishment" (Humphreys, 1979). With regard to the general concept of therapist as role model, "identification with the therapist" was cited by Marmor (1964/1974) as one of the five elements that "encompass the most significant factors on the basis of which change takes place in a psychotherapeutic relationship" (p. 305). Writing on gay therapists as role models, Woodman and Lenna (1980) recognized that "the homosexual community in general and gay clients in particular need role models" (p. 113). They added:

The gay professional who has come out is also a very important resource for the immediate gay community. . . . Responsible homosexual professionals can serve as role models for gays who are coming out . . ., provide security for those who need to see gay counselors, and act as resource consultants for other counselors. (pp. 113-114)

Riddle and Sang (1978) found "a tremendous advantage in having a gay therapist . . . who can model for the client a sense of positive identity" (p. 97). There is reward also for the therapist who can claim: "Now I could be one of the living models for young gay people I wished I could have found in my own youth" (Rochlin, 1979, p. 168).

Familiarity with the Gay World

Assessment of the gay client's need for professional help requires a gay consciousness and familiarity with current resources and events in the gay community. "Sometimes you need only serve as an information center, telling the inexperienced Gay person where to meet other Gay people and how to get involved in Gay organizations, or what sort of Gay-oriented reading material is available" (Clark, 1977, p. 174). Woodman and Lenna (1980) pointed out that "knowledge must also come from experience with the gay life-style" (p. 15) and questioned "the belief that we could be knowledgeable about gay life-styles from positions as detached observers" (p. 116). Nuehring, Fein, and Tyler (1974) reported that one of the major obstacles to satisfactory counseling with gay clients was the professional's lack of practical knowledge about homosexuality and homosexual life-styles. Many gay male and lesbian clients with uninformed therapists report that they spend a great deal of time and money educating their therapists regarding gay consciousness, life-styles, and community issues. As Riddle and Sang (1978) wrote, "Such a procedure is hardly in the best interest of the client."

In conclusion, the suitability of non-gay or undisclosed-homosexual therapists for lesbian and gay male clients warrants careful study. Clark (1977) has cautioned: "Certainly no non-Gay therapist or counselor should assume competence in serving Gay clients without retraining and Gay-oriented super—vision to unlearn the prejudices and misinformation acquired in life and in professional training programs" (p. 156). The characterization of psychotherapy as a political instrument of oppression and conformity is well-known. Szasz (1970) has shown how the homosexual has long been exploited as "the model psychiatric scapegoat." Masters and Johnson (1979) have stated: "The available evidence certainly supports the homosexual population in their general contention that if they expected the worst from health-care professionals, they would be rarely disappointed" (p. 247). Greater attention to these issues may prove salutary not only to those lesbians and gay men who seek greater personal integrity and growth through psychotherapy, but to the integrity and growth of the psychotherapeutic disciplines themselves.

REFERENCE NOTE

1. Wandrei, K. *Lesbians' experience in therapy.* Submitted as a paper for Seniors' Honors Program in Psychology, University of California at Berkeley, 1975.

REFERENCES

Bergin, A. E., & Strupp, H. H. *Changing frontiers in the science of psychotherapy.* Chicago: Aldine/Atherton, 1972.

Broverman, I., Broverman, D., Clarkson, F., Rosenkrantz, P., & Vogel, S. Sex-role stereotypes and clinical judgments of mental health. *Journal of Consulting and Clinical Psychology*, 1970, *34*, 1-7.

Calia, V. F. The culturally deprived client: A re-formulation of the counselor's role. *Journal of Counseling Psychology*, 1966, *13*, 100-105.

Carkhuff, R. R., & Berenson, B. G. *Beyond counseling and therapy.* New York: Holt, Rinehart, & Winston, 1967.

Clark, D. *Loving someone gay.* Millbrae, CA: Celestial Arts, 1977.

A Gay Male Group. Notes on gay male consciousness-raising. In K. Jay & A. Young (Eds.), *Out of the closets: Voices of gay liberation.* New York: Douglas, 1972.

Guntrip, H. *Schizoid phenomena, object relations and the self.* New York: International Universities Press, 1969.

Herron, W. G. Further thoughts on psychotherapeutic deprofessionalization. *Journal of Humanistic Psychology*, 1975, *15*, 65-73.

Hollingshead, A. B., & Redlich, F. C. *Social class and mental illness.* New York: Wiley, 1958.

Humphreys, L. Exodus and identity: The emerging gay culture. In M. P. Levine (Ed.), *Gay men: The sociology of male homosexuality.* New York: Harper & Row, 1979.

Jones, A., & Seagull, A. A. Dimensions of the relationship between the black client and the white therapist. *American Psychologist*, 1977, *32*, 850-855.

Jones, E. E. Effects of race on psychotherapy process and outcome: An exploratory investigation. *Psychotherapy: Theory, Research, & Practice*, 1978, *15*, 226-236.

Lerman, H. Some thoughts on cross-gender psychotherapy. *Psychotherapy: Theory, Research, & Practice*, 1978, *15*, 248-250.

Liljestrand, P., Gerling, E., & Saliba, P. A. The effects of social sex-role stereotypes and sexual orientation on psychotherapeutic outcomes. *Journal of Homosexuality*, 1978, *3*, 361-372.

Marmor, J. The nature of the psychotherapeutic process (1964). In Marmor, J. *Psychiatry in transition.* New York: Brunner/Mazel, 1974.

Masters, W. H., & Johnson, V. E. *Homosexuality in perspective.* Boston: Little, Brown, 1979.

Morin, S. F. Notes on formation of AGP. *Association of Gay Psychologists Newsletter*, June 1973.

Morin, S. F. Heterosexual bias in psychological research on lesbianism and male homosexuality. *American Psychologist*, 1977, *32*, 629-637.

Moss, L. Sense and the gay sensibility. In L. Richmond & G. Noguera (Eds.), *The new gay liberation book.* Palo Alto, CA: Ramparts Press, 1979.

Nuehring, E., Fein, S., & Tyler, M. The gay college student: Perspectives for mental health professionals. *The Counseling Psychologist*, 1974, *4*, 64-72.

Oden, T. C. A populist's view of psychotherapeutic deprofessionalization. *Journal of Humanistic Psychology*, 1974, *14*, 3-18.

Riddle, D. I., & Sang, B. Psychotherapy with lesbians. *Journal of Social Issues*, 1978, *34*, 84-100.

Rochlin, M. Becoming a gay professional. In B. Berzon & R. Leighton (Eds.), *Positively gay.* Millbrae, CA: Celestial Arts, 1979.

Rogers, C. R. The necessary and sufficient conditions of therapeutic personality change. *Journal of Consulting Psychology*, 1957, *21*, 95-103.

Rogers, C. R. The interpersonal relationship: The core of guidance. *Harvard Educational Review*, 1962, *32*, 416-429.

Roll, S., Millen, L., & Martinez, R. Common errors in psychotherapy with Chicanos: Extrapolations from research and clinical experience. *Psychotherapy: Theory, Research, & Practice*, 1980, *17*, 158-168.

Roman, M., Charles, E., & Karasu, T. B. The value systems of psychotherapists and changing mores. *Psychotherapy: Theory, Research, & Practice*, 1978, *15*, 409-415.

Swensen, C. H. Commitment and the personality of the successful therapist. *Psychological Bulletin*, 1971, *77*, 400-404.

Szasz, T. S. *The manufacture of madness*. New York: Delta, 1970.

Truax, C. B., & Carkhuff, R. R. *Toward effective counseling and psychotherapy: Training and practice*. Chicago: Aldine, 1967.

Voeller, B. Society and the gay movement. In J. Marmor (Ed.), *Homosexual behavior*. New York: Basic Books, 1980.

Warren, C. Homosexuality and stigma. In J. Marmor (Ed.), *Homosexual behavior*. New York: Basic Books, 1980.

Weinberg, G. *Society and the healthy homosexual*. New York: St. Martin's, 1972.

Woodman, N.J., & Lenna, H. R. *Counseling with gay men and women*. San Francisco: Jossey-Bass, 1980.

DEVELOPMENTAL STAGES OF THE COMING OUT PROCESS

Eli Coleman, PhD

ABSTRACT. Five developmental stages which describe the patterns seen in individuals with predominantly same-sex sexual orientation are described in the paper. The stages are: pre-coming out, coming out, exploration, first relationships, and identity integration.

The illness model of homosexuality has been seriously challenged by numerous researchers who have concluded there is no psychopathology inherent in homosexuality per se. (For a detailed review of this literature, see Gonsiorek, 1977.) Indeed, outcome studies of treatment based upon the illness model have indicated limited results when "heterosexual shift" was the goal (Coleman, 1978). As a result, there has been a significant change in the understanding and treatment of homosexual clients. New models postulate that homosexuality is not a definable entity but, rather, a normal variation of sexual behavior, erotic disposition, and sexual preference expressed in varying degrees and manners by different individuals (e.g., Bell & Weinberg, 1978).

The new models postulate that individuals who are homosexual to varying degrees and in various ways share similar stages of identity development (Cass, 1979; Dank, 1971; Hencken & O'Dowd, 1977; Lee, 1977; Plummer, 1975; Grace, Note 1). These models are based on developmental concepts similar to those outlined by Erikson (1956) and Sullivan (1953). Like Erikson, theorists have been suggesting that each stage of development must be resolved before subsequent stages can be completed. It is argued that the adjustment and socialization of the individual is greatly influenced by social forces (Erikson, 1956) and, most importantly, that the self develops and is shaped according to the nature of interpersonal relationships (Sullivan, 1953). These developmental concepts have in turn produced new treatment models.

Dr. Coleman is the Coordinator of Clinical Services and Assistant Professor at the Program in Human Sexuality, Department of Family Practice and Community Health, Medical School, University of Minnesota. He has written a number of papers on homosexuality, bisexuality, sexual dysfunction, and adolescent sexuality. Dr. Coleman is a psychologist and an AASECT-certified sex therapist. He is also on the editorial board of the *Journal of Homosexuality*.

A Proposed Model

This model postulates that five stages describe many of the patterns seen in individuals with a predominantly same-sex sexual orientation. The stages are: pre-coming out, coming out, exploration, first relationships, and identity integration.

Before these stages are explored, several assumptions need to be made explicit. First, this model does not assume that every individual follows each stage and naturally evolves through all. Some become locked into one stage or another and never experience identity integration. It is not uncommon for individuals to work on developmental tasks of several different stages simultaneously. Some individuals will begin tasks at higher levels of development before focusing on the task of an earlier stage. The present model, however, postulates that identity integration depends on completion of tasks at earlier stages. Individuals who do experience identity integration are not static; they can attend to tasks of earlier stages when their present situation requires this. While the development of many individuals is in fact more chaotic, fluid, or complex than this model describes, the framework remains useful as a way to understand these people and can assist therapists and clients if used in a flexible manner. It is hoped that the validity of the model will be substantiated, altered, and revised through further research.

Pre-Coming Out

The etiology of sexual object choice is not well understood. Core gender and sex-role identities are well-formed by the age of 3 (Money & Ehrhardt, 1972). This is believed because attempts to reassign gender identity after age 3 result in further gender dysphoria. Money and Ehrhardt, who believe that sexual object choice is an integral component of gender identity, assume, therefore, that the origins of bisexuality, heterosexuality, and homosexuality are determined primarily during the developmental period of late infancy and early childhood, when gender identity differentiation is being established. This rationale is not well substantiated, however, and awaits further experimentation and research.

If, however, object-choice identity is indeed formed at this early age, it is possible that, on a conscious or pre-conscious level, the child and family members know even then that the child's sexual orientation "differs." This knowledge can affect the child and family in significant ways. During these early years, the child learns about the ethical values of the family and society and incorporates external rules into a personal structure. In this way, most of today's children learn that homosexuality is wrong and that everyone must marry (even if they do not produce children of their own). A major crisis is created for the individual, the family, and ultimately for society when a child appears about to break with these expectations. Minimally, the child feels "different," alienated, and alone. As they grow up, many such children develop low self-esteem. If acknowledged, same-sex feelings would mean rejection and ridicule; consequently, individuals protect themselves from awareness through defenses, such as denial, repression, reaction formation, sublimation, and rationalization. These defenses keep the individuals, their families, and society from experiencing the crisis that would occur if the issue of homosexuality were confronted directly. The consequences of this concealment can be enormously destructive. As Fischer (1972) states:

> Every time a homosexual denied the validity of his feelings or restrains himself from expressing, he does a small hurt to himself. He turns his energies inward and suppresses his own vitality. The effect may be scarcely noticeable: joy may be a little less keen, happiness slightly subdued; he may simply feel a little run down, a little less tall. Over the years, these tiny denials have a cumulative effect. (p. 249).

Because individuals at the pre-coming out stage are not consciously aware of same-sex feelings, they cannot describe what is wrong. They can only communicate their conflict through behavioral problems, psychosomatic illnesses, suicidal attempts, or various other symptoms. It is conceivable that some suicidal attempts by children and adolescents are due to this conflict.

The conflict of this stage can be resolved in several ways. Some individuals decide to commit suicide and are successful. Others hide their sexual feelings from themselves and others, continuing to suffer from lowered self-esteem and depression. A healthy resolution to this stage is to face the existential crisis of being different. This means breaking through defense barriers and acknowledging same-sex feelings.

Coming Out

Individuals move into this stage when they acknowledge their homosexual feelings. This is the first developmental task of the coming out stage. At first, it may mean simply acknowledging a thought, a fantasy. Plummer (1975) and Lee (1977) call this stage *signification* and Plummer refers to "those first conscious and semi-conscious moments in which an individual comes to perceive himself as a homosexual" (p. 135). Hencken and O'Dowd (1977) call this stage *awareness*, Dank (1971) *identification*, and Grace (Note 1) *acknowledgement*. This is not to imply that the individual necessarily has a clear understanding of the word "homosexual" and what it means. As Cass (1979) describes, this stage is filled with confusion: Indeed, she refers to it as the stage of *identity confusion*.

Research has indicated the average age at which individuals experience this awareness as between 13 and 18. Jay and Young (1979) report that the median age of awareness for the females in their sample was 18; the median age for males was 13-14. The ranges were wide, however, and many individuals in Jay and Young's sample did not realize these feelings until they were beyond chronological adolescence. A study by Kooden, Morin, Riddle, Rogers, Sang, and Strassburger (Note 2) reports that in a sample of gay male and lesbian psychologists, the average age at which males become aware of their homosexual feelings was 12.8; for females it was 13.8. On the average, the males understood the word "homosexual"at 17.2 years and females at 15.6 years. In other words, there is usually a period of time during which individuals are aware of homosexual feelings (whether they have acted upon them or not) but do not label them as such. Consequently, they cannot verbalize these feelings to a therapist. If the therapist initiates a discussion of homosexual feelings with clients, these confusing feelings can be recognized more quickly and identity confusion can be resolved sooner.

Once their same-sex feelings have been identified and acknowledged, individuals face the next developmental task of the coming out stage: telling others. The function of this task is to begin self-acceptance. (The process of disclosure does not necessarily mean public disclosure; self-recognition and the ability to share this fact with someone else are more important: Weinberg & Williams, 1974.) Recognizing the need for external validation, individuals risk disclosure to others in hopes that they will not be rejected. This is a very critical point, for the confidants' reaction can have a powerful impact. If negative, it can confirm all the old negative impressions and can put a seal on a previous low self-concept. If positive, the reaction can start to counteract some of the old perceived negative feelings, permitting individuals to begin to accept their sexual feelings and increase their self-esteem. The existential crisis begins to resolve in a positive direction.

Research has indicated that commitment to a positive homosexual identity is related to healthy psychological adjustment (Hammersmith & Weinberg, 1973). In addition, Dank (1973) found that the frequency of feelings of guilt and loneliness, as well as the felt need for psychiatric or psychological consultations, decreased as the individual spent more time with their homosexual identity. But no one can develop self-concepts such as "accepted," "valued," or "worthwhile" all alone. One must take risks to gain acceptance from others. Therapists can be helpful in discussing with their clients situations and experiences that involve risk-taking but might lead to improved self-concepts. Because of the vulnerability of the self-concept during the coming out stage, it is important that clients choose carefully those people to whom they disclose their homosexual identity. Although there is never complete certainty, individuals can often predict how friends, work associates, and family members will respond. It is important that these first persons be people who will accept the client's homosexuality. Once an individual gains acceptance from a number of persons, it is much easier to withstand rejection, or even indirect rejection by society.

The perceived status of the person disclosed to greatly affects the possibility of self-concept change in the individual. For example, acceptance from a close friend will obviously mean more than a stranger's acceptance. Some people avoid telling their close (presumably heterosexual) friends and look for acceptance solely in other individuals who identify as gay or lesbian. This can be a missed opportunity. Since an individual's original conceptions of homosexuality are mostly negative, the perceived status of other homosexual people is usually not very high, and acceptance from them can have limited impact or value. Individuals with same-sex preferences can possibly benefit more from coming out to predominantly heterosexual significant others—if these are likely to be accepting.

Just as during the pre-coming out stage an individual may have reacted negatively to the prospect of being homosexual, it should not be surprising when a parent or family member to whom the individual discloses responds negatively. Once a parent or family member is made aware that their son, daughter, brother, sister, husband, or wife has homosexual feelings, it may take a long time before they can acknowledge, let alone accept, this fact. For many homosexual people today, the chances of an immediate positive parental or family response is minimal. This does not mean that they cannot be told, but each situation should be examined separately. Usually, telling parents and family members is most successful once homosexual individuals have already built up enough positive responses from significant others to be able to withstand a negative response from home. It is important that they persevere with their parents and family members through a grieving process. Parents will often grieve the loss of the image of their son or daughter as married and having children. Homosexual individuals should find encouragement in remembering that although it took them a long time fully to accept their homosexual selves, that possibility exists for their parents and other family members, too. More and more people today are able to support their homosexual sons, brothers, daughters, sisters, wives, and husbands. Full support and acceptance, however, are probably still the exception rather than the norm.

Exploration

This is the stage of experimenting with a new sexual identity. (Plummer, 1975, and Lee, 1977, call this stage *coming out*.) This is akin to the adolescent period of exploring and experimenting and is the first major experience of sexual and social activity with others. The opportunity to interact with others who are open and honest about their sexuality furthers the development of a positive self-image. Cass (1979) sees this process as first experiencing *identity tolerance*, which then leads to *identity acceptance*. Grace (Note 1) refers to *crashing out*, a vivid description of the awkwardness and intensity of this stage.

During exploration, individuals face several developmental tasks. The first is to develop interpersonal skills in order to meet and socialize with others with similar sexual interests. Having been socialized as heterosexual, individuals with homosexual preferences may lack the skills necessary to developing same-sex relationships.

Secondly, some individuals need to develop a sense of personal attractiveness and sexual competence. By becoming involved in sexual relationships that allow them to feel attractive to members of their own sex, they can develop a sense of mastery and competence with regard to being sexual with others. As clients begin sexual relationships, it can be helpful for the therapist to provide human sexuality education, and especially information on sexually transmitted diseases. Two resources may be useful to the therapist: *The Advocate Guide to Gay Health*, by Fenwick (1978); and *The Gay Health Guide*, by Rowan and Gillette (1978). (See Gonsiorek, 1980, for further discussion of health care issues.)

Thirdly, it is helpful to some individuals to recognize that their self-esteem is not based upon sexual conquest. Some people get locked into only seeing themselves in a sexual way. Consequently, society and the individuals themselves have difficulty understanding social and sexual exploration within a developmental framework and tend to view this behavior as immature, immoral, and merely promiscuous. The exploration stage can be better understood if it is recognized that individuals with same-sex preferences are usually not afforded an adolescence during their teenage years. Grace (Note 3) has suggested the concept of *developmental lag*, or the loss of chronological adolescence. Because most people in our society are encouraged to follow a heterosexual adolescence, homosexual individuals oftentimes do not enter their true adolescence until their chronological adolescence has long past. This can be very puzzling and frightening for men and women who have matured in other ways, e.g., intellectually, vocationally, and financially (Grace, Note 1).

Unfortunately, although researchers have documented the ages at which individuals pass through the stages of coming out, they have not always differentiated clearly between first same-sex experiences and those which are definitely understood to be homosexual. Kooden et al. (Note 2) did make this distinction. They found that first same-sex experiences for men occurred at age 15 and for women at age 20; however, males did not consider themselves to be homosexual until age 21 and the females until age 23. McDonald (Note 4) found similar results in his male sample: First same-sex experiences occurred at the average age of 15, and self-labeling at 19. While adolescent same-sex experiences are common (whether the adolescent later identifies as heterosexual or homosexual), these early sexual experiences are not clearly understood to be acts of homosexual expression. After self-labeling as homosexual, however, the meaning of these experiences is quite different.

The amount of sexual experimentation may differ between females and males. For example, Nuehring, Fein, and Tyler (1974) found that homosexual male college students engaged in more one-time sexual contact than homosexual female college students. It appears that sex-role identification in our culture has led to greater sexual exploration and experimentation among males than females. With changing sex-role stereotypes, however, there may now be more permission for females to engage in exploratory sexual behavior.

Grace (Note 3) urges therapists to help clients reconstruct their behavior as an important step in the clients' growth and development. Some individuals in the exploration stage of coming out may benefit from permission to explore and experiment with their sexual identity. They may need encouragement to meet others with similar feelings and interests, to feel physical attractions, and to act on those feelings. Many individuals feel sad that they have not received encouragement from others before, and anger that much of their suffering could have been avoided. Therapists can help clients to ventilate these emotions and to channel their feelings in constructive ways. The therapist might have the client carefully consider the methods for completing the developmental tasks of this stage.

Many individuals lose sight of their goals while in this adolescent adventure. Adolescents are known to act out, rebel, and act in a self-destructive manner; adolescents whose self-esteem is low have a greater tendency to engage in self-destructive behavior. Society accepts certain amounts of this behavior from chronological adolescents, but beyond certain limits these actions can be truly harmful. While many individuals with same-sex feelings may have been victimized by societal views of homosexuality, they can come to perpetuate that process of victimization themselves. Recognizing their behavior as self-abuse can prompt them to take more responsibility for their own actions. Many learn that the obstacles to successful identity adjustment lie within them, rather than in simply feeling sorry for themselves or in blaming others. The reality is that many bisexual or homosexual persons, because they never develop positive conceptions of themselves, never get beyond these barriers. Sometimes it can be helpful for the therapist to challenge such clients and put the responsibility on them to overcome these barriers.

One common stumbling block to completing the tasks of the exploration stage successfully is the use of intoxicating agents to anesthetize pain or to shore up a weak self-concept. For many, the use of alcohol and other drugs in socializing presents no problem. Others use drugs to cope with the existing pressures of this stage and to deal with the chronic emotional pain experienced since childhood. Drugs can become associated with sexual expression, leading to problems in the development of intimacy. If alcohol or other drugs are abused chronically, individuals can experience further developmental problems. Studies by Fifield, Latham, and Phillips (Note 5) and Lohrenz, Connelly, Coyne, and Spare (Note 6) conclude that at least 3 out of 10 members of the homosexual community have or will have serious problems with alcohol. These estimates are considerably higher than estimates for the general population. Therapists need to be keenly aware of this problem and look for signs of abuse.

Sexual activity can also be a "fix," a way to bolster a damaged self-concept and temporarily feel good about oneself. Although in many ways sex can be a healthy method of building self-esteem, if it is used compulsively this can interfere with the development of an integrated self-concept. Therapists should be aware of the many different ways that sex is used by men and women.

Grace (Note 1) suggests some other areas to investigate with the client who is at the exploration stage. These include experiences of physical and sexual assault, sexual dysfunction, how well the client can identify and meet her or his social and sexual needs with others, and how well the client can place sexual intimacy in perspective with other needs, such as for affection and support.

First Relationships

After a period of sexual and social experimentation, exploration can lose its intrigue, and needs for intimacy often become more important. The individual may yearn for a more stable, committed relationship and explore relationships that combine emotional and physical attraction.

The developmental task of this stage, then, is to learn how to function in a same-sex relationship, especially in a society where the norm is opposite-sex relationships. First relationships can be disastrous for many reasons. For one thing, there is a self-fulfilling prophecy: Individuals may not believe that a relationship can work. Lingering negative attitudes about homosexuality can sabotage efforts to establish or maintain a relationship. One stereotyped notion of a gay or lesbian relationship is that it is fraught with rejection and hurt, and never lasts long anyway.

First relationships are also characterized by intensity, possessiveness, and lack of trust. The intense need for intimacy can easily create desperation: As one client stated: "I don't care what it takes, I am going to make it work and last forever." This client, as do others, expects perfection and has expectations beyond what any other individual can provide. With these kinds of expectation it does not take much to dim hopes and dreams. One or both partners usually begin to feel cramped and confined in trying to live up to all the ideals. If they attempt to assert independence, this will be interpreted as a loss of love. In addition, these pressures and expectations can cause a loss of sexual interest, further "proof" of a failing love. A common result is increased interest in sexual activity outside the relationship. This interest then becomes the final proof of lack of love and the relationship ends. First relationships can end on a very turbulent note, sometimes causing one or both partners to return to the exploration stage, convinced that long-term relationships never develop. Some never try to develop a relationship again. Others keep trying and with each relationship learn more of the skills needed.

Homosexual people are at a distince disadvantage in learning these skills. There are very few role models to emulate; very few gay couples, for example, are depicted in books, films, or television. There is also a lack of public support for these relationships. Many couples do not have the acknowledgement and support of their friends and community. There are many more forces driving couples apart than together. Therapists can help by teaching couples how to communicate and how to get needed support.

One of the most common pitfalls of first relationships is the lack of consolidated self-identity. Relationships often begin before basic tasks of coming out and exploration are completed. In working with couples, therapists can be effective if they help the partners examine developmental needs and tasks still to be completed. Being in a relationship may put a strain on any individual's identity. After all, if one is in a couple, it is more difficult to conceal one's homosexual identity from friends, family, and society. If either of the partners has not worked through her or his coming-out issues successfully, being in a relationship can be very difficult. Some relationships end in order to relieve this pressure.

Integration

Finally, there is the stage of integration. To use Cass's (1979) terminology, individuals in this stage have moved from *identity confusion* through *identity comparison, tolerance, acceptance*, and *pride*, to *identity synthesis*. Here individuals incorporate their public and private identities into one self-image.

Grace (Note 1) calls this stage *self-definition* and *reintegration*. He describes it as open-ended, an ongoing process of development that will last for the rest of the person's life. New feelings about self will continue to emerge, new labels and concepts will be discovered, new social networks will be identified and explored, and new relationships and intimacies will be enjoyed. Grace also points out that individuals attend to different tasks of different stages as life situations demand: for example, returning to the stage of exploration and experimentation after a relationship has ended, or going back to coming out to share her or his homosexuality with a family member, employer, colleague, or friend.

Relationships in this stage, because they are often characterized by non-possessiveness, mutual trust, and freedom, can be more successful than first relationships. Individuals are better prepared psychologically for the natural and sometimes inevitable terminations of relationships. Terminations are seen in perspective and handled with normal grief reactions, rather than becoming psychologically crippling events. Many individuals in the integration stage choose not to be in long-time committed relationships.

Individuals in this stage continue to face other developmental tasks and phases of adulthood, such as midlife and old age. It is reasonable to assume that an individual with an integrated identity would have a better chance of handling these stages than individuals who are still working on earlier tasks of identity development.

Discussion

Although these stages fit into a linear progressive model of identity formation, it should not be assumed that the model fits reality exactly. As stated previously, McDonald (Note 4) found in his research that many individuals do not follow a predictable pattern, executing each stage in sequence. He concluded, "Although there appears to be an orderly developmental sequence that underlines the coming out process, vis-à-vis identity formation, not all gay persons move predictably from awareness of same-sex feelings through behavioral and eventual identity" (p. 11). The model described here, therefore, gives the therapist some understanding of the process of integrated identity formation—and nothing more.

This model also oversimplifies issues related to sexual orientation per se. For one thing, many individuals are not exclusively heterosexual or homosexual: Kinsey, Pomeroy and Martin (1948) found that sexual orientation is best described on a continuum. Sexual orientation can be described even better on continua of behavior, fantasy, and emotional attachments (Coleman, Note 7). Individuals with varying amounts of same-sex feelings, fantasies, and sexual behavior still seem to fit into this model. Secondly, Bell and Weinberg (1978) have identified many types of homosexual expression and life-style. (The developmental model described here might explain how an individual gets from one Bell and Weinberg category to another.) Thirdly, people are probably neither static nor easily classified by a Kinsey number, a Bell and Weinberg category, or one of the stages outlined in this paper. All of these classifications systems, however, are useful in approaching the complexity of sexual orientation, life-style, and psychological maturity.

There is a danger in any model that oversimplifies the developmental tasks that must be completed to assure an integrated identity. Rigid rules of conformity are sometimes dictated by the gay community, and these can be harmful to the many men and women who do not comply (De Cecco, Note 8). By the same token, therapists can develop their own rigid rules and give them as prescriptions to their clients. By appreciating the complexity and diversity of homosexual individuals and homosexual expression, therapists can avoid this trap.

This model does not presume that all individuals develop an integrated identity. Many never reach this stage. In McDonald's male sample, 15% stated they do not consider themselves to have a positive identity. These men had negative attitudes about homosexuality, participated infrequently in the gay subculture, did not disclose their affectional/sexual identity to others, and felt guilty, anxious, and ashamed about being homosexual. In Kooden et al.'s sample of gay psychologists, 8% of the females and 12% of the males stated they had not achieved a positive homosexual identity. The vast majority of this sample (as did the majority of McDonald's sample) reported having acquired a positive identity, but certainly neither sample is representative of the general homosexual population. Presumably, most respondents who would even consider completing the questionnaires used by these researchers, would have already developed some positive conceptions of themselves. Individuals in a pre-coming out stage, for example, would not have been visible to these researchers. There is no research that gives an idea of the number of individual's with same-sex preferences who are, or will remain, in a pre-coming out stage. Nor is there very good research on what percentage of individuals get stuck developmentally along the way. Studies by Kooden et al. and McDonald represent some of the first research that even attempts to answer these questions. Their studies suggest that developing an integrated identity takes between 10 and 14 years after the first awareness of same-sex feelings, and that some people move through these stages more rapidly than others whereas other people become stuck and never progress, or progress very slowly. Little is known as to why a person moves from stage to stage. De Monteflores and Schultz (1978) believe the changes are caused by "feedback loop." That is, a person's actions elicit certain societal responses, which the person then evaluates; in turn, their evaluation affects their decision on how to behave in the future.

The importance of societal attitudes in affecting positive identity development has been stressed by Humphreys (1979), Plummer (1975), Smith (1980), and Minton (Note 9). As Minton states: "Indeed it would seem that the gay liberation movement over the past decade has facilitated the process of acquiring a positive homosexual identity by providing more in the way of social support system than previously existed" (p. 12). Increasingly, men and women in contemporary America are acknowledging their homosexual feelings and developing an integrated and positive identity. This may be explained by the fact that American society is gradually changing its views of homosexuality; new societal attitudes allow for homosexual expression in more open and dignified ways. In the 1940s and 1950s, public homosexuality was relegated to seedy bars, dirty steam baths, and restrooms in bus stations. Today, there are many social, political, and religious organizations that legitimize same-sex behavior. New laws prohibit discrimination based on sexual orientation. The American Psychiatric and Psychological Associations no longer view homosexuality as an illness per se. Several corporations have personnel policies prohibiting discrimination in the hiring or firing of gay male or lesbian employees. This is not to say that anti-homosexual prejudice or discriminatory practices do not persist. They do, and they continue to make self-acceptance and coming out problematic. There are many casualties of these attitudes.

Not only society affects identity development; individuals and immediate families also have their influence. Families and individuals have the potential to offset general societal attitudes. Indeed, reactions by family and individuals could possibly have a greater impact than all the direct and indirect reactions of society. The therapist is in a particularly powerful position to affect the identity development and self-concept of the client. Because the therapist usually possesses high status in the eyes of the client, a positive response from the counselor could challenge the client's negative self-concept, counteracting society's remaining negative responses and supporting its newer, positive responses.

For the therapist to be accepting of homosexuality, therefore, and acquainted with the developmental concepts outlined in this paper, can be of great help to the client when the goals of therapy are to assist homosexual individuals to recognize and accept their sexual identity, improve interpersonal and social functioning, and value and integrate this identity while living in a predominately heterosexual society.

REFERENCE NOTES

1. Grace, J. *Coming out alive*. Paper presented at the Sixth Biennial Professional Symposium of the National Association of Social Workers, San Antonio, November 1979.

2. Kooden, J. D., Morin, S. F., Riddle, D. I., Rogers, M., Sang, B. E., & Strassburger, F. *Removing the stigma: Final report, Task Force on the Status of Lesbian and Gay Male Psychologists*. American Psychological Association, 1979.

3. Grace, J. *Gay despair and the loss of adolescence: A new perspective on same sex preference and self esteem*. Paper presented at the Fifth Biennial Professional Symposium of the National Association of Social Workers, San Diego, November 1977. (Available from author at Family and Children's Services, Minneapolis, Minnesota.)

4. McDonald, G. J. *Coming out: An empirical investigation of theoretical models*. Paper presented at the meeting of the Canadian Psychological Association, Calgary, June 1980.

5. Fifield, L., Latham, J. D. & Phillips, C. *Alcoholism in the gay community: The price of alienation, isolation, and oppression*. Sacramento: California Division of Substance Abuse, 1978.

6. Lohrenz, L. J., Connelly, J. C., Coyne, L., & Spare, K. E. *Alcohol abuse in several midwestern gay communities*. Unpublished paper, 1978.

7. Coleman, E. *Assessment of sexual orientation*. Paper presented at the meeting of the Canadian Psychological Associaton, Calgary, June 1980.

8. De Cecco, J. P. *Definition and meaning of sexual orientation*. Paper presented at the conference of the American Association for Sex Educators, Counselors and Therapists ("Making it gay"), Atlanta, January 1980.

9. Minton, H. L. *Homosexual identity formation: A dialectical perspective*. Paper presented at the meeting of the Canadian Psychological Association, Calgary, June 1980.

REFERENCES

Bell, A., & Weinberg, M. *Homosexualities: A study of diversity among men and women*. New York: Simon & Schuster, 1978.

Cass, V. C. Homosexual identity formation: A theoretical model. *Journal of Homosexuality*, 1979, *4*, 219-235.

Coleman, E. Toward a new model of treatment of homosexuality: A review. *Journal of Homosexuality*, 1978, *3*, 345-359.

Dank, B. M. Coming out in the gay world. *Psychiatry*, 1971, *34*, 180-197.

Dank, B. M. The development of a homosexual identity: Antecedents and consequences. Unpublished doctoral dissertation, University of Wisconsin, 1973.

De Monteflores, C., & Schultz, S. J. Coming out: Similarities and differences for lesbians and gay men. *Journal of Social Issues*, 1978. *34*, 180-197.

Erikson, E. H. The problem of ego identity. *Journal of the American Psychoanalytic Association*, 1956, *4*, 56-121.

Fenwick, R. D. *The Advocate guide to gay health*. New York: Dutton, 1978.

Fischer, P. *The gay mystique: The myth and reality of male homosexuality*. New York: Stein & Day, 1972.

Gonsiorek, J. Psychological adjustment and homosexuality. JSAS Catalog of Selected Documents in Psychology, 1977, *7*, 45. (Ms. No. 1478)

Gonsiorek, J. What health-care professionals need to know about gay men and lesbians. In M. Jospe, J. Nieberding, & B. D. Cohen (Eds.), *Psychological factors in health care: A practitioner's manual*. Lexington, MA: Lexington Books/D. C. Heath, 1980.

Hammersmith, S. K., & Weinberg, M. S. Homosexual identity: Commitment, adjustment, and significant others. *Sociometry*, 1973, *36*, 56-79.

Hencken, J. D., & O'Dowd, W. T. Coming out as an aspect of identity formation. *Gai Saber*, 1977, 18-22.

Humphreys, L. Exodus and identity: The emerging gay culture. In M. P. Levine (Ed.), *Gay men: The sociology of male homosexuality*. New York: Harper & Row, 1979.

Jay, K., & Young, A. (Eds.) *The gay report: Lesbians and gay men speak out about sexual experiences and lifestyles*. New York: Simon & Schuster, 1979.

Kinsey, A., Pomeroy, W., & Martin, C. *Sexual behavior in the human male*. Philadelphia: Saunders, 1948.

Lee, J. D. Going public: A study in the sociology of homosexual liberation. *Journal of Homosexuality*, 1977, *3*, 49-78.

Money, J. & Ehrharadt, A. A. *Man and woman, boy and girl: Differentiation and dimorphism of gender identity from conception to maturity*. Baltimore, MD: Johns Hopkins Press, 1972.

Nuehring, E., Fein, S. B., & Tyler, M. The gay college student: Perspectives for mental health professionals. *The Counseling Psychologist*, 1974, *4*, 64-72.

Plummer, K. *Sexual stigma: An interactionist account*. London: Rutledge & Kegan Paul, 1975.

Rowan, R. L., & Gillette, P. J. *The gay health guide*. Boston: Little, Brown and Company, 1978.

Smith, J. Ego-dystonic homosexuality. *Comprehensive Psychiatry*, 1980, *21*, 119-127.

Sullivan, H. S. *The interpersonal theory of psychiatry*. New York: Norton, 1953.

Weinberg, M. S., & Williams, C. S. *Male homosexuals: Their problems and adaptations*. New York: Oxford Press, 1974.

LESBIAN CLIENT–LESBIAN THERAPIST: OPPORTUNITIES AND CHALLENGES IN WORKING TOGETHER

Bronwyn D. Anthony, PhD

ABSTRACT. The author describes her experiences as an openly identified lesbian clinical psychologist working with 50 lesbians over the past 4 years in metropolitan Los Angeles. The women she has worked with have generally been Caucasian and middle-class; half were in their 30s, one quarter in their 20s, and another quarter over 40 years of age. The most common presenting problem is difficulty with a lover relationship—either in working out problems in the relationship or in dealing with the pain of separation. Single lesbians who wish to meet other lesbians encounter problems due to limited opportunities and undeveloped social skills for initiating contact. The relative lack of courtship rituals among lesbians sometimes results in mis-matched partners who then have great difficulty separating from each other. Fears of rejection and inflexible initiator roles during love-making lead to sexual difficulties. Therapeutic approaches to help lesbians with self-esteem issues and relationship concerns are suggested. Issues of transference and countertransference are discussed in light of the fairly common occurrence of client and therapist seeing each other outside of sessions at lesbian and gay community functions and events.

In this article I would like to contribute my own perspective to the growing body of literature about psychotherapy with lesbian women. I am a clinical psychologist in private practice in the Los Angeles area. Openly identified as a lesbian, I have worked with lesbians for the past 4 years. In addition I have seen heterosexual women, gay men, and heterosexual couples as clients. My

Bronwyn D. Anthony received her PhD from the Department of Counseling Psychology at the University of Southern California in 1975. A licensed clinical psychologist, she has been in private practice specializing in therapy with lesbians for the past four years. In 1978 she was co-chair of the fifth annual conference of the Gay Academic Union in Los Angeles and is currently co-coordinator of Women's Programs of the Gay Academic Union. This is her second year on the Steering Committee of the Association of Gay Psychologists for Women and Men. She has worked with other psychotherapists in presenting seminars and workshops to non-gay mental health professionals concerning the unique life-style issues of lesbians and gay males. She is a member of the American Psychological Association and the California State Psychological Association.

The author would like to acknowledge assistance from the following colleagues: Nancy Toder for her professional and editorial advice in shaping this manuscript; Bernice Augenbraun, Betty Berzon, Lynn Brooks, Teresa De Crescenzo, and Judith Goodman for sharing their experiences with lesbian clients.

approach is chiefly psychodynamic and insight-oriented, aimed at personal growth through increased awareness of self and understanding of others. While my particular life-style gives me an advantage in understanding and establishing rapport with my lesbian clients, I think that the most important factor in therapy with lesbian and gay clients is not the sexual orientation of the therapist but, rather, the consciousness of the therapist: She or he must be aware of and sensitive to the threats to self-esteem and self-actualization that arise from societal prejudice and the status of gay men and lesbians as oppressed minorities. (Woodman and Lenna's [1980] excellent introductory text for therapists provides perceptive guidelines for work with lesbian and gay clients.)

I hope to give the reader an idea of the diversity and commonality of the lebian experience as I have observed it, bearing in mind that when discussing a hidden minority, one runs the risk of being inaccurate in making generalizations (Morin, 1977). After describing my practice, I will discuss the concerns presented by clients as initial goals in therapy, as well as issues that unfold as therapy progresses. I will summarize approaches that have been particularly helpful and examine potential problem areas, such as transference and countertransference. Finally, I will offer indications for further research.

Characteristics of the Sample

Table 1 presents the demographic characteristics of the women in the sample. Approximately half of my lesbian clients are in their 30s, one quarter in their 20s, and another quarter 40 or older. Seven women have been married; three of these have children. Only two women currently attend religious services: one, a Catholic by up-bringing, attends services at the lesbian and gay temple with her Jewish lover; another woman attends a branch of Metropolitan Community Church, a nationwide church founded by Troy Perry, a gay preacher.

The work of Cass (1979) is useful in describing members of the sample in terms of their formation of a lesbian identity. Cass describes six stages in the process of positive identity formation for homosexual men and women. Her model, based on interpersonal congruency theory, assumes that the individual plays an active part in choosing to move from seeing the self as completely heterosexual (before Stage I) to developing an integrated, positive homosexual identity (Stage VI). The stages can be illustrated by typical self-statements such as these:

Stage I: Identity Confusion: "Maybe this information I'm hearing about homosexuals pertains to me."

Stage II: Identity Comparison: "My feelings of sexual attraction and affection for my own gender are different from my peers, family, and society at large."

Table 1

Characteristics of the Sample (N=50)

Age	f	%		Racial/Ethnic Background	f	%
25 and younger	4	8		Caucasian	45	90
26-29	12	24		Black	2	4
30-35	18	36		Mexican-American	2	4
36-39	6	12		Japanese	1	2
over 40	8	16				
over 50	2	4			50	100
	50	100				

Religious Background	f	%		Educational Background	f	%
Protestant	30	60		High school or less	6	12
Catholic	15	30		College student	5	10
Jewish	3	6		Some college	13	26
Christian Scientist	1	2		College degree	17	34
Buddhist	1	2		Master's degree	3	6
	50	100		Law degree	3	6
				Professional/trade school	3	6
					50	100

Current Occupation

	f	%			f	%
Accounting	2	4		Nursing	3	6
Arts	2	4		Sales	3	6
Clerical	3	6		Self-employed,		
Computer Sciences	4	8		owns own business	2	4
Construction	3	6		Service	5	10
Counselor	2	4		Student	3	6
Lawyer	3	6		Teaching	3	6
Managerial	8	16		Unemployed	1	2
Manufacturing	3	6			50	100

Stage III: Identity Tolerance: "I probably am a homosexual, and I'm not sure I like being one."

Stage IV: Identity Acceptance: "In relating to other lesbians and gays and learning more about the gay subculture I feel validated in my sexual orientation. I try to fit into the main culture by trying to pass, to limit contacts with heterosexuals, and to keep my personal life to myself."

Stage V: Identity Pride: "I feel a strong sense of belonging to the lesbian and gay community; I want to work toward its more equal treatment."

Stage VI: Identity Synthesis: "My homosexual identity is one very important aspect of myself, but not my total identity. I feel comfortable in both homosexual and heterosexual worlds."

No woman in the sample is in the stage of Identity Confusion. Two women are in the stage of Identity Comparison, feeling different from exclusively heterosexual women by virtue of having had female lovers (both lived with their lovers for over 3 years before separating from them), but wondering whether their feelings for these women constituted just a special instance or whether some other woman might interest them.

Ten women (20%), who have had limited exposure to the lesbian community, are in the stage of Identity Tolerance; all but one are in the process of moving toward Identity Acceptance. The woman who describes herself as barely tolerating her lesbian identity for the moment firmly believes the stereotype that lesbians cannot have stable relationships. She confirms this belief by her experiences at the lesbian bar she frequents, where there is a high proportion of single women. She does not give herself a chance to meet other lesbians, partly because her shyness and her dependence on alcohol make it difficult for her to imagine meeting people without a drink in her hand. Her belief also serves as a defense: She need not look at her own inability to form relationships so long as she thinks that no one can. The other women are moving toward Identity Acceptance by learning about opportunities for varied contact in the lesbian community; increasing their social skills; and overcoming fears about going to unfamiliar places, e.g., lesbian and gay conferences, religious services, political and educational activities, and other events, such as benefits and fundraisers.

The largest percentage, 30 women (60%) have accepted their identity (Stage IV), and several are moving toward Identity Pride. Three women are presently at Stage V (Identity Pride); two women have achieved Identity Synthesis (Stage IV). These women in Stages IV to VI have more frequent and regular contact with other lesbians, both in loosely formed social groups and in various lesbian and gay organizations in the Los Angeles area. It has been an almost universal experience for my clients that their positive feelings about being lesbian grew as they participated in activities of the lesbian and gay communities. Women have reported feeling elated at having the opportunity to be with so many other lesbians and gay men at some of the local workshops and conventions. "Imagine, this gay conference was held on my old college campus!" exclaimed one woman after her first conference.

The women in my sample are not very politically active, but are not so inactive as to be labelled apolitical, either. These women contrast to the majority of women in Peplau, Cochran, Rook and Padesky's (1978) study of lesbians, who were active in the lesbian feminist community. Approximately 15% (seven women) in this sample have been active in such feminist activities as campaigning for the Equal Rights Amendment, protesting violence against women in the media, and working to educate the public concerning lesbian and feminist issues. The majority gave time and money to defeat an initiative on the California state ballot in 1978, which would have denied the right of employment to teachers suspected of being gay.

Presenting Problems

Almost half of the clients in this sample first consulted me for difficulties in intimate relationships. They reported needing help in getting along with their current lover, in separating from a lover who had terminated the relationship, or in clarifying whether to remain in a relationship. A third of the women initially entered therapy because of difficulties in working through the grieving process necessary to letting go of a former relationship. A heterosexual person going through a divorce or break-up can rally the support of family, friends, and co-workers; emotional support has been non-existent for most lesbians who have hidden their identity from those around them. Often the presenting problem of a woman encountering relationship difficulties is anxiety or depression.

Two women have consulted me with primary complaints of overwhelming anxiety. One was anxious because of her newly acknowledged lesbian identity and was fearful about what this would mean in her life. The other suffered from incapacitating anxiety attacks, which may have been caused by her fear of being over-dependent on her lover of 9 years. Her anxiety attacks have abated as she acquires interests of her own and builds her social skills. For 10% of the clients, their reason for consulting me was the need to examine career indecision and self-defeating patterns in their careers.

Though a woman may bring a single issue to therapy, such as needing to get over the pain of separation from a lover, as our work progresses other issues emerge: the need to build self-esteem; the need to be more responsible with alcohol and drugs; the need to make appropriate career decisions; the need to have more control over compulsive habit patterns, such as overeating. Two of the three women who have children had difficulties in the areas of discipline and disclosure of their life-style to their children.

Problems and Issues of Single Lesbians

Finding and maintaining a satisfying love relationship is a primary goal for most people. For the single lesbian, finding love is difficult for several reasons. For one thing, the day-to-day need for secrecy and discretion is very great. The lesbian does not have the luxury of assuming that women who do not wear wedding bands are "eligible," as heterosexual men often do. Showing an interest in dating a woman who does not share her affectional and sexual orientation would result in disclosure of her lesbian identity, with almost inevitable embarrassment and possible serious repercussions. Therefore, several lesbian social institutions serve to help lesbians meet each other in less socially dangerous ways. The traditional place to meet other lesbians has been the lesbian bar. Abbot and Love (1972) described the dreariness and desperation of trying to find love in bars. More recently the lesbian and gay communities have evolved several other ways to establish meaningful contact (De Crescenzo & Fifield, 1979). These include political organizations, gay student unions at colleges and universities, educational and social groups, business and professional organizations, and religious organizations that address the needs of lesbians and gay men seeking spiritual community. Often an organization will serve an additional social function: for example the Gay Academic Union, which has educational goals and also provides a comfortable place for people in academic and professional fields.

Women who have not had favorable experiences at lesbian functions have usually had unrealistically high expectations. The terribly human hope of finding "Princess Charming" at the very first event has brought disappointment and kept some women from going to other events. Perhaps part of this discouragement and frustration arises from being overwhelmed and somewhat paralyzed in a unique social situation—unique in that finally the lesbian has permission to make contact with other women who might interest her without fear of approaching the wrong person. Or perhaps awkwardness stems from limited social skills. Because society dictates that women wait for invitations, women are generally unskilled in extending invitations. More specifically, learning how to court and be courted is not something lesbians learn easily while still in the closet. Even though a woman does not acknowledge her lesbian identity until she is 30, 40, or 60 years old, she may then go through a form of "adolescent dating anxiety." It is not uncommon for clients to remark, "But I don't know what to say!"; "How do I show interest and not seem pushy?"; "I couldn't stand it if she said she wasn't interested!"

This fear of rejection, which keeps women from making contact with each other, even operates in subtle ways within their relationships. Again because women have usually been the ones to say "yes" or "no," and rarely have been the ones to do the inviting, hearing "no" from another woman feels very threatening. As women become experienced in lesbian social contacts, invitations are more easily extended. A second difficulty arises with women who have trouble in saying "no." In fact, it is the ethos of some women never to say "no" to another woman, believing that since it takes so much courage to ask in the first place, it would be a great transgression to refuse a sister. Unable to decline a woman's invitation comfortably, these women sometimes send out signals of coldness. Often a woman "who can't say no" eventually causes herself and the other woman pain and embarrassment, when a clear "No, thank you, I'm not interested" would have been more appropriate.

Couple Concerns

Toder (1979) has outlined many of the challenges and opportunities that confront lesbian couples, such as different levels of openness and disclosure of lesbian identity to family, co-workers, and friends; handling money and decision-making; managing to share time and attention equitably with children and lovers; dangers of overloading the couple; and issues of monogamy.

The problems of the couples who have consulted me for couple counseling have centered around issues of commitment to each other and difficulties in communicating in non-hurtful, open ways. Often these women need help in clarifying what is good in their relationship and deciding whether or not to commit themselves to working on their relationship. Some seek assistance in ending their relationship in as non-punitive a manner as possible. Berzon's (1979) article has been very helpful reading for couples, as it encourages them to discover their unspoken contracts regarding the relationship. Sometimes individuals are very surprised at how inaccurate have been their assumptions about their partners' needs.

That lesbian couples have trouble communicating and require help in identifying their needs and the needs of their partners should come as no surprise; such difficulties plague all couples. Sometimes, however, their difficulties arise not from a deficiency in communication skills but, rather, from basic incompatibility. An inadequate process of partner selection is prevalent in the lesbian community. As Sang (1977) noted, lesbians choose one another as partners too quickly for fear that they will not find anyone else. Courtship is almost nonexistent in much of the lesbian community. Societal pressures may prompt women to "get serious" in order to "legitimatize" their sexual activity by being in a "committed relationship." It is a standing joke that "two lesbians meet and next week they move in together" precisely because it is such a common occurrence. For the majority of women, finding a partner as quickly as possible is serious business. As one woman put it, "I love to flirt, but I really can't do it with women because they take everything so seriously." Some of my work with lesbian couples is in helping them to let go of each other when they should not have become attached in the first place. With the usual romantic expectation that love will conquer all, two women may rush into living together, sometimes buying property together. After the initial "honeymoon" stage, they find they have little with which to build an enduring and satisfying relationship in the face of dissimilar values, incompatible personalities (once they let down their "good behavior"), and unwillingness to compromise.

Sexual Problems

A dangerous myth that prevents lesbians from enjoying their full potential for sexual satisfaction is the myth that women "naturally" know what pleases their female lovers. This myth reinforces one of the most common barriers to sexual satisfaction, i.e., open communication between partners before, during, and after lovemaking. Women interested in facilitating communication should read Toder's (1978) article, which is excellent in defining areas of sexual dysfunction, its causes, and treatment. Toder recommends how to seek competent professional help and suggests how couples and individuals can feel more comfortable and fulfilled in their sexuality. Barbach (1975); Heiman, Lo Piccolo, and Lo Piccolo (1976); and Kaplan (1974) are also useful reading.

Some women experience difficulties because of a tacit assignment of inflexible roles as to who initiates lovemaking and who accepts or declines this offer. Often the woman who is the accustomed initiator becomes extremely sensitive to the least hesitance on the part of her lover. The woman who is being approached may not know how much sexual interest her lover actually has, and, before she has a chance to respond, her lover has retreated after reading some "sign" connoting "lack of interest." Each woman needs to allow her lover the right to say "no" as well as "yes" without interpreting lack of sexual interest as being absolute rejection. This feeling of rejection then becomes a source of bad feelings about one's self. Women may unwittingly keep themselves from experiencing more sexual interest and excitement because of their readiness to "take no for an answer." The woman who is saying "no" may really want to be "persuaded," to be courted and wooed. If her partner does not understand that a "no" (and especially not the merest hint of "no") is not absolute, they both lose the opportunity to express their caring for each other sexually. Some women who are rejection-phobic after very few times of hearing or interpreting a "no" close themselves down and stop being initiators.

Open discussion by the lovers of their sexual fantasies can help to identify ways to heighten sexual arousal. Play and imagination can enrich lovemaking and may include a broad range of themes and scenarios. It may be that the woman who prefers to be "persuaded" has a favorite theme of "resisting/persisting." The use of fantasy may also help couples who have experienced a decline in the frequency or intensity of their lovemaking attributable to increasing feelings of familiarity or sisterliness. As a result of this developing family (sibling) feeling, which has its very real satisfactions in terms of intimacy and closeness, incest taboos might subconsciously keep women from expressing their sexual love together comfortably.

Another source of misunderstanding due to lack of communication can occur between two women when one has been lesbian for a long time and her lover has only recently come out. If she has had relations with men who moved quickly from kissing to intercourse, the inexperienced lesbian may feel hesitant to kiss or cuddle with her lover when she is not truly interested in sex. It takes a while for lovers to learn to read each other's "love signals," and for the woman who is used to "kisses = sex" to see that kissing can be an enjoyable, non-demanding affectionate activity.

Sometimes women become less sexually expressive with each other because they feel inadequate regarding their sexual attractiveness. They interpret a minor variation of desire in their partner as the end of all sexual interest and close themselves off in order to protect their own self-esteem. The belief that "lovemaking must be spontaneous" has left many women sexually isolated from each other, waiting for the "right moment" suddenly to happen. Women can talk with each other and take an active part in creating that right moment together by planning and looking forward to lovemaking.

Useful Approaches in Therapy with Lesbians

In reviewing my experiences with lesbian clients, I see them struggling with the same issues as other people: that is, how to live self-actualizing lives through gaining a strong sense of self-esteem, establishing and maintaining meaningful relationships, and pursuing satisfying work. There is no particular psychotherapy for lesbians but, rather, psychotherapy with women who happen to be lesbian. Because extremely negative views toward homosexuality are still all too common in our society, the lesbian's capacity for growth is continually challenged and thwarted (Riddle & Sang, 1978). Clinicians who would work with lesbians need to have an understanding of the consequences of social, political, and economic oppression upon the psychological development of their clients and be able to help them understand the ramifications of this oppression. Clark (1977) and Hall (1978) describe how negative social attitudes affect the self-esteem of gay men and lesbians.

I encourage my clients to read widely in the growing body of lesbian and gay literature—both non-fiction and fiction, for instance, M. Cruikshank (Ed.), *The Lesbian Path* (Angel Press, 1980); J. P. Stanley and S. J. Wolfe (Eds.), *The Coming Out Stories* (Persephone Press, 1980); and N. Toder, *Choices* (Persephone Press, 1980). Vida (1978), Berzon and Leighton (1979), and Woodman and Lenna (1980) provide useful starting bibliographies. I also urge my clients to participate in the varied activities of the lesbian community. Social skills can be improved by attending workshops; going through assertiveness training; reading books on shyness, such as Zimbardo (1977) and Girodo (1978); and rehearsing behavior in therapy sessions in order to overcome fears of initiating contact with other lesbians.

Transference and Countertransference

For me, therapy with lesbians is different from therapy with other women in that I am much more likely to see my lesbian clients outside of sessions than I am my other clients. It is easier to maintain a "sterile field," in terms of fostering an uncontaminated transference, when there is no outside contact with clients. While the ideal may be to have no outside contact, for gay and lesbian clients and therapists who participate in community activities this "ideal" is eventually impossible to maintain. I participate in and enjoy gay and lesbian community activities for the same reasons that I encourage my clients to participate: to enjoy feeling free from hiding and "passing"; to be with gay men and other lesbians in a relaxed atmosphere; and to enjoy the feeling of community and confirmation of my life-style. It is not uncommon for several of my clients to be at meetings which I chair, to attend workshops which I give, or to be at other events and places where I go.

This lack of anonymity does present some problems that must be dealt with in sessions before we meet "outside." We talk about possible feelings of awkwardness and agree to nod and greet each other and to move on to talk to others. Sometimes clients will introduce me to their friends or lovers, in which case I always leave it up to them to reveal or conceal our therapeutic relationship. I enjoy meeting the people in my clients' lives; furthermore, this makes it easier for me to understand a client in her social and interpersonal context.

There is a fine line between being friendly and being solicitous. I learned this early when I found myself being a little too helpful to a client who attended her first lesbian community function. I saw myself acting as a hostess, which was counter-therapeutic to her because she needed experiences in meeting people on her own. I realized my countertransference feelings of wanting her to have a good time at "my event," as this was a meeting of the Gay Academic Union of which I am a co-ordinator. I have to remember that I cannot meet a client's social needs, which are sometimes so glaringly evident to me when I notice her sitting by herself avoiding eye contact with anyone. I remind myself that to learn social skills takes time and patience—for both of us.

Some clients have expressed discomfort at seeing me at meetings and functions, feeling self-conscious and that they must be on their "good behavior." We examine their transference reactions and talk about the people in their lives of whom I may remind them. Depending upon the client and the stage of our work together, I may share that I, too, feel a little uncomfortable being in a quasi-social situation with her.

My awkwardness or self-consciousness may stem in part from my countertransference feelings of concern for the client—for her social ease—or may come from my concern about her opinion of me. There are advantages and disadvantages to my participation in the gay and lesbian activities my clients attend. There are the personal advantages to myself and my lover, as we enjoy going to events and functions and being active in the gay and lesbian community. The disadvantages exist more in the form of potential threats to the therapeutic relationship: The dynamics of transference may not fully develop (as far as my being a blank screen upon which the client projects feelings regarding important people in her life). Where there is minimal or no personal contact between therapist and client outside the session, the irrational reactions of the client can be ascribed more easily to inner dynamics. If reality input does occur outside the session at informal gatherings, meetings, or discos, analysis of transference becomes complicated, but not impossible. One client who felt very uncomfortable seeing me at a meeting was able to use her reaction to examine her relationship with her mother in more immediate ways than before.

Within the context of the corrective emotional experience of therapy, there is opportunity for client growth through modeling. As the therapist accepts and affirms her positive lesbian identity, she becomes a role model for her client to value and accept her own lesbian identity. Participation in gay and lesbian social events is a concrete way of fostering and expressing this positive view of self. For some clients, however, who have had long struggles acknowledging their lesbian feelings to themselves and finding fulfilling ways to express their affectional and sexual natures, the damage due to internalized homophobia may be extensive (Clark, 1977; Weinberg, 1973). For such a lesbian, already burdened by society's negative judgements, her struggle toward self-acceptance must not inadvertently be made still more difficult by a therapist who overlooks the client's need to go at her own pace in overcoming feelings of self-hatred and alienation. The transference danger here is the client's thinking that she must feel better about herself than she actually does to please her therapist, whom she sees as so positively engaged in the lesbian community. The counter-transference problem is in a therapist colluding with this short-circuited path to lesbian identity acceptance and pride.

It sometimes happens that the client idealizes her therapist to such an extent that she is unable to tolerate less than "model" behavior from her. Some of my colleagues who have separated from their lovers have been bitterly berated by lesbian clients, who were deeply disappointed and angered that their therapist could not maintain her own lover relationship.

Another issue when a lesbian works with a lesbian therapist is that of erotic transference. Singer (1965) indicated the ways in which transference may be a form of resistance to movement in therapy. It has been my experience and that of my colleagues, however, that the erotic transference feelings of lesbian clients rarely result in a therapeutic impasse. In the few instances where impasse does occur, a woman's alienation from the lesbian community and her undeveloped ability to accept her lesbian identity cause her to focus on her therapist as the only "good lesbian," the only one "worthy" of her love, and the only safe object of her affection. With lesbians striving to understand themselves as women loving women, lesbian therapists need to be prepared for a sometimes prolonged struggle with erotic transference. It is especially important for a woman who has never expressed loving feelings for and to another woman not to be silenced with an interpretation or confrontation before she has had a chance to understand and accept her feelings on her own terms and in her own time.

Complications arising from contact outside of therapy sessions occur in group therapy as well. Presently seven women are working with me in group therapy. Early in the group, which has been meeting for 9 months, we discussed members getting together outside the group in order to support and encourage each other as they make their first tentative excursions to lesbian discos, workshops, and other events. Although my initial position was to discourage outside contact, it became apparent that the usual injunction that group therapy members not see each other outside of the therapy group could not be strictly applied. In the heterosexual world it is easier for group members to maintain distance as they pursue social contacts in different parts of the city. Although the lesbian and gay communities have evolved many opportunities for social interaction, these are finite, and avoiding people one knows becomes artificial and difficult to do.

We have a group rule that whatever goes on outside of group between group members must be brought to the group to avoid forming outside alliances that might interfere with honest communication within the group. So far "field trips" (as members call their planned activities) have not caused problems, and several members maintain that such social support has been very helpful to them in becoming more socially independent. One woman compares having some group members present at a bar or disco to having a "base camp" for her social exploration. Knowing that she would be meeting people she knew when going to a place for the first time gave her courage to go and relax enough to enjoy herself.

Conclusion

I have examined some of the issues lesbians face in establishing and maintaining lover relationships; have indicated useful approaches to helping them in their personal growth; and have discussed some problems in the area of transference and countertransference arising when therapist and client meet outside therapy sessions. Many more areas need to be explored, however. Diamond and Wilsnack (1978) have contributed to our understanding of the problems of alcoholism among lesbians, but more research is required to extend their tentative conclusions regarding treatment. Research and exploration are also needed in these areas: special problems of minority-group lesbians, adolescent lesbians, disabled lesbians, and older lesbians; bereavement among lesbians; unique issues of lesbians in areas of parenting (children from a previous relationship, or those the lesbian couple or individual has chosen to have through adoption or artificial insemination); and problems lesbians encounter in male-dominated fields where the lesbians does not have "a man in her life" to keep her co-workers at some distance, particularly in jobs non-traditional for women.

REFERENCES

Abbot, S., & Love, B. *Sappho was a right-on woman: A liberated view of lesbianism*. New York: Stein and Day, 1972.

Barbach, L. G. *For yourself*. New York: Doubleday & Co., 1975.

Berzon, B. Achieving success as a gay couple. In B. Berzon & R. Leighton (Eds.), *Positively gay*. Millbrae, CA: Celestial Arts, 1979.

Berzon, B., & Leighton, R. (Eds.). *Positively gay*. Millbrae, CA: Celestial Arts, 1979.

Cass, V. C. Homosexual identity formation: A theoretical model. *Journal of Homosexuality*, 1979, *4*, 219-235.

Clark, D. *Loving someone gay*. Millbrae, CA: Celestial Arts, 1977.

De Crescenzo, T. & Fifield, L. The changing lesbian social scene. In B. Berzon & R. Leighton (Eds.), *Positively gay*. Millbrae, CA: Celestial Arts, 1979.

Diamond, D., & Wilsnack, S. C. Alcohol abuse among lesbians: A descriptive study. *Journal of Homosexuality*, 1978, *4*, 123-142.

Girodo, M. *Shy? You don't have to be*. New York: Pocket Books, 1978.

Hall, M. Lesbian families: Cultural and clinical issues. *Social Work*, 1978, *23*, 380-385.

Heiman, J., Lo Piccolo, L., & Lo Piccolo, J. *Becoming orgasmic: A sexual growth program for women*. Englewood Cliffs, NJ: Prentice-Hall, 1976.

Kaplan, H. S. *The new sex therapy*. New York: Quadrangle Books, 1974.

Morin, S. F. Heterosexual bias in psychological research on lesbianism and male homosexuality. *American Psychologist*, 1977 (August), 626-637.

Peplau, L. A., Cochran, S., Rook, K., & Padesky, C. Loving women: Attachment and autonomy in lesbian relationships. *Journal of Social Issues*, 1978, *34*(3), 7-27.

Riddle, D. I., & Sang, B. Psychotherapy with lesbians. *Journal of Social Issues*, 1978, *34*(3), 84-100.

Sang, B. Psychotherapy with lesbians: Some observations and tentative generalizations. In D. K. Carter & E. I. Rawlings (Eds.), *Psychotherapy for women: Treatment toward equality*. Springfield, IL: Charles C. Thomas, 1977.

Singer, E. *Key concepts in psychotherapy*. New York: Basic Books, 1965.

Toder, N. Sexual problems of lesbians. In G. Vida (Ed.), *Our right to love: A lesbian resource book*. Englewood Cliffs, NJ: Prentice-Hall, 1978.

Toder, N. Lesbian couples: Special issues. In B. Berzon & R. Leighton (Eds.), *Positively gay*. Millbrae, CA: Celestial Arts, 1979.

Vida, G. (Ed.), *Our right to love: A lesbian resource book*. Englewood Cliffs, NJ: Prentice-Hall, 1978.

Weinberg, G. *Society and the healthy homosexual.*. Garden City, NJ: Anchor Books, 1973.

Woodman, N. J., & Lenna, H. R. *Counseling with gay men and women: A guide for facilitating positive lifestyles*. San Francisco: Jossey-Bass, 1980.

Zimbardo, P. *Shyness: What it is and what to do about it*. Reading, MA: Addison-Wesley, 1977.

PSYCHOTHERAPEUTIC IMPLICATIONS OF INTERNALIZED HOMOPHOBIA IN GAY MEN

Alan K. Malyon, PhD

ABSTRACT. This article describes a psychodynamic model of affirmative psychotherapy for gay men. Special note is made of the clinical issues which arise from antihomosexual attitudes that bias the psychological development of the homosexual male. In particular, the way in which identity formation is affected by heterosexual socialization is discussed. The psychotherapeutic implications associated with these developmental complications are indicated.

Certain aspects of the prevailing cultural ethos have profound developmental consequences for most gay men. In particular, the emphatic antipathy which distinguishes contemporary social attitudes toward homosexuality tends to bias the socialization process and, in turn, the intrapsychic development of gay men. This article outlines some of the specific psychological effects of biased socialization and notes several of the clinical issues and psychotherapeutic implications arising from these developmental variations.

This report is based upon research and clinical data derived from samples of gay men only. For this reason it would not be prudent to generalize these findings to women. Careful extrapolation would, doubtless, lead to meaningful parallels, but the danger of misrepresenting the developmental differences between lesbians and gay men is too great to warrant such inductive inferences at this time.

The Socialization of the Homosexual Male

Socialization can be described as the internalization of the values, symbols, regulations, beliefs, and attitudes which are inherent to the developmental

Dr. Malyon is an assistant clinical professor of psychology in the Department of Psychiatry and Biobehavioral Medicine, Neuropsychiatric Institute, University of California, Los Angeles, and is a clinical supervisor for the Psychology Clinic, Department of Psychology, University of California, Los Angeles. Reprint requests should be addressed to Alan K. Malyon, PhD, University of California, Los Angeles, Psychology Clinic, 2191 Franz Hall, 405 Hilgard, Los Angeles, California 90024. The author wishes to express deepest gratitude to Allen Chivens for his help in preparing this paper.

milieu (Schafer, 1968). Since homophobic beliefs are a ubiquitous aspect of contemporary social mores and cultural attitudes (Weinberg, 1972), the socialization of the incipient homosexual individual nearly always involves an internalization of the mythology and opprobrium which characterize current social attitudes toward homosexuality.

Internalized homophobic content becomes an aspect of the ego, functioning as both an unconscious introject, and as a conscious system of attitudes and accompanying affects. As a component of the ego, it influences identity formation, self-esteem, the elaboration of defenses, patterns of cognition, psychological integrity, and object relations. Homophobic incorporations also embellish superego functioning and, in this way, contribute to a propensity for guilt and intropunitiveness among homosexual males.

The psychological processes which comprise internalization become differentiated and operational during the pre-genital era. According to Money (1963), the precursors of sexual orientation are also established by the end of latency. It is not until the adolescent era, however, that distinct and conscious homosexual desires become manifest and that the potential for homosexual self-recognition evolves. Thus, the subjective realization of homoerotic motivation is preceded by the introjection of a miasmic anti-homosexual bias. This sequence of developmental events contaminates the process of adolescent identity formation. The internalization of homophobic partiality renders homosexual desire unacceptable even before the process of attribution begins. As a result, the maturation of erotic and intimate capacities is confounded by a socialized predisposition which makes them ego alien and militates against their integration. This, in turn, precludes a satisfactory resolution of the developmental conflicts which define psychological adolescence.

The primary psychological task of adolescence is that of identity formation (Erickson, 1950). Identity develops in an interpersonal context. Therefore, the adolescent requires extensive opportunities to engage in experimental psychosocial behavior. Primitive and undifferentiated primary ties of dependency with parents must be transformed, through maturation and experience, into the capacity for erotized and empathic attachments to peers. Under optimum psychological and social conditions the evolution of identity, with concomitant changes in the dynamics and content of object relations, eventuates in the capacity for mature intimacy.

The peer group provides the primary social context for this process. Peer-group validation is of fundamental importance in the development of autonomy and self-esteem. Conformity brings acceptance, while differences, especially stigmatized divergences, result in alienation. To consolidate an identity there must be the freedom to engage in peer interactions that incorporate the expression of needs, values, interests, and proclivities. In other words, adolescent object relations should nurture the development of all adaptive aspects of the self. This ideal is, of course, never fully realized for any adolescent, but self-actualization and psychological integrity are even more severely inhibited for the homosexual adolescent.

Peer group norms and prevailing social attitudes are not compatible with the fixation of same-sex erotic and intimate capacities, especially during the latter aspects of the adolescent era. Thus, the already complex developmental task of forming an identity is further complicated for the homosexual adolescent by the conflict between cultural expectations and deviant psychosexual promptings. Disparate object choice, then, leads to atypical adaptational demands. Homo-erotic ontogeny is shaped by a heterosexual socialization process. As a result, the adolescent psychosocial and ideational environment is not conducive to psychosexual congruency for the incipient homosexual. Instead, the adolescing homosexual is encouraged to obtain peer-group validation through the development of a false identity; that is, by the suppression of homoerotic promptings and the elaboration of a heterosexual persona.

The intrapsychic consequences of this adaptation are varied and unfortunate. The most likely developmental outcome is an interruption (sometimes temporary, but often lasting a decade or more) of the process of identity formation and epigenesis of ego integrity. Conformity to role expectations consistent with the prevailing heterosexual standard precludes psychological integrity. The ego must necessarily be fragmented and those parts that significantly define the self-concept, and furnish the basis for intimacy, must be suppressed or denied. This adaptation is inherently conflictive. As a result, psychological defenses become highly elaborated to bind the accompanying chronic anxiety and to maintain a tenuous and brittle false identity.

Other aspects of ego development may continue, but the rejection of homosexual proclivities truncates the process of total identity formation. It is resumed whenever conflicts over homosexual urges change or diminish enough to allow for the acknowledgement and partial acceptance of same-sex desires, a process known as "coming out". Coming out is the precursor to a re-emergence of many of the issues, intrapsychic conflicts, and psychological resources which were pre-eminent during primary adolescence. This rather unique developmental pattern is an aspect of the process of identity formation (Cass, 1979). Thus, psychological differentiation and identity consolidation is a bi-phasic process for most gay males (Malyon, 1981; in press). During the second epoch of identity formation, previous conflicts are attenuated and the possibility of further ego development is enhanced. With the completion of this second phase, the natural vicissitudes of the ego are restored and the maturation of intimate capacities can proceed, less impeded by developmental fixation and psychological inhibition.

The foregoing has been a summary of certain of the possible consequences of biased socialization. It should not be assumed, however, that all homosexual males are affected to the same degree or in the same way by the cultural influences described. The developmental significance of any particular aspect of the socialization experience is determined by the special vulnerabilities, needs, and defensive strategies, of each individual. Furthermore, no two people function in exactly the same developmental context. Thus, not every homosexual male becomes symptomatic. Nevertheless, the psychological and social phenomena described above can be very potent, and their psychosocial consequences must be appreciated in the assessment and treatment of gay males who do enter psychotherapy.

Clinical Issues and Psychotherapeutic Guidelines

Several diagnostic and clinical considerations are implied by the developmental circumstances just outlined. Certain of these will be noted in the discussion of treatment which follows. A gay-affirmative point-of-view forms the clinical perspective for the psychotherapeutic guidelines to be described. This theoretical disposition regards homosexuality as a non-pathological human potential. The goals of gay-affirmative psychotherapy are similar to those of most traditional approaches to psychological treatment and include both conflict resolution and self-actualization. But while the traditional goal of psychotherapy with homosexual males has been conversion (to heterosexuality), gay-affirmative strategies regard fixed homoerotic predilections as sexual and affectional capacities which are to be valued and facilitated. In addition, gay-affirmative approaches to therapy appreciate the psychological effects of the developmental anomalies noted above. Thus, one of the primary objectives of gay-affirmative psychotherapy is to provide corrective experiences to ameliorate the consequences of biased socialization. Gay-affirmative psychotherapy, however, is not reductionistic: It does not regard homophobia as the singular pathogenic element in the evolution of symptomatic conditions among gay men. Instead, gay-affirmative approaches to psychotherapy consider oppression and anti-homosexual attitudes to be just two of the many factors that influence the process of personality formation and psychological adaptation.

The following description assumes a thorough set of clinical skills, a basic knowledge of psychodynamic principles, and a sophisticated understanding of the intrapsychic and behavioral consequences of atypical socialization. This is not a prescription for how to do psychotherapy. Instead, it is a frame of reference for the accomplished clinician.

The approach to gay-affirmative psychotherapy presented here has a psychodynamic orientation. It conceives of psychotherapy as a developmental process which aims at facilitating both conflict resolution and self-actualization. The therapeutic process consists of four stages, as follows: (1) the phase devoted to building the *therapeutic alliance,* (2) the *analytic phase,* (3) the *identity consolidation phase*, and (4) the *existential phase*. The basic framework for this model is derived from Wolman's (1975) description of "interactional psychotherapy", although the phases outlined here are significantly modified to fit the special psychotherapeutic needs of the homosexual male.

Before discussing each phase of the model, it is necessary to note that conflict resolution is never complete, nor is psychological growth a process with finite limits. Dynamic and reconstructive psychotherapy always consists of several phases, whether or not they are formally articulated. The phases overlap each other; at any point in the treatment process there may be a return to clinical or therapeutic issues from an earlier phase. As increasing levels of psychological reorganization and integration are achieved, there is often greater access to repressed material and an accompanying availability of additional ego strengths and resources which would enhance problem resolution and self-actualization.

The phases to be described below, then, are somewhat reified and artificial. They do, however, represent the typical issues that must be resolved in psychotherapy with homosexual men. In addition, they serve as a general guide for the sequence of treatment.

Phase One

The initial objective for any kind of psychological treatment is to establish an effective therapeutic rapport. The first phase of treatment, then, must be concerned with promoting trust and establishing the responsibilities of both client and therapist. Most often, a non-directive or client-centered approach can achieve this. The person entering therapy must be helped to regard the therapist as a person of special knowledge, competence, and genuine goodwill who will come to care about and help the client.

When building rapport, the issue of values must be addressed, since these have such a profound influence on the therapeutic process. In the past, psychotherapy was regarded as value-free; it is no longer presumed to be so (Roman, Charles, & Karasu, 1978). Values and attitudes influence virtually every aspect of the treatment process, from *what* is interpreted to *how* it is interpreted. They determine what is considered a problem and can even have a bearing on how well the therapist likes the patient. For this reason, it is important for the therapist to consider which of her or his own values should be discussed with the client during the first phase of treatment. For example, with gay male clients, it is usually prudent for clinicians to indicate their therapeutic bias with respect to homosexuality and to discuss how this bias will influence the content and goals of therapy. Open discussion can protect against iatrogenic potentiation of internalized homophobic material.

The issue of "therapist disclosure" must also be pondered carefully during the first phase of treatment. If the clinician is gay, it is often of therapeutic value to reveal this early in the treatment process in order to help assure the client that the details of his homosexual feelings and behavior will be understood and accepted by the therapist. In addition, this revelation increases the likelihood that the therapist will, at some point, become the focus for projection, displacement, and stereotypical perceptions. This therapeutic augmentation of internalized anti-homosexual attitudes creates an opportunity for interpretation, cathartic attenuation, and cognitive reworking of these attitudes and introjects. Following the resolution of homoerotic conflicts, the known homosexual orientation of the therapist often helps the client to model attitudes and adaptations consistent with psychological integration and a positive gay identity. There are instances when early therapist disclosure would be counter-therapeutic, particularly if the client has not yet come out and is deeply conflicted over his homoerotic promptings. In this instance, therapist disclosure might be too threatening to the client and result in a premature termination of treatment.

The first phase of psychotherapy with gay men should not be limited to building the therapeutic alliance. It is also the most propitious time for information gathering and assessment. In taking a developmental history, it is useful to focus on the evolution of homosexual self-awareness and, particularly, on the conflicts, self-perceptions, and adaptations associated with it. Current attitudes and adjustments to homosexuality also need to be assessed. It is especially important to identify the presence and nature of internalized homophobia and its derivatives, both conscious and unconscious.

Since the personality is a dynamic system, any developmental input, such as homophobia, has diffuse intrapsychic consequences. That is, exogenous homophobia, once internalized, usually functions as an unconscious introject with elaborations throughout the personality structure. Its very tenacity and pervasiveness, however, should be a caveat to the clinician. It is tempting to deal with the bewildering complexity and innate imperviousness of the unconscious by relying on a single dynamic or pathogenic explanation. Therefore, the reductionistic inclinations of the therapist must be mediated by an astute appreciation of the over-determined nature of *all* psychological states and adaptations. During the early stages of treatment the task is more one of assessment than intervention. Therefore, it behooves the therapist to restrict diagnostic formulations to hypotheses, and to resist attributing too much psychological determination to oppression. The initial diagnostic aim should be to delineate a tentative developmental profile that gives credence to the full range of formative variables.

Phase Two

The analytic phase of therapy is devoted to conflict resolution and cognitive re-structuring (Lazarus, 1974). The client-therapist relationship is the generic element of this stage of treatment. As Silverman (1974) points out, the transference is a fundamentally important aspect of all forms of psychotherapy. The repeatedly tested empathic psychotherapeutic relationship encourages an attenuation of defensive operations. This allows for the emergence of repressed material, including forbidden impulses, infantile fantasies, and irrational beliefs.

This is an insight-oriented phase of therapy; its purpose is to assist the client in relating to the unconscious in a conscious way. Thus, the primary form of intervention is interpretation, and the basic goal is an attenuation of the conflicts and neurotic adaptations derived from earlier pathogenic experiences. There is a particular focus on homophobia, the purpose being to infer unconscious homophobic content and to identify conscious homophobic ideation. The object is to shift the ego-dystonic focus from homosexuality to homophobia.

Conscious attitudes are rather easily modified. Repressed anti-homosexual material, however, is much more difficult to apprehend and change. The derivatives, elaborations, and developmental consequences of introjected homophobia are as pernicious as the original internalized attitudes. Therefore, an important goal of this stage of psychotherapy is to illuminate the many complex secondary and tertiary adaptations which are abstractions of homophobia; for example, low self-esteem, lack of psychological congruity and integration, overly embellished and ossified defenses, problems with intimacy, and a particular vulnerability to depression.

The initial awareness of more-than-incidental homosexual promptings usually has profound psychological implications. It is nearly always accompanied by feelings of intense anxiety, despair, and intrapsychic conflict. This affective response brings about a dramatic potentiation of suppressive defenses. Conflict over burgeoning homosexual self-awareness also activates the process of stimulus generalization. This augments a gradual stigmatization of all intense affective phenomena (Clark, 1977), prompting an even more profound elaboration of the already established defensive motif (suppression, denial, and overcompensation). This, in turn, leads to an inhibition and compartmentalization of all erotized impulses. This psychological fragmentation of sexual and affectional proclivities interferes with the developmental process; that is, an integrated and positive identity cannot be established so long as erotized desires and capacities are repugnant and, consequently, estranged. In the absence of identity consolidation, further development cannot take adequate advantage of the maturation of more differentiated and complex psychological and interpersonal capacities. Thus, one of the more significant outcomes of homophobic bias is an arrest of the developmental process. The other major consequence is a contamination of self-concept.

The analytic phase of psychotherapy addresses both of these aberrant conditions. The transference situation is particularly well-suited for reworking biased socialization experiences and consequent developmental variations. The empathic aspects of this special relationship encourage the abreactive release and affective reworking of the exquisite psychological pain associated with the profound alienation, loneliness and self-contempt engendered by the homophobic ethos. Alexander and French (1946) and Ferenzi and Rank (1925) emphasized that reparative success often can be accomplished only through the emotional relationship with the therapist. For example, the therapist's unconditional acceptance of homoerotic capacities is a necessary countervalence for earlier anti-homosexual cultural conditioning. In turn, this acceptance enhances the possibility for a cognitive re-structuring (Lazarus, 1974) of the ideas, perceptions, and beliefs which form the self-concept. Through the use of direct confrontation, interpretation, and the principles of reinforcement, fixed homophobic ideation and homosexual conflicts can be modified. In addition, if the therapist is gay and has worked through her or his own homophobic prejudice and self-contempt, a uniquely auspicious opportunity exists for utilizing the client's capacities for identification, introjection, and modeling to modify his self-perceptions and the symbolic meaning he attributes to homosexual desire. Modeling is one of the active and empirically verifiable factors in effective psychotherapy (Bandura, 1969). The gay clinician is in a position to provide a counter-stereotypic model for the homosexual client.

Phase Three

This period of psychotherapy is distinguished by its concern with identity consolidation (viz., a gay identity) and with facilitating the capacity for intimacy. Although the therapeutic goals are quite definite, this is the least discrete stage of the treatment process, for identity formation is a rather continuous process, occurring over the duration of psychotherapy and beyond. Nevertheless, it involves a special constellation of issues and conflicts in gay-affirmative psychotherapy. As already noted, biased socialization complicates identity formation and the development of intimate capacities for homosexual men. Specifically, that aspect of ego development which has to do with the resolution of identity issues is interrupted during primary adolescence and is resumed only after homosexual self-disclosure occurs. The bi-phasic process is a developmental variation which creates certain unique diagnostic and treatment issues in clinical work with gay men.

Gay-affirmative psychotherapy places a special emphasis on the issues associated with second-epoch adolescence. The goal is to aid in the development of an integrated, congruent, and positive identity. In addition, efforts are made to analyze and modify the defensive operations that were constructed to suppress unwanted sexual and affectional impulses. The purposes is to make the defenses less inclusive and tropistic.

It is uncomfortable and confusing to experience the full press of adolescent needs and impulses as an adult. As a result, psychotherapy can be especially poignant during this era. The adolescing adult often needs guidance in selecting and understanding those experiences which will lead to accurate self-definition and positive self-acceptance. Psychotherapy provides support which helps to soothe the internal chaos experienced at this stage; astute interpretations give meaning and direction that attenuate the bewilderment.

In order for the individual to benefit fully from this second phase of primary identity formation, insight must accompany impulse and behavior. To this end, the analytic and cognitive aspects of psychotherapy are of considerable utility to the homosexual male who has just begun to establish a gay identity. Knowledgeable and sensitive interventions can mitigate the subjective bias created by internalized homophobia. Even after conscious attitudes have changed, however, the unconscious homophobic lament continues to influence interpretive processes. As a result, there is a proclivity for evaluating homoerotic experiences in a negative or self-denigrating manner. Effective therapeutic correctives can change this.

Once a mature and realistic identity—a positive gay identity—has been established, the client enters the stage of ego development which is concerned with intimacy (Erickson, 1950). Intimacy is more complicated for the homosexual male than for the heterosexual. Anti-homosexual attitudes (both exogenous and internalized), masculine sex-role stereotypy and conditioning, insufficient erotized and affectional pre-intimacy involvements with other males, and the relative unavailability of models of male intimacy, all interfere with the development of the capacity for long-term and mutually satisfying love relationships among gay men. Thus, psychotherapeutic enhancement of this capacity is often beneficial. For example, it is sometimes necessary that conflict resolution, de-conditioning, and cognitive re-structuring precede intimate involvement. The transference relationship has a special efficacy in this regard. It provides an affective interpersonal milieu in which the homophobic and neurotic misperceptions and conflicts that are sometimes stimulated by intense emotional involvement can be made manifest and transformed.

The issue of intimacy presents another clinical situation where therapeutic advantages can be derived from the clinician being of the same sexual orientation as the patient. The gay male clinician, because he is both male and homosexual, is likely to elicit intense projection, homophobic hostility, and sex-role identity conflicts in the gay male client. In general, client-therapist similarities invite the very distortions and conflicts which are likely to operate in an empathic and erotized relationship with a male lover.

It is not true, however, that competent psychotherapy with homosexual men can only be conducted by gay male clinicians. Other therapist variables can outweigh biological sex and sexual orientation in successful treatment outcomes. Nevertheless, a gay male clinician working with a gay male client can provide important opportunities for enhancing therapeutic gains.

Phase Four

During the last stage of psychodynamic gay-affirmative psychotherapy the primary issues are existential: The task is to establish a sense of personal meaning and purpose. Although identity problems are again paramount, this psychological era involves in addition issues that transcend sexual orientation and object relations. At the same time, homosexuality, by virtue of its cultural stigmatization, influences the question of personal meaning and the options available for establishing a sense of purpose and significance to life. Once again, homophobic bias influences individual psychological development.

This existential phase of psychotherapy usually follows the resolution of more primitive intrapsychic conflicts and the differentiation of identity. It deals with developmental issues which are more evident once psychological maturity has been achieved. These issues usually become most critical when the client is in his 40s and 50s, for only after pre-genital and adolescent fixations have been attenuated do existential questions tend to arise.

In Erikson's model of ego epigenesis the psychological conflicts which are addressed during this psychotherapeutic era are generativity (as opposed to self-absorption) and ego integrity (as opposed to despair). These are post-narcissistic concerns and have to do with matters of productivity, creativity, and social responsibility—with the search for personal meaning, dignity, and integrity in one's life.

This phase of psychotherapy is a psychological/philosophical/spiritual state of inquiry. The resolution of the "significance dilemma" is associated with making a conscious and freewill commitment to those values, priorities, activities, or goals which one experiences as subjectively meaningful. The culture provides the heterosexual individual a wide range of well-understood and highly valued "purposes" for life. These cultural guidelines, however, tend to be exclusively heterosexual in nature. Traditions such as the nuclear family, orthodox religious beliefs, rigid sex-role models, and conservative morality are not relevant reference points for most adult gay males in search of personal meaning and integrity. As a result, the existential crisis can be especially potent for gay men.

Gay-affirmative psychotherapy can be particularly helpful during this phase, since even under the most ideal psychosocial circumstances the question of purpose can be complicated and frightening. The support provided in psychotherapy helps to diminish feelings of despair and confusion. In addition, therapy can encourage self-exploration which, in turn, helps the client to identify that which is important to him and brings satisfaction. Gay-affirmative psychotherapy recognizes the necessity of establishing individual rather than collective solutions to these questions of meaning, direction, and purpose for men. An affirmative approach to psychotherapy facilitates the courage and integrity necessary when inner peace cannot be achieved through social conformity.

Conclusions

The foregoing discussion has been a cursory and very generalized description of one model of gay-affirmative psychotherapy. Frequently, the course of psychotherapy includes variations on the phases described. For example, sometimes special phases must be devoted to crisis intervention or attenuating refractory symptoms.

Gay-affirmative psychotherapy is not an independent system of psychotherapy. Rather, it represents a special range of psychological knowledge which challenges the traditional view that homosexual desire and fixed homosexual orientations are pathological. Gay-affirmative therapy uses traditional psychotherapeutic methods but proceeds from a non-traditional perspective. This approach regards homophobia, as opposed to homosexuality, as a major pathological variable in the development of certain symptomatic conditions among gay men. The special complications and aberrations of identity formation that have been described in this article are considered to be the result of social values and attitudes, not as inherent to the issue of object-choice.

Gay-affirmative psychotherapy has an abiding concern with the developmental consequences of biased socialization. It also appreciates the equally salient contributions of other pathogenic variables. Thus, gay-affirmative psychotherapy is not reductionistic; rather, it attempts to address the full range of developmental conditions which can lead to pathological adaptations.

REFERENCES

Alexander, F., & French, T. *Psychoanalytic therapy.* New York: Ronald Press, 1946.

Bandura, A. *Principles of behavior modification.* New York: Holt, Rinehart and Winston, 1969.

Cass, V. Homosexual identity formation: A theoretical model. *Journal of Homosexuality,* 1979, *4*, 219-235.

Clark, D. *Loving someone gay.* Millbrae, CA: Celestial Arts, 1977.

Erickson, E. *Childhood and society.* New York: W. W. Norton, 1950.

Ferenzi, S., & Rank, O. *The development of psychoanalysis.* New York: Nervous and Mental Disease Publishing Co., 1925.

Lazarus, A. Desensitization and cognitive restructuring. *Psychotherapy: Theory, Research and Practice,* 1974, *11*, 98-102.

Malyon, A. The homosexual adolescent: Developmental issues and social bias. *Journal of Child Welfare,* 1981, *60*, 321-330.

Malyon, A. Bi-phasic aspects of homosexual identity formation. *Psychotherapy: Theory, Research and Practice.* In press.

Money, J. Factors in the genesis of homosexuality. In G. Winokar (Ed.), *Determinants of sexual behavior.* Springfield, IL: Charles C. Thomas, 1963.

Roman, M., Charles, E., & Karasu, T. The value system of psychotherapists and changing mores. *Psychotherapy: Therapy, Research and Practice,* 1978, *15*, 409-415.

Schafer, R. *Aspects of internalization.* New York: International universities Press, 1968.

Silverman, L. Some psychoanalytic considerations of non-psychoanalytic therapies: On the possibility of intergrating treatment approaches and related issues. *Psychotherapy: Theory, Research and Practice,* 1974, *11*, 298-305.

Weinberg, G. *Society and the healthy homosexual.* New York: St. Martin's Press, 1972.

Wolman, B. Principles of interactional psychotherapy. *Psychotherapy: Theory, Research and Practice,* 1975, *12*, 149-159.

THERAPEUTIC ISSUES WITH LESBIAN COUPLES

Barbara M. McCandlish, PhD

ABSTRACT. Lesbian relationships are most importantly relationships between two women in a homophobic and sexist society. Women newly exploring a relationship with another woman often experience their relationship as unique, as being *the best relationship*. They base this evaluation on the honest communication and open expression of caring that usually characterize the relationship. These qualities provide the basis for a fulfilling relationship which fosters personal growth and change. Major stresses and problem areas are due both to social pressures and to difficulties in establishing a sense of self within the relationship. This article explores the unique aspects of the lesbian relationship, suggests appropriate therapeutic interventions, and explores counter-transference issues for lesbian and heterosexual therapists.

Over the years, I have heard many women-friends and clients who were in their first committed relationship with a woman comment enthusiastically that this was the best intimate relationship they had ever had. This sentiment was more strongly stated if the woman had previously related to men intimately. Months or years later, however, the same woman would become disillusioned as some real difficulties threatened the relationship. Whether or not therapy was sought, hard work was necessary if the relationship was to continue to grow. At this time, important decisions were usually made about the couple's future.

Why do women experience such relief when they begin relating to women? And what is the cause of their later disillusionment? The answer lies in the fact that a lesbian relationship is most importantly a relationship between two women. The strength of lesbian relationships lies in the value both partners

Dr. McCandlish received her doctorate in clinical psychology from Harvard University in 1976. From 1968 to 1974 she received pre- and postdoctoral clinical training in institutional settings and was a founding member of two feminist therapy collectives, one in Cambridge, Massachusetts and one in Berkeley, California.

In 1972 she moved to Berkeley and completed part of her post-doctoral training at Operation Concern, a clinic serving the San Francisco lesbian and gay male community. In 1978-79 she opened practice and was a core faculty member of Antioch's Masters in Psychology program. For the past two years she has maintained a private practice in Santa Fe, New Mexico, carried out research at the University of New Mexico medical school, and worked with the terminally ill and their families.

71

place on relating. Women who have previously related to men often report a sense of relief that the burden of keeping the relationship vital no longer rests on their shoulders alone. Equally important is the experience of being treated as an equal in a society that devalues women. The relational difficulties follow from these strengths and lie mainly in the area of separation (defined as the ability to experience oneself not in relationship to another). Disillusionment with the relationship is due to these problems and to the stress of being socially isolated in a homophobic society.

In my work with lesbians singly and in couples, it has been my experience that a firm understanding of the uniqueness of these relationships (as compared with gay male or heterosexual couples) is necessary for effective therapy. The present paper offers a theory of lesbian relationships based on my clinical experience as a lesbian therapist who has treated approximately 60 individual lesbian clients and 25 lesbian couples over the past 7 years. When appropriate, research and scholarly literature are incorporated into the presentation. Clinical applications of the theory are presented along with typical countertransference issues for the therapist working with lesbian couples.

Emphasis on closeness and communication, and difficulty with separating, are characteristic not only of lesbians but of most women in this society. In *The Reproduction of Mothering*, Chodorow (1978) develops her thesis that:

> As long as women mother, we can expect that a girl's preoedipal period will be longer than that of a boy and that women, more than men, will be more open to and preoccupied with those very relational issues that go into mothering-feelings of primary identification, lack of separateness or differentiation, ego and body-ego boundary issues and primary love not under sway of the reality principle. (p. 110)

Chodorow's argument is a combination of feminist and psychoanalytic thought based on psychoanalytic and anthropological clinical accounts. She contrasts the way women and men relate in the following statements:

> From the retention of preoedipal attachments to their mother, growing girls come to define and experience themselves as continuous with others; their experience of self contains more flexible or permeable ego boundaries. Boys come to define themselves as more separate and distinct, with a greater sense of rigid ego boundaries and differentiation. The basic feminine sense of self is connected to the world, the basic masculine sense of self is separate. (p. 169)

In many heterosexual relationships, then, it is the woman who usually expresses the need for openness and communication, while the male creates emotional distance.

If women and men relate differently, it follows that the dynamics of lesbian relationships differ from those of heterosexual and gay male relationships. Based on interviews with 108 lesbian subjects, Wolff (1971) concluded that it is the strong emotional bond, rather than the purely sexual, that leads women to relate to women. Harding (1933) was one of the first to observe her lesbian clients' difficulty in separating. Research comparing lesbian and gay male relationships (Hedblom, 1973; Loney, 1972; Saghir & Robins, 1969; Tuller, 1978) has shown that lesbians form close committed relationships of long duration, while gay men have briefer, primarily sexual relationships.

Although this paper focuses on the uniqueness of lesbian couples, in many ways these couples operate like any other. The attainment of mature intimacy—a dynamic balance of closeness and separation acceptable to both partners—is a challenge to all couples. Most individuals fear true intimacy, either the closeness or the separation or both. In the lesbian couple the strengths are more often in the area of closeness and the difficulties in separating.

In the initial phase of a lesbian relationship, couples quickly begin to share thoughts and feelings. Each partner enjoys feeling close and making the relationship an important part of her life, whether or not a long-term commitment is agreed upon. Emotional closeness and empathy accompany the sexual intimacy, making the sexual contact safe and more intense than usual. If a lesbian couple seeks therapy early in the relationship, their therapist can help by emphasizing and encouraging these strengths without being misled by them.

Case #1

Marie and Annette consulted me at the onset of their relationship. Although they had been lovers for only 4 months, they easily shared thoughts and feelings and were deeply committed to working on their relationship. For each, this was her first lesbian relationship. They turned to a lesbian therapist for help in sorting out whether each was really a lesbian. I suggested that the real issue was the dynamics of the relationship itself, especially the building of trust. The couple was willing to approach their problem in this way. Marie was ambivalent about making a commitment, while Annette felt this was *the* relationship she wanted. Yet, both expressed much caring for each other. In four sessions Marie explored her fears of closeness, especially her fear of being deserted (her mother had died when Marie was young). Annette explored her underlying anger and mistrust, which was expressed in continual demands with the unstated message, "You will fail to love me if you haven't already." This work successfully aided the couple in solidifying their new relationship.

Lesbian therapists who have affirmed same-sex relationships usually are able openly to support lesbian couples. Traditional heterosexual therapists, however, may feel uncomfortable with the couple's closeness and view it as immature and pathological. In accordance with their traditional values, they are likely to decide that the relationship is unhealthy and consciously or unconsciously contribute to a separation. In general, if heterosexual therapists find it difficult to maintain empathy for lesbian couples in this or other areas, it is advised that they not treat lesbian couples at all. Heterosexual therapists who are feminists or belong to a minority culture are apt to have less trouble being empathic, for both are likely to be familiar with the experience of being second-class citizens. Further, feminists by definition place value on women's strengths. A feminist heterosexual therapist may make quite a different, albeit less serious, error by romanticizing the couple's honest and open relationship. She is then unable to identify problem areas accurately and develop a cohesive therapeutic approach. She may wish her own relationships were as nurturing. Lesbian therapists may also face various countertransference issues, such as idealizing the relationship, overidentifying with the couple, and becoming invested in the therapy outcome.

Of course, not every lesbian couple will develop initial trust even though they are openly communicative. Should the couple seek assistance in developing such trust, the therapist must help them decide if this task can successfully be accomplished.

Case #2

Nancy and Susan came to see me with multiple complaints. They had been seeing each other for 6 months. However, Susan felt she had never been in love, not even at the beginning, and preferred a friendship. Nancy stated that the problem was *really* that Susan simply didn't have sufficient experience relating and needed Nancy's help in learning to be close. Upon hearing this, Susan would back down and not know what she felt. It seemed that each reacted to the worst of her mother in the other. I asked them to take the part of the other in role-playing a recent fight. They were completely unable to do so. Such a lack of empathy and understanding after 6 months pointed to the end of an unhealthy relationship. In fact, Nancy decided to end the relationship after the second therapy session.

Lesbians often become disillusioned when they must face society's homophobia and resulting social isolation. Even in large metropolitan areas where there are substantial supportive communities, social isolation is a serious stress for the lesbian couple. The problems become almost insurmountable, however, should the couple reside in a small town where absolute secrecy must be maintained to protect employment, custody of children, and family relationships. Some couples may have no close contacts outside of their primary relationship and may not use the word "lesbian," even to themselves. They avoid being seen in public together, which tends to complicate socializing with fellow workers. Couples often struggle with the lack of family support for their relationship and miss the acceptance that heterosexual relationships are usually given. These pressures can produce such stress for the couple that what might have been minor and even growth-producing difficulties, instead overwhelm the couple and force a premature end to the relationship. Such couples tend to look to each other for all their emotional support.

When a lesbian community is available for support, much of the therapy is devoted to encouraging partners to establish friendships outside the relationship and to explore coming out whenever possible. An underlying pattern of interdependency may be much more difficult to change. In some cases, this interdependency may become so severe that one partner attempts to block any outside friendships for the other. Eventually the other partner may find the constraints of such an arrangement too limiting for her own growth and leave the relationship.

Case #3

Another couple, Joan and Barbara, were able to work successfully on becoming less dependent on each other. Much of their interdependency was due to being isolated in a small town. After moving to a large metropolitan area and deciding to live apart, they found separate friends. When they moved back together, they entered therapy and began to challenge their lack of separateness at home. Each slowly explored saying "no" to sleeping together every night and spending all their non-work time together. Although these changes were often painful, Joan and Barbara were able to create a healthy relationship by using their well-developed communication skills and continuing to care deeply for each other.

Here again, heterosexual therapists, who downplay the importance of this society's homophobia, may fail to maintain empathy. These therapists are likely to attribute the couple's interdependency to immaturity and will support a partner's feelings that it is too burdensome to be gay. A clear understanding of society's oppression is essential to keeping the consequences of such oppression in perspective. This understanding is difficult for many heterosexual therapists; it comes more easily to lesbian or gay male therapists. Support for the couple's need to become less isolated may come best of all from a lesbian therapist who is comfortable with her sexual orientation. The main danger for a lesbian therapist is that she may attribute all of the couple's problems to homophobia and the resulting self-hatred. She may fail to see how and why the partners perpetuate the social isolation. Also, she may side with the partner who is comfortable being a lesbian and ignore the more important relational issues.

Case #4

Nancy and Lois consulted me because Lois wished to relate to men, while Nancy felt herself to be "really a lesbian." This presented several difficulties since not only did Lois fear my judgement of her, but I felt vulnerable to siding against her. Considerable restraint was required on my part. I was able to point out the underlying issue: Their need to separate within the relationship had been frustrated. Lois' need to explore relating to men and Nancy's desire to pursue her career were partly defensive maneuvers to gain distance. The only way to gain separation in this relationship was to lash out in anger and blame the other person for personal impasses. In this case social isolation was not the issue. Each had separate friends and work. In the course of therapy, each became able to "be alone" by being herself in spite of the reactions of the other. Each learned to tolerate times without support or togetherness and still remain in the relationship.

As is true of any couple, some relational problems of lesbian couples can be traced to unresolved developmental issues and family scripts. Lesbian partners in a new relationship are surprised and saddened to find that old problems appear again and again. Because of the many positive aspects of relating to women, partners are especially surprised to find they have not left behind all the problems they had encountered with men. These repeating issues are a potential problem area for any couple, heterosexual or homosexual, and must be anticipated by the therapist. Growth involves learning from each other's strengths and accepting the weaknesses.

Case #4 also illustrates the final unique aspect of lesbian relationships to be discussed here. After the initial trust has been created, difficulties can arise in being separate within the relationship. Although the couple may view the problem in other ways, the lack of acceptable ways to separate undermines the existing intimacy and forces the partners to use defensive modes to gain a sense of self. At this time the couple may focus on many different problems. Should they seek therapy, they are likely to report a loss of sexual intimacy and continual fighting, in addition to other presenting problems. Although it is possible for a stalemate to be tolerated for long periods of time, eventually the couple must learn to reestablish their separate selves, or the relationship will end. The later occurs when one or both partners find they must leave the relationship to establish a new sense of self. This option is especially important for women, who often need to learn how to grow alone.

Case #5

A couple came to see me for several sessions at an important juncture in their relationship. I had worked with Carla and Victoria a year earlier, at the beginning of the relationship. This time new problems had appeared after the couple had set up a household together. The presenting problems involved deep anger on Carla's part about the level of cleanliness in the apartment and Victoria's increased involvement in her career. Victoria experienced Carla's anger as a constant attack and often felt upset and even afraid. In the therapy they were able to realize that these feelings were the direct consequences of the deeper commitment they had just made to each other by choosing to live together.

Some of the therapy involved being able to tolerate feelings of anger and separateness. Carla and Victoria came to one session full of anger. The hour-and-a-half session was not sufficient to resolve the disagreements, and they left as upset and angry as they had come. My communication that I was comfortable with such impasses helped the two women to tolerate their unpleasant feelings.

The underlying source of Carla's anger was her deep unconscious fear of losing her sense of self. She controlled her fear by attempting to retain control of the apartment's appearance. Victoria countered by keeping it messy and sought to control the level of emotional closeness by becoming more involved in her work. By identifying these fears, each woman was able to accept her fears and her own need for separation, rather than acting out. Both had to face the fact that they were giving up some control by becoming closer. The couple was then able to tolerate more closeness and allow needs for separation within the relationship. What had seemed unsolvable problems at the onset of therapy could now be successfully solved by reasonable compromise without further therapeutic assistance. The entire intervention involved three sessions.

Lesbian couples often discover in the course of therapy that they may have assumed "rules" against being separate. Each partner will tend to treat as rejection any attempts by the other to have separate friends, be emotionally distant, or have a different world view. Sometimes even talking and dressing differently is viewed as a threat. Having secrets, thoughts, and feelings that are not shared is especially threatening. Any attempts at separation are undermined with the communication "You don't love me." Even when one partner attempts to leave the relationship or have additional intimate relationships, she will persist in undermining attempts by the other partner to be separate. In a given relationship, separation may be prohibited in some or all of these areas.

An important issue involves acknowledging and facing aloneness. As the couple is able to do this, some of the more defensive ways of separating, such as continual fighting, can be put aside. Anger, rather than meaningless bickering, becomes a viable way to express the need to separate. Often a new level of intimacy is reached. Each partner learns to tolerate not continually feeling love for the other person; that is, feeling separate. Interestingly enough, as separation is allowed, couples often report the return of sexual intimacy to the relationship.

In these struggles, the couple will need to maintain honest and open communication about their relationship. This ability, and their initial caring and intimacy, provide much of the incentive for continuing to work on the relationship.

Obviously, the therapist's attitude towards the lesbian couple's difficulties in maintaining separateness greatly affects the success of the therapy. Traditional therapists see these difficulties as indicative of intrapsychic problems. Yet, to a great extent these issues are characteristic of normal lesbian relationships. A negative view is in fact extremely detrimental, for couples need encouragement and understanding to counteract societal pressures undermining their relationships. It is helpful for them to see that their struggle is shared by many women and that real growth can occur at this time, especially because of their ability as women to maintain and value a relationship. The partners often need reassurance that continually alternating between being in a relationship and being alone is not the only way to balance closeness and separation: This balance can be achieved within a relationship.

REFERENCES

Chodorow, N. *The reproduction of mothering: Psychoanalysis and the sociology of gender.* Berkeley and Los Angeles: University of California Press, 1978.

Harding, M. E. *The way of all women.* New York: Longmans, Green and Co., Inc., 1933.

Hedblom, J. H. Dimensions of lesbian sexual experiences. *Archives of Sexual Behavior,* 1973, 2(4), 329-341.

Loney, J. Background factors, sexual experiences, and attitudes toward treatment in two "normal" homosexual samples. *Journal of Consulting and Clinical Psychology,* 1972, 38(1), 57-65.

Saghir, M., & Robins, E. Homosexuality I: Sexual behavior of the female homosexual. *Archives of General Psychiatry,* 1969, 20, 192-201.

Tuller, N. R. Couples: The hidden segment of the gay world. *Journal of Homosexuality,* 1978, 3, 331-343.

Wolff, C. *Love between women.* New York: Harper & Row, 1971.

PSYCHOTHERAPY FOR GAY MALE COUPLES

David P. McWhirter, MD
Andrew M. Mattison, MSW, PhD

ABSTRACT. Although there is no specific therapy for gay male couples, this paper outlines the more critical issues therapists must understand to provide optimal treatment for gay male dyads. Additionally, the authors present new assumptions arising from their five year research study of 156 gay male couples living together from one to over 37 years. The most therapeutically useful finding is that stages of these relationships parallel stages of clinical development. Each stage has its own unique characteristics, stresses and benefits. Stages are affected by many influences, and individuals can be at different stages simultaneously.

Until the end of World War II, the primary focus of psychotherapy was the individual. Starting in the late 1940s, however, there was a gradual inclusion of therapeutic work with couples and eventually with families. A similar pattern of development has occurred in psychotherapy specifically for gay persons, as the early focus of therapy for individuals gradually broadens to include couples' therapy. In fact, the treatment of couples has become a keystone in the psychotherapeutic armamentarium of some therapists. Treatment has assumed many forms, but all are based on or extrapolated from heterosexual dyads, mainly because there is little research with homosexual couples. Although there are many similarities among primary relationships, regardless of the sex or orientation of the participants, same-sex couples do have unique characteristics that must be taken into consideration when theortetical and clinical issues are combined to form a treatment approach.

This paper presents a theoretical construct for the psychotherapy of gay male couples and is based on research and clinical work spanning 10 years. During that time we provided psychotherapy for hundreds of gay men in relationships. We also completed a 5-year research project studying 156 gay male couples

Dr. McWhirter is Medical Director of the Clinical Institute for Human Relationships, 3821 Fourth Avenue, San Diego, California 92103, and Assistant Clinical Professor of Psychiatry at the University of California at San Diego, School of Medicine. He is a member of the Board of Examiners of the American College of Sexology.

Dr. Mattison is in private practice at the Clinical Institute for Human Relationships and Assistant Clinical Professor of Family Medicine at the University of California at San Diego, School of Medicine. He is a member of the American College of Sexology.

who had been together from 1 to 37½ years. With the knowledge and insight gained from this research and from our accompanying clinical experience, we have developed a theoretical model with broad clinical applications in the psychotherapy of gay men.

Two of the more important assumptions to emerge from our work are: (1) each relationship is a separate entity in itself with its own life, history, and development; (2) much like an individual, each relationship passes through a series of predictable developmental stages.

When Dr. Benjamin Spock (1945) popularized the developmental psychologists' discovery of stages of childhood, rebellious, difficult-to-handle 2-year-olds suddenly became manageable and acceptable because they were passing through a predictable stage labeled the "terrible twos." Spock introduced a new sanity and calmness into childrearing by assigning characteristic behaviors and factors of physical growth to specific time periods or stages. These observations were not new to Spock's audience, but the commonsense, easy-to-understand way he packaged the information normalized many of the changes of infancy that had previously been so anxiety-provoking to parents.

The same may well be true of our observations about couples: What we describe as stages of the relationships are not really new findings; nevertheless, the formulation of charcteristics common to the stages of gay male partnerships offers the potential for understanding the stages better, thereby reducing distress for the individuals and couples. Behaviors, interactions, and feelings formerly considered flaws in the relationships, or individual personality defects, are seen here as merely characteristic of a certain stage.

The Stages

Over a 5-year period (1974 to 1979), the authors interviewed in depth 156 gay male couples who were not in therapy and had lived together anywhere from 1 to more than 37 years. Some couples were interviewed once, others many times. The research design was a descriptive study using an interview schedule of 256 single items and 72 open-ended questions. The couples all lived in California, mostly in San Diego County. Men's ages ranged from 20 to 69 years, the mean age being 37.4 years. The mean time in a relationship was 8.7 years, with median being slightly over 5 years.

The significant data relating to stages of the relationships emerged in themes extracted from the interviews. Many factors, such as the age of the partners, their previous relationships, personalities, and backgrounds, affect relationship stages; but considering all the possible variables, there are enough similarities among the couples as their relationships progress to recognize individual stages and to suggest that most gay male relationships pass through them.

We have identified six stages, with the first four occurring within the first 10 years as a couple. The stages are presented as tentative formulations needing further clinical trial and research validation. Even though we have found wide variations within our own practice, the conceptualization of developmental stages has been very helpful in the clinical approach to therapy with gay male couples.

Stage One: Blending (First Year)

Characteristics:
1. Blending
2. Limerence[1]
3. Equality of partnership
4. High sexual activity

Blending is experienced as the intensity of togetherness gay men feel early in their relationships. Their similarities bind them, their differences are mutually overlooked. They tend to do everything together, almost to the exclusion of others. Limerance is intense and most often reciprocal, although there are variations here. Equality is usually manifested in shared financial responsibility and equal distribution of the chores of daily living, but most importantly as a shared attitude of equality. Sexual activity varies but usually includes several encounters weekly and *de facto* sexual exclusivity.

Stage Two: Nesting (1 to 3 Years)

Characteristics:
1. Homemaking
2. Finding compatibility
3. Decline in limerance
4. Ambivalence

During the first year together men appear to have limited concerns about their living environment. By the second year, however, attention to their surroundings takes the form of homemaking activities, decorating a new home, or rearranging an old one. Couples in this stage also tend to see each other's shortcomings and discover or create complementarities that enhance compatibility. The partners' decline in limerance is usually not simultaneous and is often a cause for worry and concern. The search for compatibility and the decline in limerance set the stage for the mixture of positive and negative feelings about the value of the relationship that we call ambivalence.

Stage Three: Maintaining (3 to 5 Years)

Characteristics:
1. Individualization begins
2. Risk-taking

3. Dealing with conflict
4. Relying on the relationship

Maintaining the relationship depends upon establishing balances between individualization and togetherness, conflict and its resolution, autonomy and dependence, confusion and understanding. The intense blending of Stage Two clears the path for the re-emergence of individual differences, identified here as individualization. As this process begins, individualization is accompanied by some necessary risk-taking—whether in outside sexual liaisons, more time apart, greater self-disclosure, or new separate friendships. These risks often result in conflicts, including jealousy and differences of opinion, interest, or tastes that are dealt with either by confrontation and resolution or by avoidance. The fourth characteristic of the stage (relying on the relationship) may well be the ingredient sustaining the other three characteristics. After 3 or 4 years together, two gay men tend to look upon their relationship as if it were a third person possessing certain dependable qualities, such as steadfastness, comfort, and familiarity, which sustain the momentum of their partnership. It should be noted here that recognition and support of the relationship by family and friends often begin only after a couple has been together 3 years.

Stage Four: Collaborating (5 to 10 Years)

Characteristics:
1. Collaborating
2. Productivity
3. Establishing independence
4. Dependability of partners

Besides the usual meaning of "cooperation," collaboration also implies giving aid to an occupying enemy. Couples in Stage Four can unwittingly collaborate in this sense and aid the development of boredom and feelings of entrapment. After 5 years together, couples experience a new sense of security and a decreasing need to process their interactions. On the one hand, this decline in communication frequently gives rise to making unverified assumptions about each other. On the other hand, their collaborative adjustments often lead to effective complementarity. This complementarity, combined with the coping mechanisms for dealing with conflict and boredom, yields new energy for enriching their horizons beyond the relationship. This energy leads to mutual as well as individual productivity of a visible nature, such as business partnerships, financial dealings, estate building, or achieving personal gains in professional or academic worlds. The individualization of Stage Three can progress to the establishment of independence, sustained by the steady, dependable availability of a partner for support, guidance, and affirmation.

Stage Five: Trusting (10 to 20 Years)

Characteristics:
1. Trust
2. Merger of money and possessions
3. Constriction
4. Taking the relationship for granted

Trust develops gradually for most people. As the years pass, and as they gain experience, gay couples trust each other with greater conviction. The trust of Stage Five includes a mutual lack of possessiveness and a strong positive regard for each other. The slow merger of money and possessions may be a manifestation of this trust. Among men in the latter half of Stage Five, we also found a gradual isolation from the self as manifested by lack of feelings and inattention to personal needs, isolation from the partner by withdrawal and lack of communication and sometimes isolation from friends in the same ways. We have identified this characteristic as a type of constriction; it may be a result of the men's ages. The attitude of taking the relationship for granted develops as a result of the other characteristics of this stage.

Stage Six: Repartnering (20 years and beyond)

Characteristics:
1. Attainment of goals
2. Expectation of permanence of the relationship
3. Emergence of personal concerns
4. Awareness of the passage of time

The twentieth anniversary appears to be a special milestone for gay male couples. We found a surprising number of couples reporting a renewal of their relationship after being together for 20 years or more. Most men's goals include financial security; the men in our sample had usually attained this after 20 years. Other goals included business, professional, and academic success. These couples also assumed that they would be together until separated by death. Most men expressed a series of personal concerns, such as for health and security, fear of loneliness, death of partners or themselves, etc. Most were struck by the passage of time and would reminisce about their years together.

This developmental paradigm of gay male relationships is not intended as a new typology for couples but rather as a broad framework for understanding some of the developmental phases these couples experience. Although stages are organized around time periods and are presented in time-related linear sequence, there are many variations that influence the stages and make them far more dynamic than our brief outline reveals. For instance, men who have had several previous relationships may shorten Stage One to a few weeks or months and move dramatically through Stage Two in a year. Some couples may linger far longer in the warm glow of Stage One because of their similarities, while others with wide age differences may have many Stage Three characteristics after a few months or a year.

The Assessment

Most therapists agree that the accurate assessment or diagnosis of the problem is critical to the process of treatment. As we began working with gay male couples, the paradigms used for assessment were all based on opposite-sex partnerships. The inaccuracies introduced into our diagnoses by the use of values and assumptions found among heterosexual couples accounted for many early failures. Just two examples of differences from heterosexual couples are: (1) Among many gay men the expectation of sexual exclusivity diminishes rapidly after the first year; and (2) many maintain strict separation of money and possessions during the early years of their relationship. Couples and therapists can even share old myths, such as that all male relationships are short-term or that gay men assume butch/fem roles within their partnerships. (The evaluation of the anti-homosexual attitudes, discussed later in this paper, is also essential to a full clinical assessment.)

Assessment can be accomplished by a team composed of two males, by a female and male therapist, or by a single therapist of either sex. Experience with all these combinations inclines us toward a single therapist, since studies in our clinic show the outcomes are about the same and a single therapist costs less. The assessment usually requires several sessions: an initial session with the couple together, followed by individual sessions for collecting background and developmental histories. During the assessment we look for answers to four questions: (1) the nature of the presenting problems as perceived by both partners; (2) the quality and the stage of the couple's relationship; (3) a diagnosis of the personality of each individual, i.e., how each characteristically deals with anxiety, fear, anger, etc.; (4) an evaluation of any extenuating circumstances, e.g., medical or health issues, differences in ages, or other factors outside the couple itself. The following example illustrates the use of these assessment guidelines.

Jim is a 37-year-old business executive and Tom is a 36-year-old accountant. They have been together just over 8 years. Jim is more assertive and outgoing. He belongs to business oranizations and is active in public affairs, while Tom is more retiring, content to focus all his energy on the relationship and their home. In the 6 months prior to seeking therapy, Tom has been almost completely withdrawn from Jim, talking only when spoken to, staying home, having trouble sleeping, etc. Jim has two children (boys aged 9 and 11) from a prior marriage; they spend two weekends each month with Jim and Tom. The couple disagrees about childrearing—Tom is lenient, Jim is firm. There has been a marked decline in their sexual contact in the past year. Tom is interested in trying to meet new friends, but Jim is afraid that Tom will find a new lover if that happens. Jim has frequent brief sexual encounters with others, which Tom knows about. Tom gets jealous but does not interfere.

1) With this couple, the nature of the problem is different for each partner. Although both come to therapy with considerable unhappiness, each has a different laundry list of complaints. Tom wants more freedom within the relationship; he feels that Jim is too dominant and overpowering. Tom also complains bitterly about the inadequacy of their sexual activity and is angry about Jim's outside contacts. Jim complains about Tom's passivity, withdrawal, and general lack of enthusiasm. Jim is also fearful of Tom's desire for greater freedom.

2) Although this couple has been together 8 years and, according to theory, should be in Stage Four, there appears to be considerable developmental discrepancy between the two men. Tom is struggling to individualize—a process common to Stage Three—while Jim has already individualized but is not encouraging Tom to do the same. Tom's continued dependence on Jim is a problem for these men.

3) Tom is quite depressed. He uses avoidance, denial, and withdrawal as personality defenses. Jim is more assertive and demanding; he utilizes rationalization and intellectualization. He is also unaware of the degree of Tom's depression.

4) The couple has the additional pressure of Jim's children.

As this case clearly illustrates, some problems gay couples encounter can be completely separate from the stages of their relationships, and others can be stage-related.

Stage-Related Problems

Each of the stages has a unique set of problems. What follows is not intended to be a complete list of such problems, but rather some examples of common stage-related difficulties.

Couples in Stage One tend to believe that the love and togetherness of blending and high limerence are the critical indicators of their relationship; they see the least rupture in this togetherness as heralding the end of the relationship. When each partner begins to feel less intense, or when there is a mutual diminution of feeling, men withdraw from each other. This is the most common cause for gay men to end their relationship before the end of the first year. An accompanying problem is the fear of intimacy generated by the intensity of the blending. This fear, which can be as difficult as the loss of feelings of limerence, may also be manifested in the individual's resistance to the process of blending.

The most common problems in Stage Two arise from differences between the partners, in contrast to the problems caused by similarities in Stage One. High passion declines and no longer shields partners from their annoyances with each other. Familiarity brings the diversity in their values and tastes to the surface and sets the stage for disagreement. The partners begin to notice each other's failures and shortcomings. This stage also sees the onset of outside sexual interests and a resulting increase in jealous possessiveness.

The problems in Stage Three are provoked by the beginning of individualization and the consequent fears of loss. Misunderstandings arise from the partners' newly felt needs to be separate, specifically their increasing need for outside sexual activity. The risk-taking involved at this stage tends to generate new anger and anxiety.

As a consequence of the activity taking place outside the relationship, Stage Four is a time of considerable distancing from each other. This distancing generates fears of loss but is also partially responsible for cementing the dyad; for despite the distancing, there is a consolidation in the couple's efforts together. "Stage discrepancy," which will be discussed below, occurs most frequently in Stage Four.

In addition to problems related to the length of time in the relationship, (10 to 20 years), couples in Stage Five have the burden of concerns accompanying the process of aging. Routine and monotony can become the enemy in Stage Five. The tendency to become more fixed or rigid in personality characteristics while struggling to change each other can also plague men who have been together over 10 years.

Couples in Stage Six often continue to have the problems seen in Stage Five, but with the increase in age and the attainment of goals there is restlessness, sometimes withdrawal and feelings of aimlessness. Some, but not all, gay couples change partners at this point. Men in this stage grew up as homosexual men prior to the 1960s. Being products of a more repressive era, their beliefs and feelings may reflect anti-homosexual attitudes. Although at the present time they appear to be stage-related, these problems may not be found among gay men in the future.

Stage Discrepancy

More often than not, couples do not progress through the stages simultaneously. If there is a wide difference, problems arise which we have identified as "stage discrepancies." It is very common to find couples together 7 or 8 years with one partner in an individualized, comfortable position (Stage Four) and the other still dependent and clinging (Stage Two or Three). In clinical practice, regardless of the presenting problems, we find over half the couples seen in our Institute are laboring with some degree of stage discrepancy. Couples experience considerable relief when this concept is explained to them, just as the man with chest pain is relieved when the physician tells him it is only muscle strain—and not a heart attack.

When couples understand the concept of stage discrepancy they realize that their problems are not flaws in themselves or their partnerships but correctable, developmental differences in the growth of their relationships. Although all discrepancies may not lend themselves to rapid adjustment, the understanding derived from the cognitive framework of stage discrepancy makes the affective problems easier to handle and to treat. (After all, when a man with chest pain knows the exercise will not injure him, running need no longer be anxiety-provoking.)

Non-Stage Related Problems

Aside from all the difficulties found when two separate personalities combine to form a primary relationship, there are problems unique to the experience of gay persons in relationships. (Some apply both to gay men and lesbians, but in this paper we are limiting the observations to gay men.)

Anti-Homosexual Attitudes

The pervasiveness of anti-homosexual attitudes touches every person but affects gay people profoundly. These attitudes include: 1) ignorance, 2) prejudice, 3) oppression, and 4) homophobia. All together, or in some combination, are overtly or covertly present in every gay male couple we have ever seen. Many men have been able to understand and minimize their influence, but most have not completely recognized the depth of their own homophobia or the degree of their own self-oppression. A careful assessment and differentiation among the four attitudes is important as the couple's therapy begins.

Of these four anti-homosexual attitudes, homophobia is the most insidious and difficult to identify and treat. A diagnosis of homophobia is confirmed by ruling out the other anti-homosexual attitudes. Ignorance is changed by knowledge. We use extensive reading of books and articles, the viewing of video tapes, attendance at lectures, and other sources of accurate information to dispel the partners' lack of knowledge. It requires more than knowledge to change prejudice: There must be some accompanying impactful positive emotional experience, such as can occur with a group. Oppression, especially self-oppression, may take the form of unwitting assumptions about the negative attitudes of others toward homosexual persons. Homophobia is recognized by its persistence in the face of knowledge and the reduction of prejudice. The continued presence of low self-esteem and lack of self-acceptance, resistance to coming out, and the continued rejection of some aspects of homosexuality are evidence of homophobia's virulance. The clinician must be alert and evaluate the extensive hidden manifestations of these anti-homosexual attitudes. (Readers interested in the psychological aspects of homophobia should consult Dr. Malyon's chapter in this volume.)

Levels of Openness

Another issue peculiar to gay relationships is the degree to which couples are open about their sexual orientation. This openness has been called being "out of the closet." The degree to which individuals and couples are out to friends (gay and non-gay), family, employers, colleagues, etc., can be a focus for problems. It is very important to consider the coming-out process when evaluating gay couples. (See Dr. Coleman's chapter on stages of coming out, in this volume.)

Role Models

Gay couples lack role models for their relationships. Since each partner is the product of a heterosexual relationship, gay couples tend to share the expectations and rule of opposite-sex couples. As mentioned above, examples of heterosexual expectations include equating fidelity with sexual exclusivity; expecting one partner to assume the "feminine" and the other the "masculine" role; and one partner anticipating being taken care of by the other, much as the wife expects to be taken care of by the husband. Men who build their relationships on rules or expectations like these often find themselves in distress.

Even among gay couples who do not follow the heterosexual models, there is some vague uneasiness about how they function as a couple, as well as curiosity as to how other gay couples deal with their everyday lives, finances, outside relationships, family, sex, etc.

Communications

For most heterosexual couples seeking therapy, lack of communication is a major problem. Although gay men do encounter communication difficulties, especially at later stages in their relationship, in fact gay men have a tendency to over-communicate with each other. At times they process their feelings and behaviors "to the death," causing relationship fatigue and distress.

Other Causes

Socio-economics, family backgrounds, levels of education, religions, differences in values, previous relationships, illness, financial setbacks, individual emotional problems, sexual dysfunctions, and jealousy are examples of other sources of conflict between gay men that are not related to stages. These issues are also unrelated to sexual orientation.

Regardless of the causes, couples seeking therapy manifest their distress in a limited number of ways, including anger and hostility, withdrawal and depression, increased anxiety, fear, or some other form of unhappiness. Identification of the problem and its probable causes, achieved through adequate assessment, is the key to the choice of therapy and its ultimate effectiveness in improving the quality of life for those seeking assistance.

Choice of Therapy

In addition to evaluating the problem and its roots, the therapist should ask the couple about their needs and expectations. The therapeutic approach must be tailored to the individual couple. 1) For those with stage-related problems, a short-term counseling approach that may include explanations, reading, and a few group sessions with other couples in similar circumstances, can send them on their way with renewed confidence. 2) If the assessment exposes depression, anxiety, or fear in one partner or the other, a move toward individual, dynamically oriented therapy is indicated and recommended. In instances where individual therapy is recommended for one partner only, we continue to see the couple together at intervals, to include the other partner in the treatment process. 3) Some couples have stage discrepancies based on personality characteristics of a partner. These couples require a marital-therapy approach with emphasis on their interactional dynamics. Marital therapy is also useful for couples with conflicts unrelated to sexual orientation or the stages of their relationship: for example, jealousy or differences in values and expectations. Gay male couples share with their heterosexual counterparts the flotsam and jetsam of everyday problems. 4) For couples with sexual dysfunctions, the choice of sex therapy may be specific or adjunctive to marital therapy, depending upon the results of assessment (McWhirter & Mattison, 1978; 1980). 5) Crisis intervention for couples in acute distress requires more rapid assessment with very directive short-term (two or three sessions) treatment focused on the specific causes of the crisis. 6) Group therapy for couples can be particularly effective when socialization, problem-solving, and sharpening of communication skills are major therapeutic goals. 7) Assessment may indicate no need for psychotherapy per se but rather a need for education and information accompanied by socialization with other gay men and women. The use of social, academic, and recreational groups and clubs for gay people is a valuable tool here.

The Therapist

Writing on the psychotherapy of gay couples tends to imply that there is a specific therapy for gay men. We do not believe there is. A therapist might be trained in Gestalt, behavioral modification, psychoanalysis, bioenergetics, etc., and be very able to provide effective and useful treatment for gay couples. Regardless of the specific approach, however, there are certain attitudes and levels of knowledge the therapist must possess in order to be minimally competent on the job. We believe that therapists need to know about their own anti-homosexual attitudes, especially their own homophobia and how it affects them and their clients. Therapists must also see gay relationships as viable and desirable life-styles in general, if not necessarily for each and every couple seeking help. Therapists who believe that homosexuality represents a distinct psychopathological condition in itself are encouraged to refer gay couples to colleagues who do not share that belief.

Most gay men will be able to appraise the level of a therapist's knowledge about homosexuality and gay life-styles in a very short time. A therapist's honest admission to a lack of knowledge enhances that therapist's value to gay clients. At the very least, however, therapists do need to know the resources that are available to gay persons in the form of books, films, periodicals, organizations, etc. They need to know that there are differences between gay and heterosexual couples and ought to be open-minded enough to recognize the effects of these differences.

Conclusion

Since so little has been written on the subject of therapy with gay male couples, we must continue to rely on those in therapy to teach us more about themselves and their relationships. It appears that gay male couples have learned lessons about coupling that may be useful to heterosexual couples in untraditional relationships. In particular, the concept of developmental stages has extensive therapeutic ramifications. Although couples therapy with gay men is just now moving toward full-fledged legitimacy in the therapeutic community, it has much to contribute to the body of knowledge.

NOTE

1. In *Love and Limerence* (1979), Dorothy Tennov introduces the word "limerence" to describe the state of falling in love or being romantically in love. Tennov describes the basic components of limerence, which include: 1) intrusive thinking about the desired person (who is the limerent object); 2) acute longing for reciprocation of feelings and thoughts; 3) buoyancy (a feeling of walking on air) when reciprocation seems evident; 4) a general intensity of feelings that leaves other concerns in the background; and 5) emphasizing the other's positive attributes and avoiding the negative (or rendering them, at least emotionally, into positive attributes). Tennov includes sexual attraction as an essential component of limerence, but admits exceptions. Sexual attraction alone, however, is not enough to denote true limerence.

REFERENCES

Coleman, E. Developmental stages of the coming out process. *Journal of Homosexuality*, 1981/1982, 7(2/3).
Malyon, A. K. Psychotherapeutic implications of internalized homophobia in gay men. *Journal of Homosexuality*, 1981/1982, 7(2/3).

McWhirter, D. P., & Mattison, A. M. The treatment of sexual dysfunction in gay male couples. *Journal of Sex and Marital Therapy*, 1978, *4*, 213-218.

Whirter, D. P., & Mattison, A. M. Treatment of sexual dysfunction in homosexual male couples. In S. R. Leiblum & L. A. Pervin (Eds.), *Principles and practices of sex therapy*. New York: The Guildford Press, 1980.

Spock, B. *Baby and child care*. New York: Simon and Schuster, 1945.

Tennov, D. *Love and limerence*. New York: Stein and Day, 1979.

BISEXUAL AND GAY MEN IN
HETEROSEXUAL MARRIAGE:
CONFLICTS AND RESOLUTIONS IN THERAPY

Eli Coleman, PhD

ABSTRACT. This paper describes 31 men who at the time of entering therapy were married and expressed concern about their same-sex feelings and activity. Each of these men was treated in a "bisexuality group" designed to help him to be more comfortable and accepting of his same-sex feelings and to explore ways of incorporating same-sex and opposite-sex feelings into his life. Following treatment, 11 of the 31 men (36%) decided to end their marriage; twenty men (64%) decided to remain married. In a follow up study, there was a further attrition of marriages so that 14 remain married. The paper further describes attitudes and behavior prior to therapy, immediately following therapy, and at the time of follow up (up to three years). Factors that seem to be important ingredients of successful adjustment are discussed.

Between 5 and 10% of the population report having predominant same-sex feelings (Hunt, 1974; Kinsey, Pomeroy & Martin, 1948; Kinsey, Pomeroy, Martin, & Gebhard, 1953). A much smaller percentage actually live a life-style congruent with their same-sex preferences. Many men and women marry and attempt to live a life-style more consistent with traditional norms. Until recently, very little has been known about these people.

In their study of homosexuality, Masters and Johnson (1979) were surprised to find that 23% of homosexual females and males had previously been married. This statistic is consistent with the finding of the extensive study conducted by Bell and Weinberg (1978) of the Institute for Sex Research. To date, the only systematic study of married men with predominately same-sex feelings is that of 11 couples interviewed in Belgium in 1969-1970 (Ross, 1971). A few case studies of treatment approaches have been reported (e.g., Gochros, 1978; Hatterer, 1974), and very recently a number of books have described bisexual

Dr. Coleman is the Coordinator of Clinical Services and Assistant Professor at the Program in Human Sexuality, Department of Family Practice and Community Health, Medical School, University of Minnesota. He has written a number of papers on homosexuality, bisexuality, sexual dysfunction, and adolescent sexuality. Dr. Coleman is a psychologist and an AASECT-certified sex therapist. He is also on the editorial board of the *Journal of Homosexuality*.

and gay men who are married (Klein, 1978; Kohn & Matusow, 1980; Malone, 1980; Nahas & Turley, 1979). Basically, however, little is known about these men, their wives, or their gay relationships.

The concept that an individual may be married and yet have a significant amount of same-sex feelings seems in particular to have eluded many mental health professionals. For example, in assembling their original heterosexual study group, Masters and Johnson (1966) never considered including individuals who had varying amounts of same-sex experience, and yet when they studied homosexuality, they included individuals with a complete range of heterosexual-homosexual experience (Masters & Johnson, 1979).

This paper describes 31 men who at the time of entering therapy were married and expressing concern about their same-sex feelings and activity. Their beliefs and behaviors before entering group therapy, directly after having completed treatment, and several months after treatment, are compared.

METHOD

The 31 men in this study came from the author's private practice. Men were selected for a 10-week "bisexuality group" if their clinical needs met the following objectives of the group:

1. To be more comfortable with and accepting of their same-sex feelings.
2. To explore alternative ways of incorporating same-sex and opposite-sex feelings into their lives.
3. To examine myths and stereotypes of homosexuality, bisexuality, and heterosexuality.
4. To create better knowledge and understanding of human sexual functioning.
5. To deal with issues of sexual performance in both same-sex and opposite-sex relationships.

It was intended to accomplish these objectives by:

1. Creating an atmosphere of acceptance for variance in sexual activity.
2. Creating an opportunity for members to share concerns with one another and to receive support from one another.
3. Educating the members on the subject of homosexuality, bisexuality, and heterosexuality.
4. Learning the principles of taking responsibility for self in sexual activities.
5. Building assertiveness skills.
6. Creating an atmosphere of experimentation to explore feelings, attitudes, fantasies, and behaviors.
7. Teaching basic sex education on the sexual functioning of men and women.

Through sexual history and clinical observation, information was gathered about reasons for getting married, awareness of same-sex feelings and behaviors, wives' knowledge of husbands' same-sex feelings, marital and sexual conflicts, sexual behavior, extra-marital liaisons, effects upon the children, modes of adjustment, decisions following treatment, and self-esteem. Follow-up questionnaires (designed to assess more of the long-term effects of the therapy), were sent to all the men. The length of time at follow-up varied from a few months to 2-½ years after treatment.

RESULTS

Attitudes and Behavior Before Therapy

Reasons for Getting Married

Except for one man, all were (to some degree) aware of same-sex feelings, and all but four had acted on these feelings before they were married. Most of this activity could be labeled as normal adolescent exploratory behavior, except that it had a very different *meaning* to these individuals. Very few understood themselves to be "gay"; confusion is a more apt description of their feelings about their same-sex desires. Without exception, they decided to get married because of societal and family pressures and the perceived lack of intimacy in the gay world. Again without exception, they reported that they had married their wives because they loved them. Several men mentioned their interest in having and raising children as one significant motivating factor. Some felt that marriage would help them overcome their same-sex feelings. While the specific reasons varied, the overall motivating factors were love of their wives, societal and family pressures, and negative feelings about "gay life."

Attempts to Eliminate Same-Sex Feelings

All 31 men in the Bisexuality Group reported having previously in some way attempted to eliminate their same-sex feelings, which were a source of intense guilt and shame. Eleven (36%) had actually tried to eliminate these feelings and behaviors through psychotherapy with counselors, psychiatrists, or ministers. The length of time spent in therapy varied from 6 months to 17 years. Obviously, not one of these men had been successful in his attempt. Although all the men felt extreme guilt over their feelings and behavior, and many reported having suffered from depression and anxiety over the years, it was clear that except for one man, who had a history of psychiatric hospitalization, none suffered from any serious psychopathology.

The Wives' Knowledge

Only five wives (16%) knew of their husbands' same-sex feelings before they were married: In one case, the wife felt that those feelings were normal; in the other four cases, the wife assumed that her husband's same-sex feelings would not be a factor in the relationship. The remaining women did not find out about their husband's feelings until after they were married. Only four wives did not know about their husband's feelings before they entered therapy; all four were told by their husbands during the process of treatment. Most of the wives in this study were unsuspecting at the time of disclosure. Their responses ranged from calm concern, to extreme upset, to revulsion and disgust. It proved just as difficult for the wives to accept their husbands' same-sex feelings as it had originally been for the men.

The scope of this study did not include collecting much information about the wives' histories of reaction or modes of adjustment. Wives were recommended to attend a spouses' support group, but only eight were willing to talk with other wives about their situation. More information needs to be gathered on the spouses of bisexual and gay people.

Sexual Relationship

Sexual problems occurred in 19 (61%) of these marriages. There were a number of relationships, however, where there seemed to be satisfactory sexual activity and no reported sexual dysfunctions. Seven men had a history of erectile difficulty (problems with erection more than 50% of the time). The remainder of the problems were with frequency of sexual activity and low sexual desire.

Extra-Marital Liaisons

All but two men had engaged in sexual activity with other males outside of their marital relationship. The frequency of this activity varied greatly, from a single incident to sexual encounters at least once a week. One man had never had a single same-sex experience before or after being married.

AFTER TREATMENT

Following treatment, 11 of the 31 men (36%) decided to end their marriage. (See Table 1 for a summary of results.) It should be noted that of these 11 men, 5 had entered treatment already separated or seriously considering separation. The remaining 20 men (64%) decided to remain married. Three of these, however, openly admitted that their decision to remain married was temporary and that they would probably eventually leave their wives to pursue

TABLE 1

SUMMARY OF DATA

(N = 31)

	f	%
Average Age	38.58	
Average Length of Marriage (in years)	13.06	
Average Number of Children	2.03	
Awareness of Same-Sex Feelings Prior to Marriage	30	97
Acted on Same-Sex Feelings Prior to Marriage	27	87
Had Had Therapy to Eliminate Same-Sex Feelings	11	36
Wife Knew of Husband's Same-Sex Feelings Prior to Marriage	5	16
Sexual Conflicts Within the Marriage	19	61
Extra-Marital Liaisons	29	94
Commitment Following Treatment		
Marriage	20	64
Divorce	11	36
	31	100
Commitment at the Time of Follow-Up Study		
Marriage	14	45
Divorce	17	55
	31	100

same-sex relationships. In other words, 17 (55%) of the 31 men decided to re-commit themselves to their relationship. Only five of these men planned a monogamous relationship with their wives. Seven were definitely going to act on their same-sex feelings without the wives' knowledge, two were still undecided whether they would act on their feelings or not, and three men had developed relationships that allowed extra-marital activity by the husband with the wife's knowledge and consent.

Effects of Children

The decision whether or not to leave the marital relationship might have been related to or influenced by the fact that children were involved. Of the men studied, 24 (77%) had children. All 24 men had truly wished to be fathers and expressed a deep sense of love and admiration for their children. Five of these men had decided to communicate with their children about their same-sex feelings; there was no immediate negative effect reported. In the end, 16 of the 24 men with children decided to stay married.

FOLLOW UP RESULTS

The 20 men who remained committed to their marriage at the end of the Bisexuality Group have made a number of changes in the months and years since then. Six of these men are now divorced or are in the process of separation or divorce. Of the 14 men still married, three express grave doubts concerning the future of their relationships. Only two men are committed to a monogamous relationship with their wives.

Six married men are pursuing same-sex relationships. Their feeling is that "what my wife doesn't know won't hurt her, me, or our relationship." All of these men originally planned not to get emotionally involved with any of their sexual partners, in order to avoid threats to the primary relationships with their wives. Several men, however, have developed close emotional relationships with males; this causes difficulties in their marriages. Most of the married men continue to keep in contact with other married men with same-sex feelings, for emotional support.

Three men have open-marriage contracts with their wives. In all three cases, the husband has the freedom to seek out sexual partners but the wife has chosen not to do the same. A few other couples have tried this type of arrangement. In the past, this appeared to be a stepping-stone to divorce. It is still uncertain if any of these marriages will last.

A number of married couples have entered a couples' group or have sought marital counseling for additional support in their adjustment. Several of the fathers have joined a "Gay Fathers" group to share similar concerns and to gain support. Several wives have been getting together informally to support each other.

Of the eighteen men who decided to leave their relationship, seven were involved at the time of follow-up in a "steady relationship with another man." Two men were involved in primary relationships with women and continued to have same-sex activity and relationships. The remaining nine men were primarily pursuing same-sex relations; two of these nine expressed an interest in exploring opposite-sex relationships at some future date.

Kinsey-type ratings [A continuum from 0 (exclusive heterosexuality) to 6

TABLE 2

CHANGES IN KINSEY-TYPE RATINGS (MEANS)

	Before Group	Follow-Up
Sexual Behavior	2.42	4.26
Erotic Fantasies	4.52	4.67
Emotional Attachment	2.57	3.55

(exclusive homosexuality)] of sexual behavior, erotic fantasies, and emotional attachments were obtained from each man as he entered the group and again at the time of follow up. (See Table 2.) A significant change seems to have occurred in terms of increased same-sex sexual behavior (pre-treatment, 2.42; follow up, 4.26). There has been essentially no change in the content of sexual fantasies.

The mean score for *self-esteem* as measured by the Tennessee Self Concept Scale (TSCS) (Fitts, 1965) was 351. This score is within one standard deviation of the standard mean. It is also consistent with typical post-treatment scores of individuals who have received some type of sexual counseling (e.g., Coleman, 1978). The mean score for *personality integration* as measured by TSCS was 9.07, which is also within one standard deviation of the standard mean and is consistent with post-treatment scores of others seeking sexual counseling (Coleman, 1978).

When the TSCS scores of men who have remained married are compared with those who have separated and divorced, some differences are noticed. The mean self-esteem score for the married men was 346. The mean self-esteem score for the divorced men was 359. This difference does not represent a statistically significant difference.

The results from the sexual behavior survey (Jeddeloh, Aletky, & Coleman, Note 1) provide some additional information. As a group, the men in the sample had had, in the past, more homosexual partners than heterosexual partners. The average number of female partners was between 1 and 5, versus 20 or more male partners. Sixteen reported their only heterosexual partner was their wife. The average frequency of sexual activity with a partner was once a week. These men reported more sexual dysfunction with females than with males, and more anal stimulation with males than females.

CASE STUDIES

The following three case studies illustrate some of the concerns encountered in the process of therapy.

Case 1

Fred was a 35-year-old man who had been married for 10 years and had two children. He had been aware of his same-sex feelings before he was married but didn't think he would be happy living a gay life-style. He became emotionally involved with a woman when he was 23 and married her.

It was after the birth of their second child that Fred began to feel a greater urge to act on his same-sex feelings. These feelings had never disappeared, but until then he had decided not to act on them. He entered therapy trying to figure out if he should stay with his wife and suppress his homosexual desires, or separate and develop same-sex relationships. His wife was clear: If he decided to pursue same-sex relationships, she wanted a divorce.

In the course of therapy, Fred reported that since his adolescence all his erotic fantasies had been of males. He also was aware of strong emotional attachment to males. He discovered in therapy that his love for his wife was waning. He decided he wanted to pursue same-sex relationships and informed his wife. They discussed this in therapy together, deciding to separate.

Case 2

Drake was a 39-year-old man who had been married for 15 years and had three children. Drake had been aware of his same-sex feelings since he was very young and had some "exploratory" same-sex experiences in adolescence. He was concerned about these experiences and thought he might be gay. He was somewhat reassured, however, when he developed a loving relationship with his present wife.

For a few months after he was married he thought his same-sex feelings had disappeared, but he soon began to experience the erotic fantasies again and the urge to act on those feelings. He began having sex with men in anonymous situations without his wife's knowledge. He felt extremely guilty about these experiences. Drake maintained this "double life" for most of his marriage.

In the year before entering therapy, he fell in love with another man. This greatly disturbed Drake because up until that point he had never felt emotional attachment to any of his sexual partners. This created the crisis that finally led Drake to therapy.

Over the years as he became more committed to pursuing same-sex relationships, Drake had lost his feelings of love for his wife. However, he feared the reaction of children, family, and people at work to a divorce.

His wife was willing to stay married under any circumstances. There was little pressure for him to make a decision, other than his own guilt and depression. He vacillated back and forth, unable to decide. Although after therapy he decided to remain married, he knew that eventually he would leave.

In the year following treatment there was no change. Drake was still unhappy with his marriage and talked of leaving, but he had made no firm commitment. Meanwhile there was evidence of continued discord and that the children were aware of the uncertain status of the marriage.

Case 3

Ray was a 50-year-old man who had been married for 25 years. At the time he married, he was aware of his same-sex feelings but thought that marriage would be a "cure." He loved the woman he married and enjoyed their sexual activity, but his interest in sex with men never waned.

He sought out sex in steam baths, bookstores, and restrooms. For twenty-five years, no one knew about this activity. He never knew any of his sexual partners. Ray felt extreme guilt and shame about his behavior but was unable to discontinue it. At one time, he had tried through therapy to eliminate his same-sex thoughts and activity. This therapy was unsuccessful.

Ray entered the Bisexuality Group feeling depressed, guilt-ridden, and lonely. In the course of therapy he developed some of his first male friendships. Ray continued to seek out sexual activity with men, but with less guilt and shame and less compulsively.

While in treatment, he decided to tell his wife about his same-sex feelings. She was shocked but did not reject him. This opened up communication between them and helped to rebuild an intimate relationship. They joined a couples' support group with other couples in similar situations. Ray's wife joined a support group for wives of bisexual and gay men.

His continued sexual activity outside of marriage occurred without his wife's knowledge. She assumed that some activity might be taking place but really did not want to know about it.

DISCUSSION

At present there is no clear model for a married man with same-sex feelings who wishes to maintain his marriage. Based upon clinical experience, here are some of the factors that seem to be important ingredients of successful adjustment:

1. Both people love one another.
2. Both people want to make the relationship work.
3. There is a high degree of communication in the relationship.
4. Both people have resolved feelings of guilt, blame, and resentment.
5. Physical contact is necessary. The husband has to touch, and desire to touch, his wife.
6. The wife has a sense of worth outside the marriage.

7. If there is outside sexual contact, the wife does not know about it, or the husband and wife have worked out an open-marriage contract.
8. The wife is willing to work on understanding and accepting her husband's same-sex feelings.
9. The husband continues to work on his own acceptance of same-sex feelings.

There is now more support available in the gay community for those men who decide to leave their marriages and pursue same-sex relationships. There is also more information on factors for successful adjustment:

1. Acknowledging same-sex feelings to oneself and to significant others (see Hammersmith & Weinberg, 1973). This does not necessarily mean complete public disclosure but, more importantly, self-recognition and the ability to share this fact with someone else (Weinberg & Williams, 1974).
2. Be willing to explore and experiment with the "new" sexual identity. This means developing contacts with other men and women of similar sexual orientations. It also means permitting oneself to be sexual with members of one's own sex, exploring ways of meeting others, and learning new interpersonal skills.
3. Utilizing available support systems, such as friends, gay social groups, church group, political groups, or counseling opportunities.
4. Trying to work on establishing a new relationship with the ex-wife. It is helpful if this relationship is based upon mutual respect and cooperation, especially if children are involved.
5. Look for ways to insure continued parenting of children, possibly considering joint-custody arrangements.
6. During this stage of exploring and experimenting, it is often a mistake to get involved immediately in a long-term committed relationship. This should be an important stage of experimentation, not commitment.
7. When same-sex relationships are explored, some perspective on these relationships is helpful. Learning to be in a same-sex relationship is new for most and often does not work initially. Individuals need to keep this fact in perspective and view "first relationships" as learning experiences.
8. Look for possible support from friends, family, or people at work. This may be difficult to obtain at first; however, it is important not to neglect opportunities for support from these significant people and areas of one's life.

These suggestions have come from 3 years' experience in working with married men with predominantly same-sex sexual preferences. This study represents a beginning in understanding this phenomenon. More information is needed, however; specifically, information about non-patient populations, and about spouses. There is, of course, some question as to whether these findings can be generalized to non-patient populations or even other clinical populations. For example, it would be especially helpful to know about modes of adjustment in marriages wherein both husband and wife express satisfaction with the relationship, and the husband is bisexual.

REFERENCE NOTE

1. Jeddeloh, R., Aletky, P., & Coleman, E. *A sexual behavior survey.* Unpublished manuscript, 1980. (Available from the authors at Program in Human Sexuality, 2630 University Ave., S.E., Minneapolis, MN 55414.)

REFERENCES

Bell, A. P., & Weinberg, M. S. *Homosexualities: A study of diversity among men and women.* New York: Simon and Schuster, 1978.

Coleman, E. *Effects of communication skills training on the outcome of a sex counseling program.* Unpublished doctoral dissertation, University of Minnesota, 1978.

Fitts, W. H. *Manual, Tennessee self concept scale.* Nashville: Counselor Recordings and Tests, 1965.

Gochros, H. Counseling gay husbands. *Journal of Sex Education and Therapy,* 1978. *4,* 6-10.

Hammersmith, S. K., & Weinberg, M. S. Homosexual identity: Commitment, adjustment, and significant others. *Sociometry,* 1973, *36,* 56-70.

Hatterer, M. The problems of women married to homosexual men. *American Journal of Psychiatry,* 1974, *131,* 275-278.

Hunt, M. *Sexual behavior in the seventies.* New York: Playboy, 1974.

Kinsey, A., Pomeroy, W., & Martin, C. W. *Sexual behavior in the human male.* Philadelphia: W. B. Saunders, 1948.

Kinsey, A., Pomeroy, W. B., Martin, C. W., & Gebhard, P. H. *Sexual behavior in the human female.* Philadelphia: W. B. Saunders, 1953.

Klein, F. *The bisexual option.* New York: Arbor House, 1978.

Kohn, B., & Matusow, A. *Barry and Alice.* Englewood Cliffs, NJ: Prentice-Hall, 1980.

Malone, J. *Straight women/Gay men.* New York: Dial Press, 1980.

Masters, W. H., & Johnson, V. E. *Human sexual response.* Boston: Little, Brown & Company, 1966.

Masters, W. H., & Johnson, V. E. *Homosexuality in perspective.* Boston: Little, Brown & Company, 1979.

Nahas, R., & Turley, M. *The new couple: Women and gay men.* New York: Seaview Books, 1979.

Ross, H. L. Modes of adjustment of married homosexuals. *Social Problems,* 1971, *18,* 385-393.

Weinberg, M. S., & Williams, C. J. *Male homosexuals: Their problems and adaptations.* New York: Oxford University Press, 1974.

GROUP PSYCHOTHERAPY FOR GAY MEN

David Conlin, MSW
Jaime Smith, MD

ABSTRACT. Group psychotherapy has been employed in past years for the purpose of extinguishing homosexuality. Recent changes in nosology have allowed mental health professionals to develop groups designed to enhance or facilitate sexual expression in the context of minority sexual orientation. This paper describes one such group model presently in operation as a psychiatric outpatient service of a general hospital in Vancouver, Canada.

Group psychotherapy is a powerful instrument for effecting cognitive, affective, and behavioral changes. When considering group psychotherapy for homosexual clients, the question arises, Group psychotherapy for what purpose? Until recently, the agenda had been a reflection of the official (pre-1974) psychiatric nosology, which regarded homosexual adjustments as pathological per se. The purpose of therapy, both individual and group, was the eradication of homosexual thoughts, feelings, and behavior, and the substitution of heterosexual counterparts. More recently, however, models of group therapy have been developed to facilitate "coming out," rather than to eliminate homosexual feelings. This paper will discuss the literature on group therapy for gay people and then propose a model for such therapy.

In 1976, Rogers, Roback, NcKee, & Calhoun published a comprehensive review of the literature on group psychotherapy for homosexual clients published between 1952 and 1975. Our own re-investigation of most of these reports, as well as the three major studies not reviewed by Rogers et al.—Birk, 1974; Birk, Huddleston, Miller, & Cohler, 1971; Birk, Miller, & Cohler, 1970—confirmed the findings of Rogers et al. that the treatment of homosexuality in group psychotherapy has been directed, either overtly or covertly,

David Conlin is Outpatient Program Co-ordinator, Department of Psychiatry, St. Paul's Hospital, Vancouver, British Columbia, Canada. Jaime Smith is a psychiatrist in private practice in Vancouver, British Columbia, Canada, and is Vice-President of the Caucus of Gay, Lesbian, and Bisexual Members of the American Psychiatric Association.

Portions of this paper were presented at the 30th annual meeting of the Canadian Psychiatric Association, Toronto, Canada, October 1980.

Address requests for reprints to: Jaime Smith, MD, Suite 116A, 3195 Granville St., Vancouver, B.C., Canada V6H 3K2.

toward changing the client's sexual orientation. Methods of treatment have included traditional psychodynamic approaches (Hadden, 1971; Nobler, 1972), combined psychodynamic and behavioral approaches (Birk, 1974; Birk et al., 1971; Birk et al., 1970), and eclectic or unspecified approaches (Covi, 1972; Truax & Tourney, 1971).

Reports that do not specify a change in sexual orientation as the primary goal of treatment nevertheless regard homosexuality as disordered or pathological per se; several clinicians (e.g., Hadden, 1971; Nobler, 1972) maintain this as a covert goal, even when a homosexual patient presents with complaints unrelated to sexual orientation or clearly states a desire not to change her or his sexual orientation. Not surprisingly, homophobia—either in the patient or in the clinician—is not mentioned by these reports, much less considered to be a problem. There is no consideration of healthy homosexual functioning nor of group treatment directed toward remediation or enhancement of such functioning.

The chapter on "problem patients" in Yalom's (1975) well-known monograph on group psychotherapy includes a brief discussion of the homosexual patient. Yalom considers only mixed groups (i.e., those heterogeneous with respect to sexual orientation) and observes that successful treatment is possible only when the gay patient and group no longer consider homosexuality to be a special problem. Although he notes that one pitfall of mixed groups is that the heterosexual members tend to exert pressure on the homosexual member to "convert" to heterosexuality, Yalom also sees an advantage in that the homophobia elicited in some heterosexual members can be identified and treated.

A search of the literature published between 1975 and 1980 revealed only one article (Russell & Winkler, 1977) reflecting the change in viewpoint associated with the revision of psychiatric nosology in 1974. Russell and Winkler suggest that clinicians should feel obliged, "if only by the demands of consistency, to accept that individuals may need and request assistance to improve their homosexual functioning" (p. 3). Their outcome study comparing effectiveness of assertiveness training and lay "consciousness-raising" groups in Australia showed that significant positive change did occur in both groups, indicating that such procedures are effective, at least in the short term.

Over the last decade, the majority of the groups exclusively for homosexual clients have been generated by gay community service organizations. They have ranged from professionally led therapeutic groups to "consciousness-raising" and rap groups led by paraprofessionals and lay persons. Initially, many of these were devoted to "coming-out" agendas, i.e., the fostering of self-acceptance of a homosexual identity, the learning of social skills, the establishment of friendship networks among peers, and mobilization within the community. A second generation of all-gay groups arose in the late 1970s with more specific foci; groups for young persons, for the elderly, for men or for women specifically, for alcoholics, for couples, and for gay parents. Groups for parents and for spouses of gay people have also been formed. Many such groups have been described in gay-oriented lay periodicals, but, as is frequently the case, little professional attention has been paid to the phenomenon until recently.

A Model for Group Therapy

Since January 1980 the authors have conducted, as co-therapists, a series of groups designed to facilitate psychosexual maturation ("coming out") for gay men. The rationale for these groups is a developmental schema for minority sexual orientation described in an earlier paper (Smith, 1980). Participants are referred to the program from community mental health teams, private practitioners, and a counseling service sponsored by a local gay community organization. None of the group members has requested a change of sexual orientation; all, however, have been either disturbed by or in conflict with their homosexual feelings, and have been socially inhibited as a consequence of their internalized homophobia.

In our experience in working with both mixed and all-gay groups, we have found that mixed groups can be useful to the homosexual patient who is already functioning at a high level of self-acceptance and adaptation as a gay person, and presents with problems unrelated to sexual orientation, such as anxiety or depressive disorders. It is crucial that the group leader(s) be non-homophobic themselves and alert to the possibility of group pressure from the heterosexual members, as described by Yalom. On the other hand, when internalized homophobia is the major issue for the homosexual patient, all-gay groups are better suited to facilitating homosexual adjustment. For this reason, the members of our therapy groups are all gay men.

Our sessions are held weekly for 20 weeks, each 2-hour session being held in the early evening at the psychiatric outpatient department of a big downtown hospital located in a neighborhood with a large concentration of homosexual residents. Each group has eight participants. The age range has been from early 20s to mid 50s. Intake assessments are conducted with each applicant to determine his appropriateness and to exclude individuals with major psychopathology, such as psychosis, severe anxiety states, or borderline personality organization. These conditions are rarely amenable to short-term, problem-focused treatment approaches.

The two therapists, who are trained in psychiatry (Smith) and social work (Conlin), identify themselves as gay at the first session of each group. In all-gay groups such as ours, where the primary focus is the facilitation of homosexual adjustment, it is essential that at least one of the group leaders be identified as gay. This rapport provides role models of well-adjusted peers and offers sources of information about community resources for gay people. Although there is no theoretical disadvantage to having one gay and one (non-homophobic) heterosexual co-therapist, there is a specific advantage to having two gay co-therapists: Two co-therapists with contrasting gay life-styles can help to highlight the diversity of possible adjustments to the variety of social, sexual, and partnership options available to gay men. This is especially important for individuals who may view homosexuality in a stereotypical fashion, a common phenomenon among those in an early stage of reconciling themselves to being gay. Even though well-adjusted and non-homophobic, a solo therapist (or the only gay member of a duo) runs the risk of emphasizing her or his own life-style and excluding alternative, equally adaptive variants. For this reason we recommend gay co-therapists for this type of group.

The leader(s) should be at a late stage of their own "coming-out" process, having experienced and worked through full disclosure to friends, family, and colleagues. These issues inevitably surface as group concerns, and leadership is required to provide momentum in the direction of self-acceptance and, where appropriate, self-disclosure.

In our groups, techniques serve two principal goals: 1) to facilitate the actual working and process of the group itself; and 2) specifically to facilitate resolution of the tasks associated with the coming-out process.

Because gay people frequently grow up lacking trust in themselves and others, the initial group task is to engage the confidence and trust of the members, both in the therapists and in one another. This is accomplished by reinforcing norms that promote disclosure, support for risk-taking and change, confrontation of homophobia and non-adaptive defenses (e.g., inappropriate humor or sarcasm), and non-sexual intimacy. Modelling by the therapists and structured exercises, such as the trust-walk and guided fantasies, also aid in promoting trust, as does the tradition of ending each session with a hug.

As trust recedes as the central issue, the task of "how to work in the group" emerges. Comments such as, "How will what we do here apply to the outside?" or "I'm not sure if this is important to the group, but. . . ," signal the beginning of this stage. We continue to promote the norms described above and encourage group initiative in resolving this task.

A variety of techniques are useful at this stage of group development. "Sculpting" encourages members to depict symbolically their perceptions of group functioning and of the status of member relations. "Contracting," a bilateral agreement between a member and the group, specifies working arrangements for participation and goals. For instance, a group member who had never socialized in a gay club alone and who was fearful of doing so, contracted first to go with other group members and then to go alone, and to report on his success.

When the group has progressed through the stages of formation and norm-setting, members then focus on a variety of issues related to living as gay men in a gay community and in a non-gay world. Themes include love relationships and sexual fidelity, dealing with homophobia (both internal and external), problems of sexual dysfunction, concerns about aging and physical appearance, bisexuality and relationships with women, and handling families and employers.

Where appropriate we use such techniques as the empty chair, role-playing, psychodrama, or assertiveness skills (Knobloch & Knobloch, 1979; Lewis & Streitfeld, 1972). For example, one group member reported that a fellow employee, unaware he was gay, had made a homophobic remark to him. The group member had felt embarrassed and made no reply. After mentioning the incident in a group, he was asked to repeat the scene in a role-play in which he could practice responding in a variety of ways. Each group member in turn offered support or alternative responses.

Another time, a group member role-played an interview with his former psychiatrist, a homophobic professional who had refused to discuss his client's sexual orientation. This member was able to confront the psychiatrist and to express the years of accumulated anger engendered by his maltreatment. After the experience he found that he was able to express other feelings more freely and began to have a greater sense of himself as a potent, competent man.

One or two of the 20 sessions are designated as "family and friends' night." Each member is asked to bring a significant other person to the meeting. This is often anticipated with trepidation but proves to be a powerful method of extending to the world outside the gains made within the group setting. Following such a session, members almost unanimously comment on its value.

Shortly before the final meeting of the group, an all-day session is held. A series of structured exercises involving art and movement therapy is used to consolidate gains made in self-awareness and social functioning. In preparation for termination of the group, we emphasize the value of continued contact with one another for mutual support.

Termination interviews are conducted at the time of dissolution of the group. The majority of the participants report increased self-esteem, better socialization skills, and improved relations with friends, family, and significant others. Following the group treatment, a number of graduates have entered into dyadic love relationships; we feel this is an indication of success. As anticipated, the overall effect of the group is to facilitate and speed up the developmental process of psychosexual maturation (Smith, 1980).

In a larger sense the group provides community sanction and support for minority sexual orientation status as a valid life-style. Also, by reducing internal conflict over sexual orientation, it decreases maladaptive reactions, such as depressions, suicidal gestures, and dependencies on alcohol and other drugs.

Case Histories

A couple of case histories will serve to illustrate problems experienced by clients before therapy and the relative success of treatment.

I) Mr. A., a 30-year-old, white, single, successful professional man was referred to the gay men's psychotherapy group following a resurgence of internalized homophobic feelings related to the stresses of moving to a new city, changing jobs, and ending a long-term gay relationship. He felt disillusioned about his ability to live a successful gay life-style and became self-conscious in social situations where he had felt comfortable before. He expressed feelings of worthlessness and "cheapness" following casual sexual contacts. He had had same-sex feelings and fantasies as early as early grade school and had been quite active sexually throughout his adolescence. After entering the university he "decided" to abandon his homosexuality and to adopt a heterosexual life-style. In his mid 20s, however, as the conflict between his social behavior and his internal same-sex feelings and impulses increased, he sought treatment from a conservative psychoanalytic therapist. When this treatment failed to change his sexual orientation as he had hoped, Mr. A. left analysis feeling disenchanted and skeptical about therapy. By the time he reached the gay men's therapy group, he had achieved fair success in adapting to minority sexual orientation.

In group, Mr. A. was able to admit and accept his own bitterness, alienation, and distance from his family, who rejected him, and to locate other sources of support in building a new "family." The group challenged and supported him, and he began to drop his cynical and jaded perception of gay life-styles. He began participating in community-oriented organizations and found his self-consciousness receding to more manageable dimensions. At the time the group terminated, Mr. A. had visibly changed his critical, abrasive, and harsh style of interacting with others and was clearly more relaxed, empathic, and gentle. He reported improvements in his work and in his relationship with colleagues. At 6-months follow-up, he is involved in building a relationship with a new partner and continues to be active in gay community organizations. His occupational adjustment remains satisfactory.

II) Mr. B. is a 31-year-old, white, single businessman who had been seeing psychiatrists for the past 9 years, beginning as an undergraduate student at the university. At that time he had been concealing his homosexual feelings and dating women for cover. He periodically sought anonymous gay sexual encounters but experienced guilt and high anxiety over this behavior. He had been exclusively homosexual in fantasy life as long as he could remember but could perform sexually with women if he fantasized about having sex with a man.

He was seen by a psychoanalytically oriented clinician, diagnosed as psychoneurotic, and treated with psychoanalytic psychotherapy and chemotherapy for his manifestations of anxiety. He tried to raise the issue of his homosexual feelings on numerous occasions, but his therapist closed the discussion, saying Mr. B. couldn't be homosexual because he was dating and having sex with women. During the 6 years of this therapy, the dosage of medications for anxiety steadily increased to: 100 mgm diazepam daily, 60 mgm trifluoperazine daily, 150 mgm amitriptyline daily, a hypnotic at bedtime, and methylphenidate upon awakening. Mr. B. finally left the therapist over a dispute about a further increase in medication and with the help of his general practitioner, an old school friend from his "straight" days at the university, began to withdraw from the medications. After about 2 years he finally confided his homosexual feelings to his doctor, who immediately referred him for counseling at a gay community organization, which in turn recommended group psychotherapy.

At the beginning of the group treatment, Mr. B. was completely naive about resources for gay people in the community and had never discussed gay issues openly with peers. By the end of the group he had nearly withdrawn from his last medication and was taking 30 mgm of diazepam daily. He began to socialize appropriately and to establish a friendship network. At 6-months follow-up, he is still in therapy with the general practitioner and resists decreasing his iatrogenically induced diazepam dependency further. He has also increased his alcohol intake to an extent that worries his therapist. On the positive side, he is much less conflicted about his sexual orientation and has begun to experiment in forming love relationships. He has adjusted well at work and has received a promotion. Though Mr. B's success is somewhat qualified, because of his propensity for substance abuse, the group experience was able in 20 sessions to promote his self-acceptance to a degree individual therapy might be expected to accomplish only after a period of years.

Conclusion

This paper presents one model of group therapy designed to facilitate psychosexual maturation ("coming out") in homosexual men. Such services are helpful for those members of the homosexual population who experience sexual orientation dysphoria with subjective distress and social and occupational impairment. In addition to fostering adaptive and satisfying homosexual lifestyles for individuals, the model represents a legitimate and necessary component of mainstream mental health services.

REFERENCES

Birk, L. Group psychtherapy for men who are homosexual. *Journal of Sex Research*, 1974, *1*(1), 29-52.

Birk, L., Huddleston, W., Muller, E., & Cohler, B. Avoidance conditioning for homosexuality. *Archives of General Psychiatry*, 1971, *25*(4), 314-323.

Birk, L., Miller, E., & Cohler, B. Group psychotherapy for homosexual men by male-female co-therapists. *Acta Psychiatrica Scandinavia*, Supp. 218, 1970, 7-37.

Covi, L. A group psychotherapy approach to the treatment of neurotic symptoms in male and female patients of homosexual preference. *Psychotherapy and Psychosomatics*, 1972, *20*(3), 176-180.

Hadden, S. B. Group psychotherapy with homosexual men. *International Psychiatry Clinics*, 1971, *8*(4), 81-94.

Knobloch, F., & Knobloch, J. *Integrated psychotherapy*. New York: Jason Aronson, 1979.

Lewis, H. R., & Streitfeld, H. S. *Growth games: How to tune in yourself, your family, your friends*. Toronto: Bantam Books, 1972.

Nobler, H. Group therapy with male homosexuals. *Comparative Group Studies*, 1972, *3*(2).

Rogers, C., Roback, McKee, E., & Calhoun, D. Group psychotherapy with homosexuals: A review. *International Journal of Group Psychotherapy*, 1976, *26*(1), 3-27.

Russell, A., & Winkler, R. Evaluation of assertive training and homosexual guidance service groups designed to improve homosexual functioning. *Journal of Consulting and Clinical Psychology*, 1977, *45*(1), 1-13.

Smith, J. Ego-dystonic homosexuality. *Comprehensive Psychiatry,* 1980, *21*(2), 119-127.

Truax, R., & Tourney, G. Male homosexuals in group psychotherapy: A controlled study. *Diseases of the Nervous System*, 1971, *32*(10), 707-11.

Yalom, I. *The theory and practice of group psychotherapy* (2nd ed.). New York: Basic Books, 1975.

GROUP TREATMENT OF SEXUAL DYSFUNCTION IN GAY MEN

Rex Reece, PhD

ABSTRACT. Three different formats for treating gay men with sexual dysfunctions are described, with emphasis on group therapy for men who are without partners. Clients present with general sexual anxieties, lack of sexual desire, secondary erectile dysfunctions, and difficulties with ejaculatory control, both rapid and inhibited. The process of selecting a program, and in particular the factors to consider when deciding if a client should work with a lover, with a partner surrogate or in a group format, are discussed. Primary procedures of sex therapy in each of these formats are described. Some trends in the frequencies of presenting complaints are noted, as well as possible reasons for reported differences between homosexual and heterosexual men. Other special considerations for working with gay men in sex therapy are discussed. Results of a self-report survey of change, administered 6 weeks and again 6 months following the end of 5 different 10-week sex therapy groups, are reported.

The effectiveness of direct approaches in the treatment of sexual dysfunctions with heterosexual couples has been demonstrated over the past several years. Many clinicians have expanded on the models of sex therapy developed and presented by such leaders as Kaplan (1974), Lobitz and Lo Piccolo (1972), and Masters and Johnson (1970). When they adapted the familiar couples format to group treatment for couples, Golden, Price, Heinrich, and Lobitz (1978) reported success similar to that established for individual couples. Group programs for heterosexual couples, for the treatment of erectile dysfunctions and ejaculatory control, have also been described by Blakeney, Kinder, Creson, Powell, and Sutton (1976), Kaplan, Kohl, Pomeroy, Offit, and Hogan (1974), Leiblum, Rosen, and Pierce (1976), Leiblum and Rosen (1979), and McGovern, Kirkpatrick, and Lo Piccolo (1978). Lobitz and Baker (1979) and Zilbergeld (1975) have described their group work with sexually dysfunctional heterosexual men without partners. Barback's (1974, 1980) success in groups for

Rex Reece has a PhD in counseling psychology from Purdue University and has received clinical supervision in sex therapy at the Human Sexuality Program of the University of California at Los Angeles and at the Beverly Psychiatric and Psychological Center in Beverly Hills. He has a private psychotherapeutic practice in Los Angeles and works primarily with gay men, specializing in sex therapy.

113

preorgasmic women has provided a model for others, including Heinrich (1976) and Schneidman and McGuire (1978).

A search of the literature on programs responding to the sexual-dysfunction concerns of homosexual populations yields little evidence of programs that are not also directed toward some aspect of change in sexual orientation or object choice. Legal and social prohibitions against homosexual expression have inhibited the development of sexual-dysfunction treatment programs within an atmosphere supportive of gay male and lesbian life-styles. Nevertheless, many homosexual people have become aware of sex therapy in general and are assuming they can find treatment programs responsive to problems within the context of same-sex relationships and culture. Some clinicians are responding to this assumption. McWhirter and Mattison (1978, 1980), for example, have described their experience in treating sexual dysfunctions in gay male couples. In pointing out some of the differences between working with gay men and working with heterosexual couples, they suggest that the high likelihood of a gay male relationship's being open, and the fact that gay men are likely to be less rigid in their attitudes toward sex and sex-roles, should be kept in mind when working with gay male couples. McWhirter and Mattison also imply that the lack of institutional support for same-sex coupling could contribute to a couple's decision to separate and to try to find more satisfactory sexual relationships with other partners, rather than to enter therapy to solve the problem. Masters and Johnson (1979), who used a format assumed to be similar to that used with heterosexual couples, have reported on the treatment of 57 cases of impotence in homosexual male couples. After conducting a sexual enrichment program for lesbians and gay men, Meston (1979) observed that many difficulties in male homosexual relationships may stem more from being socialized as male than from being gay.

This paper describes a group sex-therapy treatment format for gay men who are not in couple relationships. The program evolved from the need to provide an alternative treatment process for those men who do not have cooperative partners and for whom therapy with a partner surrogate is inappropriate. (Couples therapy and work with surrogates are briefly described, and a rationale for the choice of format for a particular client is offered, before the group program is discussed.)

Choosing a Treatment Program

Sex therapy for gay men in couples follows a process essentially like that for heterosexual couples. After proper screening and sex history taking, the couple generally attends weekly conjoint therapy meetings, engaging in a series of specific experiences between sessions. The suggested activities include sensate focus and self-pleasuring exercises, as well as the development of communication and assertiveness skills directly related to sexual expression. The

therapy hour is typically spent in discussing individual responses to these experiences, working with relationship issues, identifying and diffusing resistance to
therapy, and planning a series of experiences for the couple to engage in during
the following week.

Although work with surrogate partners has often been described (Jacobs,
Thompson, & Truxa, 1975; Lowry & Lowry, 1975; Masters & Johnson, 1970),
some controversy, as represented by Leroy's (1972) concerns with liability,
still exists in the professional community. The American Association of Sex
Educators, Counselors and Therapists (AASECT) Code of Ethics (1980), however, supports responsible use of surrogates.

The present author has structured a treatment format with surrogates, as
follows. Most appointments last 2 hours and take place at the therapist's
office. During the first few minutes of the session, the therapist and client
discuss the client's reactions to specific between-session experiences recommended at the end of the previous session, such as self-pleasuring or body-
image experiences, or perhaps some practice directed toward developing assertiveness or social skills. Then the client, surrogate, and therapist plan together an appropriate activity for the client and surrogate during that session.
With those specifics in mind, the client and surrogate spend the next hour
together, in private, engaging in a particular activity or series of experiences;
for example, sharing a sensate focus exercise or practicing a specific process
involving successive approximation. They then return to the therapist's office
to process their time together. After difficulties have been explored and positive behaviors reinforced, the surrogate leaves, allowing another few minutes
for the client and therapist to process further the relationship with the surrogate, to integrate sex therapy with broader therapeutic issues, or to discuss
the client's between-session activities during the following week.

For a variety of reasons, some people who present for sex therapy are not
likely to benefit from such a program. Sexual problems that are physiologically
based are not apt to respond to a psychological approach. A urological examination and an exploration of past and present use of medications, alcohol, and
other drugs usually determine whether the difficulty is organic, although a
combination of causes can be involved. Kaplan (1979) has said that people
who are seriously depressed, suicidal, or psychotic are not likely to benefit
from a program of sex therapy and should be treated for those conditions with
other forms of therapy. The screening interview includes questions and observations directed toward identifying such conditions. The sexual dysfunctions of
some couples who present for sex therapy are based in their relationship conflicts; they are appropriate candidates for couples counseling, at least until they
have sufficiently overcome their conflicts to allow them to cooperate with the
sex therapy process.

After screening out clients with a physiological basis for their dysfunction,
those with serious emotional disturbances, and those with other relationship

difficulties (if in a couple), an appropriate treatment format is selected. One of the most commonly accepted conditions for the success of sex therapy is being able to work with a cooperative partner. Therefore, most gay men who are in couple relationships work with their lovers. For the therapy to succeed, however, the partners need to be relatively committed to their ongoing relationship. The process of sex therapy can bring hidden relationship conflicts to the surface, as well as intensify the degree of intimacy between the partners. In the author's experience, couples who come to sex therapy soon after beginning a relationship are not good candidates for couples sex therapy; the relationship may not have "seasoned" enough to withstand the stresses of sex therapy.

McCarthy (1980) has described a sex therapy treatment process for heterosexual men without partners that does not include the client working with a cooperative partner. A similar process has occasionally been used by the author in working with gay men without partners, but most single clients seem to respond more rapidly and dependably with a partner.

Although some clients have ethical or moral qualms about working with a surrogate, and for others the comparatively great expense of a surrogate means they must attend a group instead, many clients prefer the relative privacy of working with a surrogate, rather than opening up about their sexual fears and feelings of inadequacy to several people in a group format. For example, some gay men who are sexually dysfunctional have never had the experience of an intimate, ongoing relationship with another man; the reversal of their dysfunctions seems to be integrated with overcoming blocks in their ability to form such relationships. Working with a surrogate can put these men in a more intense setting where the focus can include overcoming some of the intrapersonal dynamics that have inhibited their ability to be intimate. By paying attention to the dynamics of his relationship with the surrogate, the client is able to learn some relationship skills which later he can generalize to other partners.

The Participants and Their Dysfunctions

The author has recently conducted five group programs for gay men without partners; a total of 31 participants completed the 10-week program. Nine other clients began the group, but dropped out. Their stated reasons for leaving included work or family crises and, for at least four of the participants (all of whom had attended more than four sessions), a fear that the process would not work for them. Three men who dropped out spoke of being uncomfortable with the idea of doing physically intimate exercises with a relative stranger, even though they had originally thought this would not be a problem. It is impossible to determine to what degree their statements accurately reflect the participants' reasons for leaving the group, but they would seem to recommend a more thorough process of screening and orientation to the group, to lessen the likelihood of participants withdrawing, perhaps leaving with an additional sense of failure in overcoming their difficulty.

The participants were referred to the groups by former clients, other therapists, and public announcements. Two groups consisted of non-fee-paying clients referred through the Gay and Lesbian Community Services Center, a nonprofit social service agency in Los Angeles.

The participants ranged in age from the early 20s to the mid 50s. Ten men were in their 20s, 10 in their 30s, 6 in their 40s, and 5 in their 50s. Table One illustrates the frequencies of their presenting complaints and the fact that many members had more than one complaint—a total of 50 dysfunctions among 31 men.

The three letters in the "General Sexual Anxiety" column represent participants who, in addition to some specific response complaints, also talked of generalized anxiety in sexual situations and awkwardness while participating sexually. It was felt that these three participants could overcome some of their anxiety and awkwardness by participating in weekly discussions about sex and engaging in the between-session sensate focus and self-pleasuring experiences.

Kaplan (1979) has separated the sexual response cycle into three phases— desire, excitement, and orgasm—and discussed the etiology and treatment of problems associated with each. The two participants represented in the "Desire" column of Table One indicated difficulty in being interested in sex generally. They were not motivated to make the necessary effort to get together with others in order to be sexually involved.

The highest frequency of complaints is represented in the "Excitement" phase column of Table One. This phase of the sexual response cycle has to do with the ability to have or maintain an erection during sex. The men in these groups reported having erections in some situations, such as upon awakening, during private masturbation, or during sensual/sexual play before undressing with a partner. Although the specifics varied for each individual, they frequently complained of having no erection during manual or oral stimulation by a partner; or, if they were satisfactorily responsive to such stimulation, their erection faded during attempts to enter their partner anally, or soon after penetration.

The "Orgasm" phase—reflecting some difficulty with orgasms or ejaculations—is broken down into two categories. The five participants who are represented in the "Rapid Ejaculation" column reported ejaculating in response to varying degrees of specific stimulation but, most of the time, too quickly for them to feel sexually satisfied. Most commonly, they reported an ability to control their ejaculation during masturbation (whether alone or in the presence of a partner) but an inability to control ejaculation when a partner directly stimulated their genitals manually or orally. They also reported the likelihood of ejaculating during attempts at anal penetration or very soon after penetra-

Table One: Frequency of Phase Disorders

General Sexual Anxiety	Desire	Excitement	Orgasm	
			Rapid Ejaculation	Inhibited Ejaculation
		A		
		B		B
		C		C
		D		D
E	E	E		E
		F		
		G		
		H		
		I		
		J	J	
				K
			L	
			M	
	N			
		O		
		P		P
				Q
		R		R
		S		
		T	T	
		U		U
		V		V
		W		W
		X	X	
Y		Y		Y
		Z		Z
		AA		
BB				BB
		CC		CC
		DD		
		EE		
3	2	25	5	15

tion. As can be seen from Table One, three of the men who presented with this complaint also had difficulty getting or maintaining erections in some situations.

Fifteen participants complained of difficulty ejaculating when involved with a partner (Inhibited Ejaculation). Again, there seemed to be little difficulty in achieving orgasms during masturbation alone. Some reported not being able to ejaculate, even with self-stimulation, in the presence of a partner, while several were able to ejaculate under these conditions. Most were unable to reach an orgasm, except occasionally, during direct stimulation from a partner, either manual, oral, or especially anal. From the Table it can also be seen that 12 of the 15 in the "Inhibited Ejaculation" column are also represented in the "Excitement" phase column. From an examination of their sexual problem histories, it was noted that for several of these 12, inhibited ejaculation pre-dated the development of secondary erectile dysfunction, which was the client's primary complaint upon entering therapy. The difficulty with ejaculation was discovered only as a result of careful questioning during the sexual history taking. This suggests that in cases where a client presents with an excitement phase disorder that has developed from an orgasm phase disorder, the client is unlikely to respond to treatment unless the earlier difficulty is discovered and treated.

The frequencies of the various dysfunctions reported here are comparable to those reported on presumably heterosexual populations, except for the approximate reversal of frequencies in the two orgasmic phase categories. Masters and Johnson (1970) reported on the diagnosis and treatment of 448 cases of sexual dysfunction among heterosexual men. Of these, 245 (54.5%) complained of primary secondary erectile difficulties, representing excitement phase disorders, while 186 (41.5%) were rapid ejaculators ("premature ejaculators" in Masters and Johnson's terminology) and 17 (4%) were categorized as inhibited ejaculators ("retarded ejaculators").

In the present study, on the other hand, 15 (30%) of the 50 complaints had to do with inhibited ejaculation, while only 5 (10%) participants complained of rapid ejaculation. Although Masters and Johnson (1979) did not report any differences between the frequencies of presenting complaints for homosexual men when compared to heterosexual men, both George (Note 1) and McWhirter and Mattison (1980) have reported that gay men more commonly seek sex therapy for inhibited ejaculation than is generally reflected in the literature regarding presumably heterosexual males. This difference is also evidenced in popular gay writing by Shilts (1977) and Whitmore (1980). Shilts interviewed several therapists in New York and San Francisco regarding sex therapy for gay men and summarized their estimates. He wrote that perhaps half the case loads involved erection problems, while 30% of the clients complained of delayed or absent ejaculation with partners and close to 20% reported too rapid ejaculation. Whitmore wrote a fictionalized account of a sex therapy process directed toward overcoming difficulty ejaculating with a partner (*The Confessions of Danny Slocum*). The surname in the title indicates the protagonist's sexual response difficulty.

The present author speculates that the apparent higher frequency of complaints of inhibited ejaculation among gay men, as opposed to heterosexual men, has to do with issues of male-male intimacy and with the male's acceptance of his own homosexual identity. Males are socialized to be (or perhaps inherently are) competitive, defensive, and emotionally inexpressive rather than yielding, vulnerable, and open with feelings toward other men. Since an orgasm is generally accompanied by an abundance of feelings that are difficult to hide from a partner, perhaps the fear of being vulnerable to another man is partly responsible for blocking the specific response. Some of the men who complain of inhibited ejaculation report being afraid that if they learn to ejaculate with a partner, it will then be possible for them to establish an intimate relationship with another man. If they were to do that, they feel, they would have finally and deeply acknowledged that they are gay. Perhaps withholding ejaculation from another man allows some part of them to hold on to the illusion of heterosexual identity. If fears of intimacy or homosexuality that inhibited ejaculation were present during the initial same-sex experience, that first failure to ejaculate could have begun a process of performance anxiety that maintains the inhibition even after the man has developed more self-accepting attitudes toward masculinity and homosexuality.

Procedures

Each participant was interviewed for at least an hour before being accepted into the group. A sexual problem history similar to that suggested by Annon (1974) was taken, and an overview of the participant's coming-out process and relationship history was recorded. As previously mentioned, the evaluation also included procedures to screen out seriously disturbed applicants or those who might find some other form of therapy or another sex therapy format more useful. The groups met for 10 2-hour weekly sessions led by the author. The importance of participants' attendance at each session was emphasized; with few exceptions, attendance was perfect.

The group process generally followed that presented by Zilbergeld (1975) and Lobitz and Baker (1979) but also reflected the first three phases suggested in Annon's (1974) P-LI-SS-IT model. Annon has taught that many sexual difficulties can be overcome with relatively little time and interaction. For example, his first level of therapy, "permission giving," might be accomplished by using facts and figures to illustrate that many people share the client's feeling or behavior.

Through "limited information," the second level in Annon's model, it may be possible to overcome other kinds of sexual problems. If a client is anxious because he does not maintain an erection constantly during a sexual encounter, to teach him that the waxing and waning of arousal is normal may reduce his anxiety significantly.

"Specific suggestions," Annon's third level of treatment, involve the sensate focus exercises, self-pleasuring techniques, cognitive restructuring interactions, and other therapy processes that make up the core of the group treatment discussed here. (Annon's "intensive therapy" level is intended for work with sexual "problems," such as fetishistic, transvestite, or voyeuristic behavior and is not appropriate for use in this particular group treatment program.)

At group sessions, each participant reported to the leader and the other group members about his homework experiences. The rest of the time together was devoted to informational or permission-giving activities. Short explanations or brief simulated demonstrations of activities suggested for homework were given at the end of each session. For the first few meetings, these suggestions were general, but later they were tailored to each participant's presenting complaint and his weekly report of response to activities. The importance of having no sexual involvement between sessions, except as a part of the homework exercises, was underscored.

Primary Techniques

Early in the sequence a review of sexual physiology and anatomy and a description of the sexual response cycle (Masters & Johnson, 1966) were presented. Sexual performance anxiety was explained and the rationale for the treatment discussed. Permission-giving activities included desensitization to sexual terminology, discussion of attitudes, history, habits, and styles of masturbation, and sharing of participants' fantasy material. Specific suggestions for activities between the sessions centered around individual self-pleasuring activities described by Zilbergeld (1975) and adaptations from Masters and Johnsons's (1970) sensate focus exercises with partners.

Excitement Phase Disorders

The men who were concerned with erectile failure generally did some nongential, sensual awareness exercises alone, gradually progressing to genital pleasuring and to masturbating with an erection. Next they practiced interruption of stimulation to let the erection subside, stimulating to erection again; and again allowing the erection to subside. This last activity was designed to teach the value of concentration on the sensations and the futility of direct attempts at maintaining an erection. Participants learned that even if an erection goes away, tumescence will often return when one focuses on pleasurable sensations rather than performance. After a client had been successful alone, he tried the same sequence of exercises (involving non-genital pleasuring, then genital, then having and losing an erection) with a partner. Once the man was less anxious about having and losing an erection when alone or when manually stimulated by a partner, he was encouraged to masturbate to fantasies of being fellated or anally penetrating his partner. He was urged to let go of the fantasy only if he became so anxious that his erection began to subside. Typically, the sequence moved from oral to anal sex, since for most participants oral stimulation evoked less performance anxiety than did attempts at anal penetration.

When he could move through the originally fearful episodes in his fantasy with relaxation and arousal, it was suggested that the client either receive fellatio from his partner or anally penetrate his partner from the sexual position least threatening to the client. After containment, he was to allow his erection to subside. Once the anxiety associated with this procedure had diminished appropriately, the client proceeded through the remaining progressive steps: thrusting, experimentation with various positions during containment, and insertion from various positions. The directions included interrupting the activity if performance anxiety began to distract from the pleasure, and moving to an activity not associated with pressure until an attitude of pleasure was re-established. Participants were repeatedly urged to identify performance anxiety in themselves and to replace it with an awareness of pleasurable sensations, either through sensate focus skills, focus on the partner's pleasurable response, or fantasy material.

Orgasm Phase Disorders

The early homework suggestions for men desiring more control over ejaculation were similar to those for the men with erectile dysfunctions.

Rapid ejaculation. The men who were rapid ejaculators moved through the non-genital pleasuring sequences to the stop-start process developed by Semans (1956), first alone and then with a partner. Each participant then masturbated through the anxious aspects of sexual fantasy, which included oral and then anal penetration of a partner. With subsequent oral or anal containment, the sequence included no movement at first, then stimulation or thrusts by the partner, then movement by the participant with the partner simply receptive, and eventually both moving more freely.

Delayed ejaculation. In the sexual problem histories gathered by the author from gay men who cannot ejaculate with a partner or who experience delayed ejaculation with a partner, a noticeable masturbation pattern has emerged for some. Generally, these men consciously increase muscle tension in their bodies, especially in the lower abdomen and thighs, as they approach ejaculation. They often describe using a great deal of pressure in grasping their penis when masturbating, stroking very rapidly and often holding their breath for several seconds, intermittently gulping for air. These habits, if sufficiently extreme, can create a problem when the man has sex with a partner, for rarely is the pressure from oral or anal stimulation sufficient to recreate the degree of intensity familiar in self-stimulation. In addition, rapid motion, which is easy enough in masturbation, and the muscle tension that seems to facilitate the ejaculatory response during masturbation, are difficult to simulate and coordinate in sex with a partner.

The treatment of delayed ejaculation frequently included attempts to change masturbatory habit patterns (Roberts, Note 2). This was accomplished in two types of exercises performed progressively, alone and with a partner. First, the participant practiced pleasuring himself with a light touch while keeping his muscles and breathing relaxed. Then he practiced the same relaxation while being stimulated by a partner.

The second, and later, set of exercises involved a process that was based on the principal of successive approximation described by Wolpe and Lazarus (1966). In the solo activities, the group member stimulated himself in his habitual way while focusing on the sensations in his penis. Close to the point of ejaculation, he varied his position or method of stimulation (such as rolling from his back to his side, or switching hands), relaxed his breathing and muscles, and lightened his touch as the orgasmic contractions began. If he was unable to ejaculate with self-stimulation in the presence of a partner, successive approximation was utilized: the partner gradually moving into the room, becoming physically closer and more sexually involved with each experience. Sessions with a partner alternated between (1) receiving non-demanding, relaxed manual, oral, or anal stimulation; and (2) having the recipient stimulate himself almost to ejaculation and then relax, with the partner stimulating him progressively earlier in the sequence.

Other Activities and Issues

As mentioned earlier, emphasis was placed on learning to identify one's own anxiety and on creating the conditions (Zilbergeld, 1978) necessary to alleviate it. One homework exercise involved having the participant write a letter to himself from his penis, an exercise developed by Zilbergeld. Participants were also encouraged to disclose progressively more about their sexual concerns and needs to other people, first to acquaintances or friends, and then to potential partners.

Other homework assignments were designed to assist the participants in becoming more sexually assertive. They practiced refusing sexual requests with which they really did not wish to comply, asking their potential partners for the stimulation they desired, and initiating specific behaviors during sex.

Hartman and Fithian (1972) have recognized the relationship of a self-accepting body image to sexual satisfaction and response. In these groups for gay men, one series of suggestions included activities intended to improve this self-acceptance.

One of the discussions that seemed to relieve much anxiety was stimulated by a reading assignment from Zilbergeld (1978), specifically chapters 3 and 4, which described the fantasy model of sex and the unrealistic expectations that are placed on men as a consequence. This was followed by an exploration of some of the myths and realities of the gay subculture and a discussion of how they can result in even more performance pressures.

One of the major differences between groups for heterosexual men without partners (as reported by other authors) and these sex therapy groups for single gay men involves the exercises with cooperative partners. Men in groups for single heterosexual males must find partners on their own. In the five groups described here, most of the participants were encouraged to arrange sensate focus and other homework exercises with fellow group members. It was felt that a partner who understood the concepts and procedures of sex therapy as a result of his own participation in the group would be more cooperative. A committed couple participated in one group, so they worked together; a few other members have worked with people outside the group with whom they were in special relationships.

An opportunity to express the feelings that arise from involvement in such a group, reassurance that the exercises are highly structured and safe, and role-playing in being assertive when making plans to get together and in coping with the fear of rejection have resulted in a spirit of support and cooperation among group members. The anxieties expressed became material for exploration and growth when practicing assertive social-sexual skills with potential extra-group partners.

Sensate focus and other exercises with others in the group seem to be easier if the participant feels attractive, is comfortable refusing requests, is able to be sexually open to a wider variety of "types" of partners, and has a value structure that permits sexual involvement outside the context of a committed relationship.

Results

A total of 28 participants out of 31 attended the 6-week follow-up sessions; 21 returned for the 6-month follow-up. Forms to evaluate progress were filled out at each follow-up session. Four other evaluation reports (one for the 6-week follow-up, three for the 6-month follow-up) were obtained by mail. These participants had been sent a stamped, self-addressed envelope, along with a request to complete the report and return it to the author.

The two follow-up sessions consisted of participants' reports of experiences, problems, and progress, as well as some suggestions on how to continue progress. Table Two shows the frequency of self-report ratings on a 5-point scale measuring the degree to which participants felt their sexual problems had been overcome, at both 6-week and 6-month follow-up sessions.

Some progress was reported on at lest 93% of the returned forms at the 6-week meetings; 83% reported progress at the 6-month interval. Even if the worst is assumed—that those who neither attended the follow-up sessions nor

Table Two: Frequencies of Degrees of Success in Overcoming Sexual Problems

	6-Week Follow-up		6-Month Follow-up	
	N	%	N	%
Evaluations Returned				
	29	93.5	24	77.4
Problem worsened	0	-0-	0	-0-
Remained the same	2	7.0	4	16.7
Somewhat overcome	12	41.5	8	33.3
Significantly overcome	12	41.5	10	41.7
Completely overcome	3	10.0	2	8.3

returned the questionnaires had made no progress—87% reported progress after 6 weeks, while 65% reported some continued progress after 6 months.

At the 6-month interval, each respondent was also asked to indicate the degree to which he felt his particular sexual problem had been overcome. Table Three shows those results.

Of those participants responding, all reported progress in overcoming their general sexual anxieties, half in overcoming problems of desire, 65% in overcoming erectile dysfunctions, 80% in overcoming rapid ejaculation, and over 66% in overcoming inhibited ejaculation. Again, if it is assumed that those who did not respond had made no progress, the figures go down to 67% reporting success in overcoming general sexual anxieties while the results for the desire category remain the same: 50%. Continuing with this assumption, 52% of the men with erectile dysfunction reported success after 6 months, while 80% of the rapid ejaculators did and 53% of the inhibited ejaculators did.

Among others, Derogatis and Melisaratos (1979) have assumed that other attitudes and skills not only influence sexual functioning but may be altered as a result of change in sexual response. At the 6-month interval, the group members were asked to respond to three questions regarding how they saw themselves or felt about themselves now, as compared with the beginning of the group. Table Four shows those results. Over 83% reported some positive

Table Three: Frequencies of Degrees of Sucess Reported in
Overcoming Specific Sexual Problems

	Anxiety		Desire		Erectile		Rapid Ejaculation		Inhibited Ejaculation	
	N	%	N	%	N	%	N	%	N	%
Presenting Problem	3	6.0	2	4.0	25	50.0	5	10.0	15	30.0
Evaluations Received	2	66.7	2	100.0	20	80.0	5	100.0	12	80.0
Problem has:										
Significantly increased										
Somewhat increased										
Remained the same			1	50.0	7	35.0	1	20.0	4	33.3
Been somewhat overcome	1	50.0			11	55.0	2	40.0	6	50.0
Been significantly overcome	1	50.0	1	50.0	2	10.0	2	40.0	2	16.7

Table Four: Change Reported in Attitudes and Skills

	Somewhat Lessened		Remained the Same		Somewhat Increased		Significantly Increased	
	N	%	N	%	N	%	N	%
Self-confidence has:	1	4.2	3	12.5	13	54.2	7	29.1
Comfort level in potentially intimate situations has:	2	8.3	5	20.8	13	54.2	4	16.7
Ability to function in social situations has:	1	4.2	9	37.5	10	41.6	4	16.7

change in self-confidence, over 70% said they were more comfortable in intimate situations, and almost 60% said their ability to function in social situations had increased.

Even though this method of evaluation is by no means a controlled study, indications are that sex therapy for gay men without partners can be conducted with results comparable to those reported for other formats and with heterosexual populations.

Assessment of Sexual Response in Gay Men

Assessment of change in the sexual response of the men in these groups was little more than impressionistic. Many currently available measures of sexual functioning were recently listed and reviewed by Schiavi, Derogatis, Kuriansky, O'Connor, and Sharpe (1979). Few, if any, of these devices are appropriate for use with homosexual populations, however, since the various items usually refer to sex in a male-female relationship. Instruments need to be developed on a homosexual assumption. Perhaps then, more dependable evaluations can be made of various treatment modalities for overcoming sexual dysfunctions in gay men.

REFERENCE NOTES

1. George K. *Sex therapy with gay men*. Paper presented at the conference of the Society for the Scientific Study of Sex, San Diego, California, 1979.
2. Roberts, B. Personal communication, Los Angeles, 1977.

REFERENCES

Annon, J. S. *The behavioral treatment of sexual problems, Volume 1: Brief therapy.* Honolulu: Enabling Systems, 1974.

Barback, L. G. Group treatment of preorgasmic women. *Journal of Sex & Marital Therapy,* 1974, *1*, 139-145.

Barback, L. G. *Women discover orgasm: A therapist's guide to a new treatment approach.* New York: Free Press, Macmillan Publishing Co., Inc., 1980.

Blakeney, P., Kinder, B. N., Creson, D., Powell, L. C., & Sutton, C. A short-term, intensive workshop approach for the treatment of human sexual inadequacy. *Journal of Sex & Marital Therapy,* 1976, *2,* 124-129.

Derogatis, L. R., & Melisaratos, N. The DSFI: A multidimensional measure of sexual functioning. *Journal of Sex & Marital Therapy,* 1979, *5,* 244-281.

Ethics Committee, American Association of Sex Educators, Counselors and Therapists. *AASECT code of ethics.* Washington, D.C.: Author, 1980.

Golden, J. S., Price, S., Heinrich, A. G., & Lobitz, W. C. Group vs. couple treatment of sexual dysfunctions. *Archives of Sexual Behavior,* 1978, *7,* 593-602.

Hartman, W. E., & Fithian, M. A. *Treatment of sexual dysfunction: A bio-psycho-social approach.* Long Beach, CA: Center for Marital and Sexual Studies, 1972.

Heinrich, A. G. *The effect of group and self-directed behavioral-educational treatment of primary orgasmic dysfunction in females treated without their partners.* Unpublished doctoral dissertation, University of Colorado, 1976.

Jacobs, M., Thompson, L. A., & Truxaw, P. The use of sexual surrogates in counseling. *The Counseling Psychologist,* 1975, *5,* 73-76.

Kaplan, H. S. *The new sex therapy.* New York: Brunner/Mazel, 1974.

Kaplan, H. S. *Disorders of sexual desire and other new concepts and techniques in sex therapy* (*Vol. II: The new sex therapy*). New York: Brunner/Mazel, 1979.

Kaplan, H. S., Kohl, R. N., Pomeroy, W. B., Offit, A. K., & Hogan, B. Group treatment of premature ejaculation. *Archives of Sexual Behavior,* 1974, *3,* 443-452.

Leiblum, S. R., & Rosen, R. C. The weekend workshop for dysfunctional couples: Assets and limitations. *Journal of Sex & Marital Therapy,* 1979, *5,* 57-69.

Leiblum, S. R., Rosen, R. C., & Pierce, D. Group treatment format: Mixed sexual dysfunctions. *Archives of Sexual Behavior,* 1976, *5,* 313-322.

Leroy, D. H. The potential criminal liability of human sex clinics and their patients. *St. Louis University Law Journal,* 1972, *16,* 586-603.

Lobitz, W. C., & Baker, E. L. Group treatment of single males with erectile dysfunction. *Archives of Sexual Behavior,* 1979, *8,* 127-138.

Lobitz, W. C., & Lo Piccolo, J. New methods in the behavioral treatment of sexual dysfunction. *Journal of Behavior Therapy and Experimental Psychiatry,* 1972, *3,* 265-271.

Lowry, T. S., & Lowry, T. P. Ethical considerations in sex therapy. *Journal of Marriage and Family Counseling,* 1975, *1,* 229-236.

McCarthy, B. W. Treatment of secondary erectile dysfunction in males without partners. *Journal of Sex Education and Therapy,* 1980, *6,* 29-34.

McGovern, K. B., Kirkpatrick, C. C., & Lo Piccolo, J. A behavioral group treatment program for sexually dysfunctional couples. In J. Lo Piccolo & L. Lo Piccolo (Eds.), *Handbook of sex therapy.* New York: Plenum Press, 1978.

McWhirter, D. P., & Mattison, A. M. The treatment of sexual dysfunction in gay male couples. *Journal of Sex & Marital Therapy,* 1978, *4,* 213-218.

McWhirter, D. P., & Mattison, A. M. Treatment of sexual dysfunction in homosexual male couples. In S. R. Leiblum & L. A. Pervin (Eds.), *Principles and practice of sex therapy.* New York: The Guilford Press, 1980.

Masters, W. H., & Johnson, V. E. *Human sexual response.* Boston: Little, Brown and Company, 1966.

Masters, W. H., & Johnson, V. E. *Human sexual inadequacy.* Boston: Little, Brown and Company, 1970.

Masters, W. H., & Johnson, V. E. *Homosexuality in perspective.* Boston: Little, Brown and Company, 1979.

Meston, J. T. The use of a sexual enrichment program to enhance self-concept and interpersonal relationships of homosexuals. *Journal of Sex Education and Therapy,* 1979, *1,* 17-20.

Schiavi, R. C., Derogatis, L. R., Kuriansky, J., O'Connor, D., & Sharpe, L. The assessment of sexual function and marital interaction. *Journal of Sex & Marital Therapy, 1979, 5,* 169-224.

Schneidman, B., & McGuire, L. Group therapy for nonorgasmic women: Two age levels. In J. Lo Piccolo & L. Lo Piccolo (Eds.), *Handbook of sex therapy.* New York: Plenum Press, 1978.

Semans, J. Premature ejaculation: A new approach. *Southern Medical Journal*, 1956, *49*, 353-358.

Shilts, R. Sexual dysfunction: Its ups and downs. *The Advocate*, August 24, 1977, pp. 32-34.

Whitmore, G. *The confessions of Danny Slocum or gay life in the big city*. New York: St. Martin's Press, 1980.

Wolpe, J., & Lazarus, A. A. *Behavior therapy techniques: A guide to the treatment of neuroses.* New York: Pergamon Press, 1966.

Zilbergeld, B. Group treatment of sexual dysfunction in men without partners. *Journal of Sex & Marital Therapy*, 1975, *1*, 204-214.

Zilbergeld, B. *Male sexuality: A guide to sexual fulfillment*. Boston: Little, Brown and Company, 1978.

COUNSELING THE PARENTS OF YOUNG HOMOSEXUAL MALE PATIENTS

Michael F. Myers, MD

ABSTRACT. This paper describes the author's practice of interviewing the parents of young homosexual men in therapy; specifically, parents who are in crisis after having recently learned their son is homosexual. A review of the literature on the "old" and "new" schools of thought in this area is presented, as well as an analysis of motivations for disclosure to parents. The importance of thorough patient assessment and preparation is emphasized. Therapist roles and functions in assisting parents are described and discussed in detail.

Although there is no definitive empirical evidence of an increased incidence of homosexuality, more openly gay men are now requesting or are actually receiving psychotherapy than ever before. This does not imply increased symptomology. One study, of gay volunteers (contacted through a homophile organization) and matched controls, showed no significant difference in the prevalence of neurotic disorders between heterosexual and homosexual respondents (Saghir & Robins, 1971). Several articles on homosexuality and adjustment written since that study (e.g., Hart, Roback, Tittler, Weitz, Walston, & McKee, 1978; Siegelman, 1972) have reinforced its conclusions. Gonsiorek (1977) has undertaken an excellent, comprehensive review of this area.

That greater numbers of gay men appear to be seeking psychotherapy does represent an increase in self-disclosure among homosexual men. Hooker (1972)

Michael F. Myers graduated from the University of Western Ontario School of Medicine in 1966. After completing his internship at Los Angeles County General Hospital, he did post graduate residency training at Wayne State University, Detroit, Michigan; Los Angeles County - U.S.C. Medical Center, Los Angeles, California; and the University of British Columbia, Vancouver, British Columbia. He completed his psychiatric training in 1973, and is a Fellow of the Royal College of Physicians and Surgeons of Canada.

Dr. Myers is a Clinical Assistant Professor, Department of Psychiatry, University of British Columbia, and is also in private practice. He is with the Department of Psychiatry, Shaughnessy Hospital, where he is actively involved in the teaching of medical students and the training of residents in psychiatry. He has a clinical and academic interest in marital therapy, psychotherapy with gay persons and their families, and women's issues within the care-giving professions.

Dr. Myers is a member of the Canadian Psychiatric Association, the American Psychiatric Association, and the American Association for Marriage and Family Therapy.

has commented on "heightened visibility" as a reflection of radical changes in the attitudes of the public and of homosexual men and women themselves. Similarly, Bell and Weinberg (1978) have cited the rise in homosexual candor since Bieber, Dain, Dince, Drellich, Grand, Gundlach, Kremer, Rifkin, Wilbur, and Bieber's study in 1962.

For many gay people, an important manifestation of candor is disclosing one's homosexuality to one's parents. Unfortunately, this can precipitate symptoms in the parents (e.g., anxiety, guilt, anger, bewilderment) and may enhance interpersonal conflict between the son and his parents. The purpose of this paper is to underscore the importance of interviewing and counseling the parents of young gay male patients who have recently revealed their homosexuality. Motives for telling parents will also be presented. (Whether to tell parents, when to tell them, and how to tell them, have been discussed elsewhere by Weinberg, 1972.)

This article is based on the author's experience with homosexual male *patients* and their parents, not on homosexual males in general. The age range of the patient sample is approximately 17–30 years. Most are of middle- to upper-middle-class socioeconomic status and are engaged in a wide range of occupations. Most came to therapy with neurotic symptoms: anxiety, depression, relationship conflict, sexual dysfunction, etc. Most could be defined as "obligatory homosexuals" (Freud, S., 1905).

With the exception of Freud's famous letter to the American mother of a homosexual son (Freud, S., 1951), most of the important traditional theories and treatments of homosexuality (Bieber, 1971; Cappon, 1965; Ferenczi, 1909/1955, 1912/1956, 1914/1956; Freud, A., 1951; Freud, S., 1905/1953, 1911/1958; Hadden, 1958, 1971; Hadfield, 1958, 1966; Hatterer, 1970; Ovesey, 1954; Ovesey & Gaylin, 1965; Socarides, 1968; 1970; 1972; 1978; West, 1967) do not address the issue of working with families. The work of Bergler (1956), who believes that homosexuality is a curable neurotic disease, illustrates traditional psychiatric attitudes toward homosexuality. He accuses Kinsey, Pomeroy, and Martin (1948) of grossly exaggerating their statistics on homosexual behavior and then proceeds to make frankly pejorative statements about homosexual people in general. Bergler has the following to say about the parents:

> I am also thinking of the unhappy parents of these young homosexuals, and especially of their mothers, who are horrified and shocked by the sudden and unsuspected revelation of their sons' and daughters' troubles. . . .These poor parents accuse themselves of having failed in their duty, or, leveling mutual accusations, search both family trees for "faulty inheritance" (p. 10).

Perhaps the most well-known study of male homosexuality is that of Bieber et al. in 1962. Their oft-quoted family description is of a "close-binding intimate mother"; a hostile or detached or brutal or absent father; a poor relation-ship between the parents; and frequent rejection or hostility by the sibs of their homosexual brother. One criticism of their methodology questions the validity of data about families the analysts had never seen. In a more recent paper, Bieber and Bieber (1979) state that examination of 100 pairs of parents con-firmed the findings reported in their original study. However, they do not explain how they "examined" the parents or whether any attempt was made to counsel them.

The NIMH Task Force on Homosexuality: Final Report and Background Papers (1972) makes notable recommendations in areas of research and treat-ment relevant to this topic: attitudinal patterns of parents, significance of family structure and ideology, the effects on the family of having a homosexual member, innovative treatment techniques, treatment centers for gay people and their families, reducing of the taboo against seeking help, etc. To date, few of these recommendations have been carried out.

There are, however, authors who do not adhere to a "disease model" of homosexuality and do not have "heterosexual shift" as their therapeutic goal, a trend reviewed in a paper by Coleman (1978). For example, Weinberg (1972) has itemized factors to consider when contemplating disclosure to parents, including possible reactions and guidelines for parents. Clark (1977) describes the effects of disclosure on parents, spouses, children, siblings, and friends. Jones (1978) has written about his experiences as a minister counseling gay people, their relatives, and friends. Silverstein's (1977) book, which is specif-ically for parents of gay people, urges meaningful dialogue between parents and their gay daughter or son. Fairchild and Hayword's (1979) work has been advertised as "the first book written for parents of gay children by parents of gay children." Berzon and Leighton's (1979) book on being gay contains an excellent chapter on telling the family. Gilberg (1978) describes how the changing culture has affected homosexual adolescents and the attitudes of their parents toward therapy. He stresses a family approach to the treatment of the homosexual adolescent. The issue of whether attitudes toward homosexuality are changing or not, particularly the attitudes of families and the helping pro-fessions, is reviewed by Gross (1978). In a strong position paper, Lawrence (1977) has emphasized the therapeutic value of gay paraprofessionals counsel-ing other gay people and their parents in the Homophile Community Health Service of Boston.

Occasions and Motivations for Telling Parents

Homosexual male patients disclose their sexual orientation for a variety of reasons and in a number of different situations. Research has shown that young single subjects are more disclosing to their mothers than to their fathers, and that this is an index of the "closeness" of the relationship (Gelman & McGinley,

1978; Jourard, 1964, 1971). As one would predict, therefore, many gay men have "come out" to their mothers first—or solely to them.

Consequence of the Gay Liberation Movement

With its emphasis on self-acceptance, self-esteem, and dissemination of information, the movement has undoubtedly affected the feelings and thinking of many gay people. Many contemporary young men, particularly in urban settings, elect to tell their parents of their homosexuality for political reasons.

Inner Torment

Lee (1977) has written about the psychological costs of "passing" as heterosexual. Many gay people cannot tolerate the double life, deception, and psychological distance from their families that result from attempts to pass. Some young men look to disclosure as a way to reduce these strains.

The "Coming-Out" Process

The transition to a homosexual identity—i.e., identifying and accepting oneself as homosexual—has been described by Dank (1971), Roesler and Deishler (1972), Lee (1977), Cass (1979), and by Coleman in this volume (1981/82). A man may self-disclose to his parents at any stage in the process of coming out.

The Psychotherapeutic Process

A patient in therapy may become more open and honest with others, especially with family and friends. As symptoms recede and self-regard improves, his trust and confidence may increase sufficiently for the patient to reveal his homosexuality to his family.

Development of a Serious Love Relationship with Another Male

Union with another person, a phase of the maturation process, is most probable following resolution of separation-individuation conflicts with the patient's family of origin. The patient is particularly likely to self-disclose to his parents if there are practical considerations, such as plans to cohabit with a lover in the same locale as the parents.

Destructive Motives

These are less common but deserve mention. Destructive motives attend premature disclosure by someone who has many ambivalent feelings and considerable inner conflict about being gay. Revealing one's homosexuality to parents as an act of angry rebellion, or as an attempt to lay blame and induce guilt, sets the stage for confrontation, bilateral defensiveness, and increased alienation.

Assessment of the Patient

It is not unusual for a gay person to be overt with friends, neighbors, employer, and fellow workers, but covert with parents. In the Saghir and Robins (1973) study, close to half the homosexual men stated that their families definitely knew about their homosexuality, although only one-third had actually told the parents on their own volition. Saghir and Robins report: "Surprisingly, over one-half of the parents who became aware of their son's homosexuality (52%) reacted with compassion, understanding and acceptance while 48% reacted in a variety of other ways." These "other ways" were anger, condemnation, self-blame, disbelief, alienation, and ignoring the issue. In the Bell and Weinberg (1978) study, more mothers of respondents were reported as knowing about their sons' homosexuality, followed by the sibs, and then the fathers.

Before broaching the subject of meeting with the parents, the therapist should consider the following checklist of important questions:

—How much do the parents know?
—Were they told by the patient?
—If so, how were they told—i.e., with sensitivity or anger, by letter or face-to-face, individually or together?
—If the patient did not tell his parents, how did they find out?
—Did they find out against his *conscious* desires while he left many clues for discovery?
—Do both parents know?
—If only one parent was told by the patient, why?
—Does the patient suspect that the other parent has been told?
—Does he actually fear the other parent knowing?
—Do his siblings know?
—If so, did he tell them himself?
—How did the parents react initially?
—Did their feelings change or fluctuate with time?
—Did each parent react the same?
—How understanding, tolerant, or accepting are they at present?
—How long have they known?
—What has been the state of the patient's relationship with his parents since telling them?
—How concerned is the patient about this and does he want to do anything about it?

If the patient's preoccupation with the family continues for several sessions and does not abate with ventilation and reassurance, an interview with the parents is proposed. The therapist should pledge to maintain confidentiality, for there are many patients who fear or even expect that the therapist will discuss their personal psychotherapeutic work with their parents. If the patient is hesitant or totally opposed to a meeting, the matter is best dropped for the time being. This is consistent with a psychodynamic approach to therapy. The issue may be discussed again in future sessions—perhaps in more detail and with a renewed statement of professional trust. With the patient's consent, the parents may then be interviewed.

Interview with the Parents

If the patient is not present at the parents' first visit, they may be less defensive and therefore able to answer and ask questions more frankly. It is important to follow up this visit with one or more meetings at which the parents and the patient are all present, in order to address basic communication issues.

Some examples from the author's experience with patients may help to illustrate the variety in parents' attitudes and behavior during meetings.

Case #1. M. was a 19-year-old middle-class youth, living at home. When he told them he was gay, his parents urged him to see a psychiatrist. Although M. denied any conflicts or regret about his homosexuality, 3 to 4 months later he reluctantly consented to see the author. The patient emphatically stated that he was "OK," but that his parents needed help. A visit was scheduled for his parents, but his mother refused to join the meeting. M. came in with his father, and they were seen together. M.'s father stated that since the disclosure he had felt closer to his son, and although not approving of M.'s homosexuality, he was slowly accepting him. They had visited a gay bar together and the father had met some of M.'s friends. The father expressed concern about his wife and how she was reacting. The interview ended with a second invitation for M.'s mother to come in, alone or with her husband. It was arranged that M. could return alone if necessary. There has been no subsequent contact with M. or his parents, however.

Case #2. Dr. and Mrs. A. came in together. Two years previously, their 23-year-old son had told his father he was gay. The father, with the son's encouragement, told the mother. Although 2 years had passed, Mrs. A. stated that she still had trouble accepting her son's style of living. Her reaction had caused estrangement and a great deal of secretive behavior on the son's part. Mrs. A. disapproved of most of her son's friends and refused to meet them if he brought them by the family home. (He had been living on his own for 3 years.) During the interview, Mrs. A. confided, with her husband's coaxing, that she felt responsible for the son's sexual orientation and could not help but feel it was all her fault. Dr. A., who stated that he felt more accepting than his wife, explained his acceptance as the result of having met and treated gay people in his practice. Mrs. A. admitted she had had no exposure whatsoever. She said she felt as if she were living in the Dark Ages.

Case #3. Mr. T. came in alone. Mrs. T. felt too phobic actually to come to my office but did express her concerns over the phone: i.e., guilt, ambivalence, the hope her son would marry again, feelings of distance from her son and husband. Three years previously, at the age of 30, their son had confided that he was leaving his wife and infant son to live with his male lover of several months' duration. To say that this led to family chaos would be an understatement.

What was most obvious in the interview was the intensity of surface feelings still experienced by the father. He alternately expressed rage, bitterness, sorrow, rejection, guilt, and disappointment. He admitted feeling sad that his son would be "alone" when the father and mother die. Mr. T. described family get-togethers as awkward and longed for the family parties they had had when his son had been married. He confessed to feeling ashamed in front of his friends and colleagues and stated that their children were "healthy normal, married with kids. None of them have sexual aberrations." He frankly admitted that he longed to be closer to his son yet did not wish to know more about his personal or social life.

Purposes of the Meeting

The interview with the parents serves many purposes.

Parent Assessment

The interview provides the therapist an opportunity to observe and assess each parent. In particular, examining how the parents relate to each other can help to clarify the therapist's dynamic understanding of the patient and his problems.

Obtaining More Information

With certain patients, it may be important, as part of a comprehensive assessment, to have collateral information from the parents. This might range from data about infancy and developmental milestones, to anxieties the parents may have had about their parenting. Long before any overt disclosure was made by their son, many parents have had fears or concerns about his sexuality, social skills, and capacity for same-sex and opposite-sex friendships. Almost consistently they have denied, rationalized, or avoided frank discussion of these issues with their sons.

Background and developmental history can be obtained in the interview directly or indirectly by inference.

Affording the Parents an Opportunity to Meet the Therapist

This consideration is more important than one would realize, particularly if one subscribes to a general systems theory of family homeostasis. It is crucial that the parents have an occasion to meet their son's therapist; in a sense, to assess her or him as a competent, mature, and respected professional. This is especially important with late adolescent and young adult patients with problems of delayed separation-individuation from their families of origin.

Counseling for the Parents

The role of the therapist in the interview is chiefly supportive, particularly in the following areas:

Problem identification. The parents' definition of the problem areas may be quite different from their son's. It may be necessary to clarify expectations of therapy and behavioral changes, and to identify realistic and tangible goals. The parents may be expecting therapy to produce a change in sexual orientation, while their son wishes to remain homosexual—but with less conflict. Depending on their level of psychological sophistication, the parents may see therapy in very limited or concrete terms. The current controversy about homosexuality as illness vs. normal variant generates important treatment considerations (Freund, 1977). For example, depending on the situation, it may be important to point out to parents that their son appears to have accepted his homosexuality, has no desire to change, and is in therapy for unrelated issues. It has been the author's impression that most parents are operating from a "homosexuality as disease" mind set. This of course must be respected, but they may also need to be reminded that their son's differing perception of himself needs to be respected, too.

Catharsis. It is wise to encourage ventilation of feelings during the interview. The extent to which parents are able to do this depends on many factors, including their underlying personalities and whether or not they are in crisis. The symptoms of people in crisis and the various stages of adjustment are well documented (Caplan, 1964). Often the parents, if seen relatively soon after the disclosure, are in a state of mourning. That is, they are attempting to work through a loss, usually of a dream of seeing their son meet the "right girl," fall in love, get married, and have children. Many parents react with denial, sometimes forever. Others are full of anger and may be temporarily (or, more rarely, permanently) rejecting of their son and his style of living. Still others are guilt-ridden, blame themselves totally, and have embarked upon an obsessive process of self-scrutiny to discover where they "went wrong."

Parents vary in how they react to the disclosure. Initially, one parent may be affected more than the other; later, the roles may switch. Or both may be devastated. The reaction to the revelation is highly personal, and parents need time to adjust.

The therapist should attempt to facilitate this process by empathy, by responding as directly as possible to the parents' questions, and by attempting to allay their guilt or feelings of failure as parents. Normalizing helps; i.e., pointing out that it is quite common for parents to feel all of what they are feeling, that those feelings will diminish in time, and that increased understanding and intimacy with their son should ensue.

Parents frequently express disillusionment. This is especially true among families with an only child, in which case the parents may be deeply upset about never having grandchildren; or in families where an only son is gay, and the parents fear the family name will not be carried on into the next generation. The topic of generation requires a great deal of attention by the therapist, for two reasons. First, it is an almost universal concern of all parents approaching mid-life; and second, it is virtually impossible for the son and parents to discuss it, because of the son's guilt or because of guilt-induction by the parents.

Explanation. In order to preserve therapeutic confidence, specific inquiries about their son's homosexuality or style of living are best answered in general terms. Most parents have a host of questions and fears, often very sophisticated and insightful, which they will express with amazing candor if given the opportunity. When indicated, a brief discussion about current theories of homosexuality may go a long way toward allaying some of their fears and guilt. The parents should be told that the precise cause of homosexuality is still unknown despite major biological, psychological, and sociological insights. Their soul-searching ruminations as to how they went wrong are counterproductive; the parents need encouragement to focus on the present and the future.

It is essential to emphasize to parents that the gay culture is far from monolithic. Their image of a "homosexual" may be of a very sad, lonely, desperate figure engaging in repeated perverse sex acts with anonymous partners and forever flirting with venereal disease and violence.

Inquiries about coupling among homosexual men are best responded to in a direct, affirmative manner. Parents need to know that many gay people establish long-standing and healthy relationships. The author stresses to parents that they can play a major part in fostering such a relationship if they exhibit understanding and acceptance of their son's friendships. Often parents do not fully grasp how strong an influence they may have had, or still do have, over their homosexual son and his future adjustment. Gross (1978) has emphasized that parents' remarks and attitudes in the home can do much to "closet" homosexuality if they have not worked through their anger, condemnations, disbelief, and self-blame.

Many parents will ask about the future of their son's present sexual orientation. Is it fixed or may it change with time? Obviously, it is important for the therapist to have assessed the patient for prognostic variables (Bancroft, 1970; Ovesey & Gaylin, 1965; West, 1967). Even then, in some cases it is difficult to be certain. At all times the therapist must be aware of the "hidden agenda" behind this query—i.e., the parents' hopes and fears and uncertainties —so that he or she may respond with emphathy, tact, and honesty. Caution and reservation about prognosis are particularly critical when discussing the homosexuality of an adolescent. Adolescence is a crucial and often turbulent period of development, and one must recognize that the beliefs, values, feelings, and outlooks of many teenagers change rapidly. Glasser (1977) insists that not before late adolescence can homosexuality become firmly established as the individual's permanent way of relating and functioning sexually. Slater and Roth (1969) take this position even further: "It is unwise to assume that exclusively homosexual behaviour is established until the age of 25 has been passed" (p. 174). Many observers and therapists would take issue with this view. In any event, each patient must be assessed on his own merits with these and other variables in mind.

Reassurance. Many parents require soothing or comfort. The therapist's attitude toward them, as people and as parents, should serve to validate their parenting. (Other aspects of reassurance have been referred to above, in the discussion of attempts to debunk stereotypic myths about homosexuality.)

Confrontation. What about those parents who are exerting an adverse influence over their son or who are thwarting his adjustment to homosexuality? Parents who appear to be overinvolved, overprotective, or frankly controlling may need to be urged to ease up. The degree of their psychopathology will determine if they can respond to this very superficial intervention; if not, subsequent sessions may be necessary for reinforcement. Those parents who have been detached or passive over the years should be encouraged to attempt some occasional one-to-one activity or dialogue with their son. Again, this may require reinforcement in a later session.

Suggestion. The stress of acknowledging that a son is homosexual may exacerbate preexisting relationship problems between the parents, in addition to raising new issues in the home. In some cases, the therapist may suggest couples therapy or family therapy.

Guidance and recommendations. "What can we do?" Parents often ask directly for assistance. It is helpful to reaffirm basic parental responsibilities, such as to supply their son's need (often disguised to them) for their continued caring, love, understanding, support, and respect. Reading material on the subject (e.g., Clark, 1977; Fairchild & Hayward, 1979; Leo, 1979; Silverstein,

1977) or a community support-group for families of gay people may be recommended. Meeting other parents with a gay daughter or son can be a very enlightening experience, and extremely supportive. This will serve to diminish their sense of isolation, sharpen their perceptions, and perhaps improve a strained relationship with their son.

Follow-Up Interviews

These may be conducted at any time with the patient's permission, or perhaps at his request. A follow-up interview can help to reinforce previous suggestions or give the therapist an opportunity to focus on any new tensions that have arisen between the patient and his parents. It is important to arrange at least one session with the patient together with his parents, so that the therapist can observe their style and form of communication, their problem-solving ability, their relative comfort or discomfort with each other, their cohesiveness, and their general sense of family. These insights will then facilitate more accurate and appropriate therapeutic interventions, not only in the family session itself but also in later individual therapy.

Conclusion

When a patient has elected (for whatever conscious or unconscious reasons) to tell his parents of his homosexuality, and when the patient and his parents have experienced or are still experiencing some difficulty with the disclosure, meeting with the parents is an extremely important part of individual therapy. It is critical that the patient be involved and cooperate in arranging for counseling with his parents. Interviews with parents almost always enhance the therapist's rapport with the patient and may expedite movement in therapy. Most importantly, a parents meeting can serve to minimize or to alleviate conflict in one area of overall functioning.

REFERENCES

Bancroft, J. H. J. Homosexuality in the male. *British Journal of Hospital Medicine*, February 1970, 168-181.

Bell, A. P., & Weinberg, M. S. *Homosexualities: A study of diversity among men and women.* New York: Simon & Schuster, 1978.

Bergler, E. *Homosexuality: Disease or way of life?* New York: Hill & Wang, Inc., 1956.

Berzon, B., & Leighton, R. (Eds.). *Positively gay.* Millbrae, CA: Celestial Arts, 1979.

Bieber, I., & Bieber, T. B. Male homosexuality. *Canadian Journal of Psychiatry*, 1979, *24*, 409-421.

Bieber, I., Dain, H. J., Dince, P. R., Drellich, M. G., Grand, H. G., Gundlach, R. H., Kremer, M. W., Rifkin, A. H., Wilbur, C. B., & Bieber, T. B. *Homosexuality: A psychoanalytic study.* New York: Basic Books, 1962.

Bieber, T. B. Group therapy for homosexuals. In H. I. Kaplan & B. J. Sadock (Eds.), *Comprehensive group psychotherapy.* Baltimore: Williams and Wilkins, 1971.

Caplan, G. *Principles of preventive psychiatry*. New York: Basic Books, 1964.

Cappon, D. *Toward an understanding of homosexuality*. Englewood Cliffs, NJ: Prentice-Hall, Inc., 1965.

Cass, V. C. Homosexual indentity formation: A theoretical model. *Journal of Homosexuality*, 1979, *4*, 219-235.

Clark, D. *Loving someone gay*. Millbrae, CA: Celestial Arts, 1977.

Coleman, E. Toward a new model of treatment of homosexuality: A review. *Journal of Homosexuality*, 1978, *3*, 345-359.

Coleman, E. Developmental stages of the coming out process. *Journal of Homosexuality*, 1981/82, 7(2/3).

Dank, B. M. Coming out in the gay world. *Psychiatry*, 1971, *34*, 180-197.

Fairchild, B., & Hayward, N. *Now that you know*. New York: Harcourt Brace Jovanovich, 1979.

Ferenczi, S. [More about homosexuality.] In *Final contributions to the problems and methods of psychoanalysis*. London: Hogarth, 1955. (Originally published, 1909).

Ferenczi, S. [On the part played by homosexuality in the pathogenesis of paranoia.] In *Sex and psychoanalysis (contributions to psycho-analysis)*. New York: Dover Publications, 1956. (Originally published, 1912.)

Ferenczi, S. [The nosology of male homosexuality (homo-erotism).] In *Sex and psychoanalysis (contributions to psycho-analysis)*. New York: Dover Publications, 1956. (Originally published, 1914.)

Freud, A. Clinical observations on the treatment of manifest male homosexuality. *Psychiatric Quarterly*, 1951, *02*, 337-338.

Freud, S. [*Three essays on the theory of sexuality*.] *Standard Edition* (Vol. 7). London: Hogarth, 1953. (Originally published, 1905.)

Freud, S. [Psychoanalytic notes upon an autobiographical account of a case of paranoia (dementia paranoides).] Standard Edition (Vol. 12). London: Hogarth, 1958. (Originally published, 1911.)

Freud, S. A letter from Freud. *American Journal of Psychiatry*, 1951, *107*, 786-787.

Freund, K. Should homosexuality arouse therapeutic concern? *Journal of Homosexuality*, 1977, *2*, 235-240.

Gelman, R., & McGinley, H. Interpersonal liking and self-disclosure. *Journal of Consulting and Clinical Psychology*, 1978, *46*, 1549-1551.

Gilberg, A. L. Psychosocial considerations in treating homosexual adolescents. *American Journal of Psychoanalysis*, 1978, *38*, 355-358.

Glasser, M. Homosexuality in adolescence. *British Journal of Medical Psychology*, 1977, *50*, 217-225.

Gonsiorek, J. Psychological adjustment and homosexuality. JSAS *Catalog of Selected Documents in Psychology*, 1977, *7*, 45.

Gross, M. J. G. Changing attitudes toward homosexuality—or are they? *Perspectives in Psychiatric Care*, 1978, *16*(2), 70-75.

Hadden, S. B. Treatment of homosexuality by individual and group psychotherapy. *American Journal of Psychiatry*, 1958, *114*, 810-815.

Hadden, S. B. Group therapy for homosexuals. *Medical Aspects of Human Sexuality*, 1971, *5*, 116-126.

Hadfield, J. A. The cure of homosexuality. *British Medical Journal*, 1958, *1*, 1323-1326.

Hadfield, J. A. Origins of homosexuality. *British Medical Journal*, 1966, *1*, 678.

Hart, M., Roback, H., Tittler, B., Weitz, L., Walston, B., & McKee, E. Psychological adjustment of nonpatient homosexuals: Critical review of the research literature. *Journal of Clinical Psychiatry*, 1978, *39*, 604-608.

Hatterer, L. J. *Changing homosexuality in the male*. New York: McGraw-Hill, 1970.

Hooker, E. Homosexuality. in *National Institute of Mental Health: Task Force on Homosexuality: Final report and background papers*. DHEW Publ. No. (HSM) 72-9116, 1972.

Jones, C. R. *Understanding gay relatives and friends*. New York: Seabury Press, 1978.

Jourard, S. M. *The transparent self*. New York: Van Nostrand, 1964.

Jourard, S. M. *Self-disclosure: An experimental analysis of the transparent self*. New York: John Wiley and Sons, 1971.

Kinsey, A. C., Pomeroy, W. B., & Martin, C. E. *Sexual behavior in the human male*. Philadelphia: Saunders, 1948.

Lawrence, J. C. Gay peer counseling. *JPN and Mental Health Services*, 1977, *15*(6), 33-37.

Lee, J. A. Going public: A Study in the sociology of homosexual liberation. *Journal of Homosexuality*, 1977, *3*, 49-78.

Leo, J. *Time* Essay: Homosexuality: Tolerance vs. approval. *Time*, January 8, 1979, pp. 34-35.

National Institute of Mental Health: Task Force on Homosexuality: Final report and background papers. DHEW, Publ. No. (HSM) 72-9116, 1972.

Ovesey, L. The homosexual conflict. *Psychiatry*, 1954, *17*, 243-250.

Ovesey, L. Pseudohomosexuality, the paranoid mechanism, and paranoia. *Psychiatry*, 1955, *18*, 163-173.

Ovesey, L., & Gaylin, W. Psychotherapy of male homosexuality. *American Journal of Psychotherapy*, 1965, *19*, 382-396.

Roesler, T., & Deishler, R. W. Youthful male homosexuality. *Journal of the American Medical Association*, 1972, *219*, 1018-1023.

Saghir, M. T., & Robins, E. Male and female homosexuality: Natural history. *Comprehensive Psychiatry*, 1971, *12*, 503-510.

Saghir, M. T., & Robins, E. *Male and female homosexuality*. Baltimore: Williams and Wilkins, 1973.

Siegelman, M. Adjustment of male homosexuals and heterosexuals. *Archives of Sexual Behavior*, 1972, *2*, 9-25.

Silverstein, C. *A family matter*. New York: McGraw-Hill, 1977.

Slater, E., & Roth, M. *Clinical psychiatry*. London: Bailliere, Tindall, and Cassell, 1969.

Socarides, C. W. *The overt homosexual*. New York: Grune and Stratton, 1968.

Socarides, C. W. Homosexuality and medicine. *Journal of the American Medical Association*, 1970, *212*, 1199-1202.

Socarides, C. W. Homosexuality: Basic concepts and psychodynamics. *International Journal of Psychiatry*, 1972, *10*(1), 118-125.

Socarides, C. W. *Homosexuality*. New York: Jason Aronson, 1978.

Weinberg, G. *Society and the healthy homosexual*. Garden City, NY: Anchor Press/Doubleday, 1972.

West, D. J. *Homosexuality*. Chicago: Aldine, 1967.

West, D. J. *Homosexuality re-examined*. Minneapolis: University of Minnesota Press, 1977.

Willis, S. E. *Understanding and counseling the male homosexual*. Boston: Little, Brown, and Co., 1967.

MALES AS SEXUAL ASSAULT VICTIMS: MULTIPLE LEVELS OF TRAUMA

Craig L. Anderson, MSW

ABSTRACT. The definite and persistant phenomenon of sexual assault upon males is virtually ignored in the literature, although incidence data reported here suggest the greater scope of the problem. The avoidance of the subject of sexual assault on males creates a negative environment for victims. While the motivation of assailants is briefly discussed, the article focuses on the psychological aftermath for sexual assault victims. A paradigm is offered, consisting of "Set-up," "Attack," and "Aftermath" phases. Male victims suffer "Rape Trauma Syndrome" as described for females, as well as various forms of stigmatization and secondary trauma. Differences and similarities between male and female victims are identified. Victim responses are discussed as they proceed through several stages, with implications for appropriate interventions on both the clinical and community levels. The article concludes with an extensive bibliography.

Sexual assault on men by men may or may not involve genital contact or penetration prior to or during the assault. Though some sexual assaults against men do fall into this narrower, traditional definition of rape, other physical assaults may be generally sexualized, usually through accompanying verbal abuse. In a sexual assault, the victim perceives that his actual or presumed homosexuality is targeted for attack (as distinguished from crimes with other motivations, for example, robbery or "mugging"). Such an attack can be extremely damaging to the victim's self-image. Whatever their actual sexual identity, men may share very similar reactions to this type of assault.

A graduate of Macalester College, Mr. Anderson received his MSW from the University of Minnesota in 1981. He lives in St. Paul, Minnesota, where he is a mental health social worker. Among his former professional positions were urban and social planning, and advocacy. His work with gay male and lesbian issues includes social action in the areas of politics, religion, community development, and sexuality. Mr. Anderson took a leading role in the campaign to retain civil rights coverage for gay men and lesbians in St. Paul. He co-created the *Twin Cities Gay and Lesbian Resource Guide* (1980) and was a member of Minnesota's No More Assault Project. This paper is adapted from presentations given at the Fourth National Conference on Men and Masculinity, Washington University, St. Louis in November 1977, and at Hennepin County Mental Health Center, Minneapolis in January 1980. The author wishes to acknowledge Doug Elwood; as well as Leo Treadway and other members of the *No More Assault Project*, especially Terrie Couch, John Grace, Gregg Riley and Gary Wilson.

The purpose of this paper is to discuss a subject that has historically been unmentionable and disbelieved, and whose victims have as a consequence been underserved, ignored, and further abused. The focus will be on the clinical effects for victims; appropriate clinical or community interventions will be recommended. Practitioners in this area have found themselves working in a vacuum. The relevant literature is sparse, and clinical studies have only recently begun to be published. Therefore, a bibliography has been compiled and is printed at the end of the article. The bibliography covers assaults on men; rape, where the victims are female; and the newly emerging discipline of victimology. Works on male assault come mostly from the popular press, which reflects the community impetus of the issue and the grass-roots demand for professional response. This popular attention has generally been pioneered by the gay and lesbian press across the country. Many case histories can be gleaned from these primary source reports.

Neither sado-masochism ("S&M") in sexual behavior, nor assaults by police, nor sexual or physical abuse of male children is within the scope of this article. Nor will this paper examine sexual assault in prisons, county jails, or other places of incarceration. (Although unwilling to recognize most male assaults, the public does acknowledge that rape occurs in prisons. It is often wrongly assumed, however, that gay men are invariably the assailants.)

Whether popular or scholarly, much of the literature on sexual assault has focused on the assailants, often regarding them from a political perspective. John Money (see Ireland, 1978) has identified the "exorcist syndrome" in which the attackers, usually young men, are in some way attracted to homosexuality but are also repulsed and need to destroy that part of themselves and others. Discomfort with their own desires and needs is acted out in a violent homophobic reaction against what they see as a threat. In cases where there is more than one assailant, the behavior of group members has been explained (e.g., Weissman, 1978) in terms of peer pressures and the need to maintain in-group power and status, even if an individual member does not want to participate in an attack. Broader explanations (e.g., Rofes, 1978) see sexual assault as an agent of social control: either as the physical extension of societal attitudes; or as punishment for those who reject traditional "masculine" roles and thereby cause others to question themselves; or as a form of misogyny. In various cities, community agencies have reported that certain political events or climates (for example, civil rights referenda) appear to lend external permission to act out in sexual assaults, and that attacks increase at these times. In behavioral terms, the lack of consequences for attackers serves as reinforcement for future assaults.

Statistics on male sexual assault are rare, encouraging disbelief in the phenomenon. Evidence from agency staffs and from informal reports suggests the low official figures are more indicative of flaws in the reporting system than of actual incidence rates. In their official records, most criminal justice or social service bodies do not separate by sex of victim those incidents for which they do receive reports. What data are available are specific to agency or locality (e.g., Kaufman, DiVasto, Jackson, Voorhees, & Christy, 1980). For example, Gay Community Services in Minneapolis included several questions on assaults in its broader advocacy needs assessment survey distributed informally to non-clients in the Twin Cities during December 1978 - February 1979. The questionnaire was returned by 289 gay men and lesbians. Verbal harassment because of sexual orientation had been experienced by 72.3% of the respondents; 23.2% had suffered physical assault; 5.9% had been raped because of their sexual orientation (this figure includes 10 men). Of these three types of incidents, 63.7% occurred during 1978. Of the respondents who were victims of assault, 9.3% reported the incident to the police, 2.4% to a gay/lesbian agency, 1.7% to a rape center, and 0.7% to a victim compensation program. Most telling is that 22.5% talked to a friend and 5.5% to a family member, but 66.4% took no action at all.

More of a mainstream program, Sexual Assault Services of the Hennepin County (Minnesota) Attorney's Office reports that in 1977 (the first year in which the sex of the victim was recorded) 22.7% of 185 victims served were male; 15.9% of 164 in 1978 and 11.4% of 141 in 1979 were male. In most of these reported cases, the male victim was younger than 17; by contrast, nearly half the female victims are under 17. In the social services system, the Rape & Sexual Assault Center of Neighborhood Involvement Program in Minneapolis reports that in 1979, 35 (6.6%) of 534 victims served were male, 42 (5.6%) of 748 in 1980. In Saint Paul, Sexual Offense Services of Ramsey County reports that in 1980, the first full year they kept records of the sex of victims, 5.3% of 454 victims were male (this includes some child victims). Statewide in Minnesota, among 20 programs surveyed by the Minnesota Program for Victims of Sexual Assault of the state's Department of Corrections, 125 (6%) of 2103 victims served in 1980 were male. (The total figure, 2103, includes 10 victims whose sex was unreported.)

A Paradigm

Although patterns can be discerned, individual cases of assault vary in their particulars. Some variety can be accounted for by geography or the demographics of a locale, or by the ideology of the observer. Predictions as to which individuals will be victimized are dubious: No one is entirely protected by their "image," their behavior, or the behavior of others. Indeed, establishing a typical or normative case and victim-profile may furnish a new set of blinders when dealing with "atypical" victims.

Nevertheless, it is useful to recognize a general paradigm for assaults on men. Not only does this counteract the idea that such attacks are beyond the range of comprehension (an idea which places a tremendous onus of responsibility on the victims), it also suggests that differing interventions are called for in different situations and at different stages. In brief, a victim can be characterized as going through a "set-up," the attack itself, and the aftermath. Much of the paradigm will be familiar to readers acquainted with the literature on female rape, and, in fact, studies of women as victims can be extremely useful in working with men. There are important differences between the two experiences, however, and these will be discussed.

The Set-Up

When male victims are set up for the subsequent attack, they are subjected (as are women) to dynamics both personal and political in nature, with no rigid boundary dividing the two aspects. Sex, violence, and power are often confounded within our culture; in sexual attacks this confusion is focused and acted out by hostility and aggression. Violence is the prominent theme; power becomes the "transaction." Though sexuality (both the stereotypic masculinity of the attacker and his perception of his victim's sexual orientation) is the method of expression, sexual gratification is not generally the focus of these attacks.

Victims are not selected entirely at random from the larger society. Rather, just as with women, there is a significant pattern of certain men being more often preyed upon. This group includes gay men, men who engage in varying amounts of homosexual behavior but who are not gay-identified, and predominantly or exclusively heterosexual men who are perceived by their attackers as gay. The minority group status of gay men encourages violence through the mechanisms of scapegoating (Rofes, 1978). Gay males are at risk in the culture and live with the constant threat of violence. Chronic implied threat (to which certain other groups are subject as well, for example, the elderly, blacks, and women) may have some of the same effects as experience of actual attack. That is, multiple factors can breed a fear that cripples and isolates members of such groups. All gay men are traumatized by the oppression in a homophobic society, though only a few may be identified in the victim role, having actually suffered a sexual assault.

Gay people are perceived by many as a danger to cultural values. The counteracting role of "prey" has received general sanction by society. Police assaults are a blatant manifestation of this. "In God We Trust, Inc.," a San Francisco affiliate of the "Moral Majority," has unveiled its campaign to eliminate local civil rights protection for gay men and lesbians, while encouraging violence against, and advocating the death penalty for, homosexual persons. Factors associated with group membership can lead to some victims playing into their victimization. It is crucial to bear in mind, however, that a victim is not to blame or deserving of an assault. Rather, how an individual copes with the oppression surrounding sexual identity can increase his vulnerability and be used against him by assailants. In the face of homophobia, some men may be isolated, suffering feelings of low self-esteem, and may even engage in self-punishment.

A pattern of social or sexual contacts in anonymous settings can make an individual particularly vulnerable and cause a set-up to become an attack (Miller & Humphreys, 1980). For example, when a man is "cruising" his level of anxiety may be raised. In his internal efforts to block the anxiety, he may also block important environmental and emotional cues that could have warned him that "something is wrong here." This can be exacerbated if the man is already feeling lonely, disappointed with himself, angry, etc. A "closeted" man knows that simply to cruise is to be in high jeopardy, and so he sets that risk aside even before setting out to cruise. His subsequent feeling of unreal excitement may make him even more oblivious. In addition, some individuals are inexperienced in this pattern of interaction and have no "street sense."

Once the victim is in this frame of mind, an entrapper may make overtures that are more enticing than usual, in fact overly seductive. The entrapper mimicks seductive behavior in an intentional game or "theatre." Because his goal is other than sexual fulfillment, he jumps over many of the usual steps in a seduction. The process becomes abbreviated and therefore very intense. The man being set up, if his need is high and he consciously represses internal or external messages of caution, may respond to this exaggerated seductiveness. Many victims report that they thought at first that the other person was a "hustler" (a prostitute) but then decided he was not. The set-up often ends with an implicit non-verbal agreement or contact between the parties. The victim is led to a place where others are waiting, or perhaps others come out of hiding, and the victim is attacked.

Heterosexual men can also be targeted, especially if for some reason attackers are able to project their own notions of homosexuality onto them. For a man to be in a place (neighborhood, street, parking lot, park, etc.) at a time (usually at night) when it is identified as "gay turf," is often enough to label the man as homosexual. Expressiveness, particularly of feelings, in a way that is inappropriate to traditional male socialization, can also elicit such projections. It is important to remember, however, and especially important that clinical practitioners remember, that anyone can become a victim—whether or not they appear or behave to society's stereotype of the gay man; whether or not they seek social or sexual contacts; no matter where they happen to be.

The Attack

Attacks vary in their details, such as the numbers involved and the degree of force used, but a common pattern is of multiple assailants attacking a lone man. There is evidence that this pattern occurs more frequently in male rape than in assaults on women (Kaufman et al., 1980). The attackers are often a group, even a gang, of adolescent males who affect extremes of stereotypical male ("macho") behaviors. Just as in attacks on women, in one-on-one assaults the assailant is frequently slightly older and larger than his victim. One-on-one attacks may be preceded by genital sex, even though the assailant does not self-identity as gay (as in the case, for instance, of hustling). Group attacks may follow diversionary interactions with the victim, such as a "decoy" member asking for directions, making a sexual proposition, etc. All forms of sexual assault are usually characterized by a good deal of verbal abuse, as well as physical violence. A weapon is used more often, and the violence results in more severe physical injuries than when women are victims. Not surprisingly, the assailants are more often strangers to their male victims than is the case when women are raped.

Because the attack is unprovoked but obviously premeditated, because the victim knows he has been set up, and because he is overpowered and often outnumbered, the assault is not just upon the victim's body: His sense of self and his identity are also attacked.

At the time of the assault, the issue of power is inherent in the victim's terror. His fear for his life, and his recognition of powerlessness in the face of a life-and-death situation, can prove overwhelming. The feelings of being violated and devalued, coupled with a sense of having lost the ability to control his circumstance, his body, or his own life, can also have an emotionally immobilizing effect on the victim. Whether the victim is actually subjected to life-threatening assault or not, he directly experiences his own helplessness and dependence on the mercy of others. "I thought I was going to die" is a common recollection of victims. The effects of trauma result in the unravelling of the victim's psychological defenses, for the feeling of vulnerability is devastating to his ego. This can be a particular shock to men who have internalized the societal belief that sexual assault of men is beyond the realm of possibility. They may have trouble accepting their rape experience as real, a problem exacerbated by the common initial reaction of denial. It is expecially hard to talk about the assault, since the phenomenon has rarely been articulated in this society. One effect of middle-class socialization is that a victim may "freeze" during an attack—and later be beset by self-incrimination. For those with working-class socialization, a more acceptable response is to fight back.

The Aftermath

In this society, the aftermath for victims is usually far more disruptive than for the perpetrators. Although our system focuses much time, energy, and expense on processing and protecting the rights of those few actually charged with criminal acts, victims are very seldom compensated for the crime, and may in fact be punished by subsequent proceedings. This is particularly true for male victims of sexual assault, who are subject to stigmatization. The set-up and attack are usually the prelude to a process of secondary trauma, a revictimization.

In the rare instances when a victim is able and willing to report the assault, he is usually greeted with disbelief or outright hostility by the police, who are the first line of formal intervention. This hostility may be directed at the victim's homosexuality. Even if he is not gay, the police may take it for granted that he is, the same assumption made by the assailant; or they may assume that his victimization was deserved and brought about by his own behavior. The victim is further humiliated and may be deterred from seeking any additional assistance, whether medical, psychological, or judicial.

Emergency room staffs can demonstrate insensitivity, either to the possibility that such an incident actually occurred, or to the victim himself when he presents for treatment. County Attorneys, too, in their discretionary role as prosecutors, can make the victim's experience unbearable.

Many victims are left without the support of friends or of their community. This is especially true for "closeted" or married homosexual men whose overriding concern is a fear of exposure, even more than a fear of physical attack (except as this is a direct threat to their secret). The pre-attack isolation of many victims is worsened by their decision not to report the rape or to seek medical/helping services. In repressing or hiding the incident, they minimize the physical and psychological injuries they have sustained—a dangerous avoidance.

Other victims, especially openly gay men, may be faced with their gay friends' or significant others' fear and subsequent denial of the seriousness of what has happened. This denial shields the others from having to acknowledge the vulnerability they share with the victim as gay men and helps them to forget their own role as potential victims. The victim's community, whether mainstream or subcultural, may ostracize him. Gay men may receive overt or covert messages that their particular social or sexual style is "politically incorrect" or an embarrassment to the gay community. If the community can believe the victim's behavior was peculiar or bad, it is then easier to imagine that an assault cannot happen to others. All these reactions are proof of the pervasiveness of internalized homophobia among gay men. (See Alan Malyon's article, "Psychotherapeutic Implications of Internalized Homophobia in Gay Men," in this volume.) Heterosexual victims, on the other hand, are especially vulnerable to accusations that "A man should be able to defend himself," etc.

No matter what form it takes, this "protective etiology" serves only to punish and blame the victim, while ignoring his real needs and distress in crisis. If a victim cannot rely on the people close to him for support, he usually questions his own innocence, feeling guilty and shameful. The others may feel that if they talk or think about sexual assault in personal terms, they must also be the "type" who asks to be assaulted; but if they are "good," they will have nothing to worry about. The situation begs a fundamental question posed by both the gay movement and the men's awareness movement: How willing are men to support other men?

Victim responses. This description has thus far focused on how other people, whether professional or lay, have responded to the victim during the aftermath period. It is also important to study victims' responses to the trauma, responses which can be helped or hindered depending on the appropriateness of other peoples' reactions. Of general clinical importance is the ego-developmental level of victims; and for gay men, the stage of gay identity formation—where they are in the "coming out" process. (See Eli Coleman's article, "Developmental Stages in the Coming Out Process," in this volume.) The victim's competence in areas of sexuality, interpersonal relationships, and support systems is critical (Sutherland & Scherl, 1970). Especially in earlier developmental stages, assault trauma can increase psychological distance between a gay man's public and private selves, adding to the distress surrounding his identity. Further, such a victim may "freeze" or regress developmentally. For men who are not gay-identified, same-sex assault can be devastating to their personal identity.

Responses by victims of sexual assault have been organized into patterns proceeding through stages and extending over a period of time, which may last several years (MacDonald, 1971; Sutherland & Scherl, 1970). These responses resemble psychological responses to sudden unexpected loss, the death of a loved one, and other life crises. The immediate, shorter-term responses constitute the "Acute Reaction" or "Impact" stage. Various forms of reaction and feeling are evident at this stage.

Shock and *denial* may present themselves jointly, in which case the victim will either disclose no information or will indicate little emotion while reporting serious physical or emotional injuries. This response is adaptive insofar as it protects a victim from facing an intolerable situation he is not yet able to work through. Confronting the denial too early may not be helpful. Different victims may express their emotions in a variety of behaviors, such as laughing or crying hysterically.

Shame, guilt, self-blame, and *embarrassment* often occur as a result of the societal predisposition toward blaming the victim, or because the victim is uncomfortable with matters of the body and sexuality, or because he experienced stripping away of his privacy during the assault or in the aftermath. Victims may feel ashamed that they were unable to protect themselves or to overpower their assailants. The male ego and socialization tell them that a "real man" is strong and would be invincible in such a situation. An assault can force to a crisis any ongoing struggle with internalized homophobia or stereotypical masculine sex-roles. Guilt, too, will more than likely be induced by the trauma. This can range from "If only I hadn't been in that place" to "I shouldn't have had sexual needs" to "Why do I have to be gay?" This guilt is reinforced by the culture and probably by the victim's immediate peers as well. The victim comes to blame himself for his assault and may take his aggressor's side, i.e., "I got what I deserved." The assailants are relieved of responsibility, while the victim focuses solely on himself as being somehow at fault.

Fear and *suspicion,* with accompanying *anxiety reactions,* may be targeted towards the assailants or generalized to things that remind the victim of his assault. In either case, there is, not surprisingly, a fear of being assaulted again. This can reach the levels of paranoia as the environment, previously perceived as benign, is subjectively transformed into a "jungle." In extreme cases, the victim's feeling that he has lost control over his life can develop into a chronic disability, such as agoraphobia or a fear of the future. Many victims may have had a sense of invulnerability before the assault. This generalized trust is usually shattered after their resistance has been forcibly overcome in an attack. The realization that they are vulnerable and mortal can impede the victims' daily routine or general life-style. Victims may be particularly threatened by other men; their development of intimacy, especially with men, is usually impaired. Gay men will often disavow their sexuality and their right to enjoy sex, devaluing their own needs in the process. General withdrawal, fatigue, and isolation are common, straining relationships and emotional supports. Pan-neurotic symptoms can occur at the same time. Victims may abuse alcohol and other chemicals. The residue of emotional scarring, which is sometimes repressed or delayed until triggered by later circumstance, will often continue for years, well beyond the range of crisis intervention services. In some cases, the victim associates any sexual arousal by men with terror and fears of violence. For "closeted" men there is no support in fighting off these associative terrors or dealing with their homosexual feelings.

Depression and chronic *low self-esteem* may often be manifestations of *underlying anger.* Feelings of rage towards the assailants, towards society for condoning or encouraging his victimization, and toward his own gay community for being insensitive to him as a victim, are common among victims and frequently the most appropriate response. Reporting the rape, prosecuting, and self-defense training are three constructive ways to ventilate anger. However, it may be extremely difficult for male victims to express their anger verbally if they suffer a great deal from self-blame or dwell on anger directed against themselves. When the victim's multifaceted rage at having been violated is displaced, focused inward, or otherwise kept from conscious awareness, the result can be depression or even self-destructive actions. These men need help to channel their rage into direct, outward expressions. If untreated, a longer term depression may result in which the victim presents secondary problems as a direct consequence of the assault (e.g., reclusiveness and insomnia) but at so late a date that the victim is less likely to realize that his victimization is the reason for these symptoms.

Victims frequently report *somatic symptoms*, which can be either *stress related* or *hypochondriacal*, or both. Of the former, tension headaches, ulcers, difficulty in eating, colitis, upset stomach, as well as extremes of sleep or appetite, are common. A general malaise or overconcern and preoccupation with physical problems are more common in the case of hypochondriasis. Most people have the ability to repress the possibility that they might suffer bodily harm. After the assault, however, this repression may break down, causing the victim to ruminate about bodily harm in a hypochondriacal or obsessional-phobic way. This will usually be exaggerated if certain organ systems already have a special meaning to the person: for example, a man who has a "hymen-like" attitude towards his anus and is ill at ease with anal intercourse or sensual activity, and who then suffers anal penetration during an assault. Any premorbid *issues of body image* may be exacerbated by an assault. *Phobias* may also result that relate to any characteristic of the assault, e.g., fear of strangers, of walking alone or being approached from behind, of being in a park or out at night. It is useful to explore such phobias with the victim and link these feelings to the assault.

The feelings and reactions discussed above are struggled with, submerging and reemerging, throughout the victim's longer-term response stages. A second distinct stage, lasting from days to years, can be called "Outward Readjustment." It is a pseudo-adjustment in which the victim returns to his usual, seemingly secure, activities in order to regain some sense of normalcy. Though it may appear as if he had resolved his victimization, the victim is actually reacting with denial, suppressing his anxiety, pain, or despair over things ever getting better. Since he will seldom want to deal with or even talk about the assault, the victim is likely to terminate professional services during this period. The traditional, insensitive attitudes towards male victims of sexual assault can cause men to remain in the Outward Readjustment stage. (This may be less true for female victims of rape.)

Some victims may enter a subsequent stage of "Substitution," signalling the beginnings of resolution. Though the individual may be sufficiently uncomfortable to seek some help, the presenting concern will often not be the primary issue (the assault) but instead a substitute issue. A successful outcome regarding the complaint may not alleviate the client's distress, but if he realizes this and has gained sufficient confidence, he can then pursue the underlying issue, the assault.

Finally, there may come a stage of "Resolution and Integration," beginning with a need that can no longer be denied, avoided, or substituted: to talk about the sexual assault itself. This stage may be precipitated by a specific incident that is somehow related to a victim's own assault, or to someone else's. During this period, the victim learns to accept his own feelings about himself, and his reactions to the assault and his assailants. The victim learns to express and direct these emotions where they appropriately belong, and to put them to rest so that he no longer must repress or be dominated by them. Psychosocial (as well as psychosomatic) functioning can improve as helplessness, ambivalence, despair, or self-destructive acting-out are identified and self-esteem boosted. At last the person can feel he has some personal control and that things can improve.

Interventions

A useful trend in recent years has been a shift away from preoccupation with "victim participation" in a victim/criminal dyad (which posits a "victim personality") to focusing on the suffering of the victim. Since an assault is neither an isolated incident nor merely someone's "personal problem"—"something that goes on between a victim and an assailant," much as wife-beating was formerly conceptualized—there are at least two levels of intervention required: clinical and community. Victims require immediate direct services, focusing on the aftereffects of assault. But a longer-range approach that addresses the broader issues, causes, prevention, education, and public policy is also needed. In many locales practitioners may find service development to be their first task. It may be necessary to link available services in an effective network, based on agency capabilities, to make them truly responsive to the situation. The development of a clear continuum of response from first report through on-going therapy has been useful in Minneapolis and St. Paul.

Crisis Intervention

Crisis intervention therapy is of particular importance, and has been the most developed part of this continuum. Initially developed as a therapeutic approach to working with female rape victims, it is transferable to male victims, if allowance is made for public disbelief, for the male socialization of the victims, and for the double stigma of victimization and homosexuality attached to same-sex assaults.

Being always alert to the possibility of such an incident is the crucial first step for a practitioner. Also important are a knowledge of symptoms and clues and the ability to put a name onto the victim's experience while reassuring and listening to him. The therapist must also be prepared to take necessary steps to insure the immediate safety of a victim and alleviate the client's concern for his safety. Early in the contact, the practitioner must check for physical and medical needs. A goal of this intervention is to prevent secondary trauma; therefore, identifying the victim's significant others and ascertaining his support system are recommended.

This intervention approach calls upon the qualities Truax and Mitchell (1971) posit as characteristic of an effective therapist and caseworker: nonpossessing warmth, accurate empathy (understanding), and genuineness free of attempts to dominate or make final decisions for a client. Crisis intervention is focused, with the relatively limited goals of getting the client to utilize the coping behaviors in his repertoire and returning him to his prior level of adjustment. Therapists are most useful when they are directive and active in their approach, and use supportive, teaching, confrontive (see Truax & Mitchell), and "advice-giving" (see Reid & Shapiro, 1969) techniques. Being passive, vague, or reflective is usually not as helpful under such highly emotional conditions.

Many clients in this situation will be seeking psychological help for the first time. Most are not basically "sick"; the psychopathology (symptoms, behavior) manifested in these instances is usually transitory and in reaction to the intensity of the stressors. Clients may need guidance, and the therapist should not be overly inhibited by worries about dependency. Victims will often exhibit a "clinging" response in the aftermath. The therapist who is distant, unavailable, or who immediately shuttles the client to several different service providers, is rarely helpful. As the intervention progresses, however, it is useful for the therapist to be aware of "letting go" and actively discourage continued dependence, as the time-limited structure requires that the victim quickly learn to cope. Reinforcing previous and present strengths among the client's actions and behaviors, such as something he did that helped him survive the attack, can help renew an inherently therapeutic sense of autonomy and decision-making.

Victims will usually have a need to tell others about the experience, but some may require encouragement or "permission" to talk. What will often emerge is their greatest horror, that of the close brush with death. Participatory listening can be difficult for the practitioner, and empathy could become blunted by her or his own feelings. This is a problem of countertransference, as the therapist may have her or his own fears surrounding bodily injury or have a preconceived world-view in conflict with the reality the victim presents. It is helpful to recognize and respect the victim's pain and to accept his behavior during set-up, attack, and aftermath. Questions that imply blame or challenge behaviors will usually be recognized by the client, increasing his shame, guilt, self-blame, fear and suspicion. In general, this therapeutic approach does not call for aggressively assaulting the client's defenses, though some feelings and defense mechanisms may need to be identified. The client's post-attack behavior or situation may need to undergo change, in his self-interest: for example, the common-sense decision not to walk alone or to avoid a certain area, etc. This is not the same as identifying "causal factors" within the victims themselves.

Other Direct Services

Advocacy is an inseparable part of the client's needs during the aftermath and in the face of secondary trauma. Most victims to not seek even basic medi-

cal care, unfortunately, and fewer pursue counseling or legal channels. Advocacy can reinforce those who do seek services. During crisis intervention, a
client usually needs a sympathetic intermediary to deal with emergency-room
and other medical staffs. Longer-range advocacy, including inter-agency co-
ordination, is required to assist a victim with police procedures and County
Attorneys' offices during prosecution of assailants. An alternative reporting
network of non-threatening agencies, which will respect victims' requests for
anonymity or confidentiality, should also be available for those otherwise
unwilling to report cases to the police. The higher self-esteem and reduced
depression many clients experience after filing complaints are consistent with
cognitive-behavioral theories of depression, which encourage clients to take
self-enhancing actions in the world.

Many clients will require *follow-up support* and resources. Timely reporting
of incidents is often a prerequisite for benefitting from *compensation programs*
for victims of crimes. An appropriate long-term *counseling referral* is also
important for many. Routine sex histories are ways to uncover past incidents of
assault in clients coming into longer-term counseling with other presenting
issues. (The incidence of previous assault is surprisingly high.) These unresolved situations are quite often relevant to the current treatment but might take
a long while to turn up on their own. History-taking also indicates to the client
that the counselor regards sexual assault as a legitimate concern and is open to
the issue if the client wants to bring it up later. *Confidentiality*, which is often
treated casually by agencies and professionals, can be especially important in
these cases.

Self-Defense

Assertiveness training and self-defense training that is responsive to the
threat of sexual assault are of enormous benefit to clients, either before (prevention) or after (therapeutic) experiencing an assault. Self-defense training
utilizing such components has been developed in the Twin Cities (Bera, Note
1). Assertiveness and self-defense skills can be conceptualized on a continuum
that allows the target of an attack to match the level of attack with an appropriate response. When escalation occurs (for instance, from verbal to grab-
bing, to hitting, and ultimately to the use of deadly weapons), the response
must also escalate. Teaching someone only one self-defense option, usually—
how to take an assailant's life—is neither useful nor appropriate in many situations. Indeed, it may not fulfill the primary task of safety for the attacked,
if he is reluctant to use the skill in a particular situation. It is more important
to be able to get away and actively protect oneself. The issue of whether one is
willing to take the life of an assailant if one's own life, or that of another, is
threatened, needs to be decided in advance, not at the time of an attack.

The range of attacks and self-defense is but one side of a continuum that
also encompasses positive interactions (i.e., from a compliment to love). Iron-

ically, training a person to deal with violence also has beneficial effects in helping her or him experience greater capacity for affection. When people know that they have the skill to control their privacy and their bodies, they are better able to allow others to approach in positive ways. Conversely, someone who feels vulnerable will use distance as the only defense, keeping everyone away. Such a person will be especially devastated by secondary trauma if assaulted.

Community Intervention

Organizing officials, organizations, and the media is part of a broader, longer-range strategy to reduce and eventually to eliminate assaults. Increasing the visibility of the problem is a critical indirect intervention and can result in tangible clinical benefits to clients. Breaking the silence on the issue often uncovers more victims, many of whom can then seek helping services.

Education efforts, though often tedious and highly charged politically, are nevertheless important. These can take different forms for different segments of the community. (See Elwood and Larson, Eds., 1981.) In-service *training* sessions and *consultations* can target police, service professionals and agencies, and public officials. A *consciousness-raising* approach can be employed when targeting the general or gay and lesbian communities. The focus may include an awareness of the dynamics of violence in its many forms and arenas; the goal may be to defuse fear surrounding the issue and thus encourage support for victims. How the community's character is perceived and experienced by its own members is also at issue; i.e., is it characterized as merely a hedonistic community or as a caring one? The broadening of self-definitions beyond sexual activity for some gay men, or narrow sex-roles for others, can also be addressed.

Enhancing a sense of community among the population group targeted for attacks is another important strategy. In this case, intra-community *communication* is emphasized, for violence and assaults have as one of their generalized effects the inhibition of routine communication in an unmobilized community. Particularly controversial is the matter of *group actions* aimed at protecting community members and preventing aggression and intimidation. Demonstrations have been used to combat invisibility and indifference, as part of a consciousness-raising strategy and as a mechanism to mobilize for further actions. There have been some changes in recent years. Whereas it was once usual for other gay people to flee the vicinity of an attack, now, in many instances, they will run toward the scene and, even if some do not physically intervene, will shout or try to scare the attackers away. Communities in Chicago, Minneapolis, and other cities have organized citizen groups, usually armed only with whistles, to patrol in high-risk gay ghetto areas on nights during the warm season. The continued functioning of these patrols is directly related to the immediacy of the threat felt by the community and their perception of non-response by mainstream institutions.

Community intervention with regard to sexual assault draws upon both community organization and practical clinical skills. Those men more likely to be preyed upon are largely an anonymous and secretive population. Though they may be most in need of services, they are least likely to be informed or to respond to offers of help. One is faced with the extremely difficult task of *outreach* to very "closeted" single or married homosexual men, readily set-up as victims of multiple levels of violence precisely because they will not acknowledge their assault. Some heterosexual men, especially those insecure in their traditional roles, may also face this isolation. The conscientious practitioner may also feel lonely when attempting to address male sexual assault in the absence of existing services, understanding, or even recognition of the problem.

REFERENCE NOTE

1. Bera, W. Personal communication, 1981.

REFERENCES

Coleman, E. Developmental stages of the coming out process. *Journal of Homosexuality*, 1981/82, *7*(2/3).

Elwood, N. D., & Larson, B. (Eds.). Same-sex assault: A handbook for intervention training. St. Paul: State of Minnesota Department of Corrections, Minnesota Program for Victims of Sexual Assault, 1981.

Ireland, D. Rendezvous in the Ramble. *New York*, July 24, 1978.

Kaufman, A., Di Vasto, P., Jackson, R., Voorhees, D., & Christy, J. Male rape victims: Noninstitutionalized assault. *American Journal of Psychiatry*, 1980, *137*, 221-223.

MacDonald, J. M. *Rape offenders and their victims*. Springfield, IL: Charles C. Thomas, 1971.

Malyon, A. K. Psychotherapeutic implications of internalized homophobia in gay men. *Journal of Homosexuality*, 1981/82, *7*(2/3).

Miller, B., & Humphreys, L. Lifestyles and violence: Homosexual victims of assault and murder. *Qualitative Sociology*, 1980, *3*(3), 169-185.

Reid, W., & Shapiro, B. Client reactions to advice. *Social Service Review*, 1969, *43*, 165-173.

Rofes, E. Queer bashing: The politics of violence against gay men. *Gay Community News* (Boston), August 12, 1978.

Sutherland, S., & Scherl, D. J. Patterns of response among victims of rape. *American Journal of Orthopsychiatry*, 1970, *40*, 503-511.

Truax, C. B., & Mitchell, K. Research on certain therapist interpersonal skills in relation to process and outcome. In A. Bergin & S. Garfield (Eds.), *Handbook of psychotherapy & behavior change*. New York: John Wiley & Sons, 1971.

Weisman, E. Kids who attack gays. *Christopher Street,* August 1978.

BIBLIOGRAPHY

Assaults on Men

Books and Articles

Bell, A. Hunting gays in Central Park. *Village Voice*, July 17, 1978.

Bell, A. *Kings don't mean a thing: The John Knight murder case*. New York: Morrow, 1978.

Califia, P. Queer-bashing. *The Advocate*, April 2, 1981.

Dezutter, H., & Fahey, P. Knights on Broadway: Gays fight back in New Town. *The Reader* (Chicago), July 21, 1978.

Durand, R. Male rape. *GPU News* (Milwaukee), February 1977.

Elwood, N. D., & Larson, B. (Eds.). *Same-sex assault: A handbook for intervention training*. St. Paul: State of Minnesota Department of Corrections, Minnesota Program for Victims of Sexual Assault. 1981.

Engle, M. Rape of males—The picture is blurred. *Honolulu Star-Bulletin*, August 15, 1978.

Gays: Targets for violence. *Metro Times* (Dallas), September 18, 1980.

Giteck, L. A good defense. *The Advocate*, April 2, 1981.

Groth, A. N., & Burgess, A. W. Male rape: Offenders and victims. *American Journal of Psychiatry*, 1980, *137*, 806-810.

Hardy, R. Overkill. *Body Politic*, February 1979, pp. 19-21.

Hudgins, C. Most male rape victims are silenced by emotional strain. *Minneapolis Star*, April 13, 1979.

Ireland, D. Rendezvous in the Ramble. *New York*, July 24, 1978.

Kaufman, A., DiVasto, P., Jackson, R., Voorhees, D., & Christy, J. Male rape victims: Noninstitutionalized assault. *American Journal of Psychiatry*, 1980, *137*, 221-223.

Klibanoff, H. Hatred, fear, spur gay-basher. *Boston Sunday Globe*, December 9, 1979.

Kohl, L. Assault season here, gays say. *St. Paul Dispatch*, June 18, 1979.

Kokopeli, B., & Lakey, G. More power than we want: Masculine sexuality and violence. *WIN: Peace and Freedom through Non-Violent Action*, 1976, *12*(27).

Lipsyte, R. The closet, a violent and subtle prison. *New York Times*, August 1, 1978.

McNaught, B. Anti-gay violence rising. *Metro Gay News* (Detroit), August 1977.

Miller, B. Adult sexual resocialization: Adjustments toward a stigmatized identity. *Alternative Lifestyles: Changing Patterns in Marriage, Family and Intimacy*, May 1978, *1*, 207-234.

Miller, B., & Humphreys, L. Lifestyles and violence: Homosexual victims of assault and murder. *Qualitative Sociology*, 1980, *3*(3), 169-185.

Parsons, J. Gays fight against unprovoked assaults. *Minneapolis Tribune*, November 26, 1978.

Rofes, E. Queer bashing: The politics of violence against gay men. *Gay Community News* (Boston), August 12, 1978.

San Miguel, C. L., & Millham, J. The role of cognitive and situational variables in aggression toward homosexuals. *Journal of Homosexuality*, 1976, *2*, 11-27.

Simon, R. A walk on the wild side of gay life. *Chicago Sun-Times*, July 14, 1978.

Swigert, V., Farrell, R., & Yoels, W. Sexual homicide: Social, psychological, and legal aspects. *Archives of Sexual Behavior*, 1976, *5*, 391-401.

Weissman, E. Kids who attack gays. *Christopher Street*, August 1978.

Willenbecher, T. Male rape. *The Advocate*, October 30, 1980.

Pamphlets

No More Assault Project. *Men beating men: What you don't know about same-sex assault can hurt you*. Available from: Gay Community Services, Inc., 2855 Park Ave. South, Minneapolis, MN 55407; or Minnesota Committee for Gay and Lesbian Rights, P.O. Box 993, Main Post Office, Minneapolis, MN 55440.

Sexual assault against men—It does happen. State of Minnesota, Department of Corrections, Minnesota Program for Victims of Sexual Assault, 430 Metro Square Building, St. Paul, MN 55101.

Victims of rape. . .Not only women. Sexual Trauma Center, 50 Ivy St., San Francisco, CA 94102.

Rape

Amir, M. *Patterns in forcible rape*. Chicago: University of Chicago Press, 1971.

Brownmiller, S. *Against our will: Men, women, and rape*. New York: Simon & Schuster, 1975.

Burgess, A. W., & Holmstrom, L. L. Rape trauma syndrome. *American Journal of Psychiatry*, 1974, *131*, 981-986.

Burgess, A., & Holmstrom, L. L. *Rape: Victims of crisis*. Bowie, MD: Robert J. Brady, Co., 1974.

Burgess, A., & Holmstrom, L. L. *Rape: Crisis and recovery* (2nd ed.). Bowie, MD: Robert J. Brady, Co., 1979.

Halpern, S. *Rape: Helping the victim—A treatment manual.* Oradell, NJ: Medical Economics Co., Book Division, 1978.

Hilberman, E. *The rape victim.* New York: Basic Books, Inc./American Psychiatric Association, 1976.

Holmstrom, L. L., & Burgess, A. W. *The victim of rape—Institutional reactions.* New York: John Wiley & Sons, 1978.

Katz, S., & Mazur, M. A. *Understanding the rape victim: A synthesis of research findings.* New York: John Wiley & Sons, 1979.

Keller, E. (Ed.). *Sexual assault—A statewide problem.* St. Paul: State of Minnesota, Department of Corrections, Minnesota Program for Victims of Sexual Assault, 1975.

MacDonald, J. M. *Rape offenders and their victims.* Springfield, IL: Charles C. Thomas, 1971.

McCahill, T., Meyer, L. C., & Fischman, A. M. *The aftermath of rape.* Lexington, MA and Toronto: Lexington Books/D. C. Heath & Co., 1979.

Silverman, D. Sharing the crisis of rape. *American Journal of Orthopsychiatry,* 1978, *48*(1), 166-173.

Sutherland, S., & Scherl, D. J. Patterns of response among victims of rape. *American Journal of Orthopsychiatry,* 1970, *40*, 503-511.

Symonds, M. The rape victim: Psychological patterns of response. *American Journal of Psychoanalysis,* 1976, *36*, 27-34.

Victimology

Baluss, M. E. *Integrated services for victims of crime: A county-based approach.* Washington, D.C.: National Association of Counties Research Foundation, 1975.

Barkas, J. L. *Victims: Violence and its aftermath.* New York: Charles Scribner's Sons, 1978.

Geis, G. Victims of crimes of violence and the criminal justice system. In D. Chappell & J. Monahan (Eds.), *Violence and criminal justice.* Lexington, MA: D. C. Heath, 1975.

Kivens, L. (Ed.). Services for victims/survivors. Program Evaluation Resource Center, Minneapolis Medical Research Foundation, Inc.: *Evaluation and Change,* Special Issue, 1980.

Symonds, M. Victims of violence: Psychological effects and aftereffects. *American Journal of Psychoanalysis,* 1975, *35*, 19-26.

Viano, E. C. (Ed.). *Victimology: An International Journal,* Quarterly. Washington, D.C.: Visage Press, Inc.

Viano, E. C. *Victims and society.* Washington, D.C.: Visage Press, 1976.

Interventions (General)

Butcher, J., & Maudel, G. Treatment of the individual in crisis. In I. Weiner (Ed.), *Clinical methods in psychology.* New York: John Wiley & Sons, in press.

Lick, J., & Bootzin, R. Expectancy factors in the treatment of fear. *Psychological Bulletin,* 1975, *82*, 917-931.

Muller, E. J., & Dumpson, J. R. (Eds.). *Evaluation of social intervention.* San Francisco: Jossey-Bass, 1972.

Rapoport, L. Crisis intervention as a mode of brief treatment. In R. Roberts & R. Nee (Eds.), *Theories of social casework.* Chicago: University of Chicago Press, 1970.

Reid, W., & Shapiro, B. Client reactions to advice. *Social Service Review,* 1969, *43*, 165-173.

Truax, C. B., & Mitchell, K. Research on certain therapist interpersonal skills in relation to process and outcome. In A. Bergin & S. Garfield (Eds.), *Handbook of psychotherapy and behavior change.* New York: John Wiley & Sons, 1971.

Prison

Boffum, P. *Homosexuality in prisons.* Washington, D.C.: U.S. Government Printing Office, 1972.

Brownmiller, S. Power: Institution and authority—Prison rape: The homosexual experience. Chapter 8 in *Against our will: Men, women, and rape.* New York: Simon & Schuster, 1975.

Carrol, L. Humanitarian reform and biracial sexual assault in a maximum security prison. *Urban Life*, January 1977.

Davis, A. J. Sexual assaults in the Philadelphia prison system and sheriff's vans. *Trans-action*, 1968, *6*(2), 8-16.

Friar, D. J., & Weiss, C. *Terror in the prisons: Homosexual rape and why society condones it*. Indianapolis: Bobbs-Merrill Co., 1974.

Gagnon, J. H., & Simon, W. The social meaning of prison homosexuality. *Federal Probation*, 1968, *32*(1), 23-29.

Giallombardo, R. Social roles in prison for a woman. *Social Problems*, 1966, *13*, 268-288.

Johnson, E. The homosexual in prison. *Social Theory & Practice*, 1971, *1*(4), 83-97.

Kleinberg, S. Prisoners: The three R's—Reading, rape, and riot. Chapter 8 in *Alienated affections: Being gay in America*. New York: St. Martin's Press, 1980. (Reprinted from *Christopher Street*, January 1979.)

Sagarin, E. Prison homosexuality and its effect on post-prison sexual behavior. *Psychiatry*, 1976, *39*, 245-257.

Scacco, A. M., Jr. *Rape in prison*. (American Lectures in Behavioral Science and Law Series). Springfield, IL: Charles C. Thomas, 1975.

Ward, D. A., & Kassebaum, G. G. Homosexuality: A mode of adaptation in a prison for women. *Social Problems*, 1964, *12*, 159-177.

RELIGIOUS AND MORAL ISSUES
IN WORKING WITH HOMOSEXUAL CLIENTS

James B. Nelson, PhD

ABSTRACT. While strict moral and religious neutrality in psychotherapy is problematic at best, the therapist working with homosexual clients particularly needs clarity about her or his own moral and religious assumptions, together with a knowledge of the Judeo-Christian tradition on the subject. This article examines the biblical evidence and current theological arguments about homosexuality. Christianity as an incarnationalist faith is a sex-affirming religion with positive resources for lesbians and gay men. An analysis of homophobia concludes, maintaining the position that the church as a whole will benefit greatly from the liberation of gay men and lesbians from oppression.

At the outset, let me offer a linguistic comment. I consider "homosexuality" an abstraction. There is no such thing as "homosexuality" per se. When we use the term we are speaking about people—people who happen to be more or less erotically oriented to their own sex; people who are more or less comfortable with this orientation; and people who experience more or fewer difficulties, personal and social, because of their orientation. Always we are speaking of concrete persons, in spite of the limitations of language (see Nugent, 1980).

Can a Therapist Be Neutral?

Can a therapist, whatever her or his own sexual orientation, be neutral when working with "homosexual" clients? Quite apart from the question of sexual orientation, when the general issue of religious and moral neutrality in counseling is considered, a distinction is sometimes made between "pastoral counseling" and "secular psychotherapy." The former is assumed to be interlaced with

James B. Nelson is Professor of Christian Ethics at United Theological Seminary of the Twin Cities, New Brighton, Minnesota, where he has taught since 1963. A graduate of Macalester College, he served in the U.S. Army before entering Yale Divinity School for his theological training. Following that he studied at the Graduate School, Yale University, for his PhD.

An ordained minister of the United Church of Christ, he has served parishes in Connecticut and South Dakota. Since its inception in 1970, he has been closely associated with the Program in Human Sexuality, University of Minnesota Medical School. Nelson is the author of five books, the latest of which is *Embodiment: An Approach to Sexuality and Christian Theology*.

His wife, the Rev. Wilys Claire Nelson, is a hospital chaplain. They have two grown children.

163

normative values and religious beliefs, since clergy are expected in all of their ministerial functions to represent and interpret the meanings of the religious group. In contrast, many people assume that the "secular psychotherapist" (whether or not committed to a religious tradition) will take an eductive counseling approach. As such, the therapist will not attempt to impose solutions but, maintaining a neutral standpoint, will attempt to educe both emotional and moral solutions from the client.

This neat division, however, is highly misleading. In recent decades many clergy have moved toward substantially psychotherapeutic models of counseling, attempting to keep their own religious and moral convictions very much in the background. At the same time, it is increasingly recognized that the professional psychotherapist is not dealing with a religiously or morally neutral process. Psychotherapy, like religion, tries to help people change their lives. In assisting clients to alleviate their emotional distress, the therapist necessarily operates with certain images of "sin" (the causative factors and dynamics of the distress), certain images of "salvation" (the dynamics of change, the hoped-for cure or pattern of growth), and some general interpretation of human fulfillment and life's meaning (see Browning, 1976).

If these observations are true of counseling in general, it is even clearer that religious and moral neutrality are impossible when one is working with homosexual clients. Although counselors will vary in the extent to which they allow their own convictions to enter the process, I believe it neither possible nor desirable for them to escape altogether a whole series of moral and religious questions, the answers to which will critically affect the pattern and course of the counseling or therapy: Is homosexuality as such good, bad, or neutral? Are certain difficulties frequently encountered by gay men and lesbians intrinsic to their sexual orientation, or are they rooted in the dynamics of social oppression? What are the ethics of genital expression; and are these criteria the same for both homosexual and heterosexual persons, or are they different? What are the purposes of human sexuality? How does one assess the varied Western religious traditions on the issue of homosexuality? Are clients likely to be helped or hindered by their particular religious belief systems and involvements? As these questions—and others—will be answered in one way or another by the therapist, it is important that the counselor be clear about her or his own commitments and knowledgeably sensitive to particular issues commonly faced by gay men and lesbians.

The following discussion will reflect a number of my own convictions which I have attempted to elaborate elsewhere: that homosexuality is a Christianly valid orientation; that homosexual genital expression should be guided by the same general ethical criteria as are appropriate for heterosexual expression, though with sensitivity to the special situation of an oppressed minority; that the church, while too frequently a participant in oppression, does have important healing resources for gay men and lesbians; and that the church deeply needs the gay and lesbian presence and witness (see Nelson, 1978). Although I shall address these issues out of my own Protestant Christian context, I believe that much of what I write is applicable to Catholic and Jewish positions as well.

Understanding the Religious Tradition

No gay or lesbian person in our society can escape responding in some manner to the ways in which the Judeo-Christian tradition has dealt with homosexuality. Likewise, it is predictable that numerous gay and lesbian clients will be working on issues of self-worth and self-esteem stemming from preconceived condemnation by organized religion. Whether the biblical and theological arguments are of personal interest to the therapist is beside the point. They *do* matter to many gay and lesbian clients. Accordingly, it can be enormously helpful if the counselor is able to respond knowledgeably to the question "But doesn't the Bible say homosexuality is a sin?" with "No, not as I understand it." Fortunately, a number of books and articles now available afford reliable, detailed treatment of the biblical and theological issues. My purpose here is limited to a summary overview.

Any specific biblical passage relating to homosexuality must, I believe, be interpreted with several things in mind. First, homosexuality *as a psychosexual orientation* is not dealt with in the Bible. The concept of sexual orientation is distinctly modern. The Bible's references are, without exception, statements about certain types of same-sex *acts*. In all probability, the biblical writers assumed all persons to be "naturally" heterosexual; hence, those who engaged in homosexual activity were doing so in willful and conscious violation of their own (heterosexual) natures.

Second, the strong link between sex and procreation, particularly in the Old Testament, must be understood in a particular historical context. A small Hebrew tribe in a hostile environment indeed needed children for its survival.

Third, both Old and New Testaments (though I believe they also contain a doctrine of radical human equality) were admittedly written in the context of male-dominated societies. The issue of *male* homosexual activity receives virtually all the attention, for lesbian activity hardly constitutes the same threat to the patriarchal mind-set.

Fourth, coupled with the procreative emphasis and patriarchal assumptions, there was a biological misunderstanding. The pre-scientific (male) mind, knowing nothing of eggs and ovulation, and assuming a special life-transmitting power for the semen alone, frequently concluded that deliberate non-procreative expulsion of semen was a serious life-destroying act.

Fifth, biblical references to homosexual acts almost always reflect a genuine anxiety about idolatrous religious practices. In the ancient Mid-East, idolatry frequently found sexual expression. In such practices (both heterosexual and homosexual), sex was depersonalized and seen as a mysterious power which one must dedicate to the deity out of fear.

Given these contextual factors, what might we make of the specific biblical passages? The answer, in short, is: not very much. In the vast spectrum of biblical material there are surprisingly few references to homosexual acts and almost all of these speak to religious and social conditions significantly different from our own. Consider, briefly, the most frequently cited texts (and those with which most gay and lesbian clients have had personally to deal).

The destruction of Sodom and Gomorrah (Genesis 19), though often believed to show God's condemnation of homosexual activity, cannot fairly be interpreted in this manner. In recent decades, many noted biblical scholars have concluded that "the sin of Sodom" actually was the general violation of Hebraic standards of social justice, including the violation of the norm of hospitality to the stranger. Even if one grants a primarily sexual focus to the story, the only reasonable conclusion is that here are condemnations of sexual intercourse with divine messengers and of violent gang rape—but not condemnations of other forms of homosexual genital activity or of homosexuality as an orientation.

In two other Old Testament passages, however, there are unmistakable denunciations of homosexual acts, both explicitly male in reference. Leviticus 18:23 and 20:13, part of the "Holiness Code," reflect an overriding concern for the separateness and purity of God's chosen people in contrast to the surrounding tribes with their idolatrous practices, including the use of female and male temple prostitutes. Selective literalists today frequently single out these texts, forget (or are unaware of) their historical context, and ignore the numerous other proscriptions in the same code, such as those against eating rare meat, having marital intercourse during menstruation, and wearing clothing of mixed fabrics.

The New Testament contains no recorded words of Jesus on the subject. Its principal references are those of Paul in Romans 1 and First Corinthians 6, and of the "Pauline" writer in I Timothy 1. The latter two texts deal with types of activity which, it was believed, warrant excluding persons from the Kingdom of God. Both passages, however, need careful linguistic interpretation and when given such appear not to be directed toward all homosexual persons but rather to specific kinds of homosexual acts, namely exploitation, homosexual prostitution, and the sexual use of boys by adult males.

Paul's words in Romans 1 are usually taken as the strongest New Testament rejection of homosexuality. (Here is the one and only biblical reference to female as well as male same-sex activity.) Paul, however, speaks specifically of same-sex acts that express idolatry and acts undertaken in lust (not tenderness or mutual respect) by "heterosexuals" who willfully act contrary to their own sexual natures. I am not inferring that the Apostle necessarily would have approved of other kinds of same-sex acts. I am simply arguing that it is inaccurate and unfair to interpret his words as directed to non-exploitive and loving acts by same-sex couples for whom mutual homosexual attraction is part of the given of *their* natures.

Clients and their counselors, therefore, need to be aware that careful examination of the biblical material renders no definitive scriptural word on homosexuality as a sexual orientation or upon homosexual genital expression in a relationship of respect and love. Specifically, what the Bible gives us is several references to certain kinds of same-sex acts in quite different religious and cultural contexts from those faced by gay men and lesbians today. Often forgotten, too, is the manner in which scripture celebrates instances of genuine love between two men or two women—David and Jonathan, Ruth and Naomi, Jesus and the Beloved Disciple. Beyond all this, a Christian approach counsels its adherents to assess every moral judgment (whether made by ancient Hebrews or later by Christians) in terms of the spirit of love and to recognize that the central question is not what constitutes a breach of divine moral law as understood in certain historical periods but rather what constitutes responsive faithfulness to God, the Cosmic Lover, who is revealed in Jesus the Christ. The Bible conveys the message that human sexuality is one of the Creator's great and good gifts, to be integrated fully into one's personhood and expressed in ways that honor both God and the human partner.

Dealing with Current Theological Opinion and Church Practice

The scriptural questions by themselves do not exhaust the theological issues with which many gay men and lesbians must deal. The church has a long and unfortunate history of homosexual oppression, which continues into the present. As John Boswell's (1980a) impressive scholarship has recently demonstrated, Christianity's opposition to homosexuality was not original but derived from non-Christian sources. Nor has it always been consistent. There were centuries of Christian tolerance. Nevertheless, most of today's gay men and lesbians have met with enormously more rejection than affirmation by the church.

Two theological issues in particular frequently surface in counseling. One is the claim that the homosexual orientation itself is contrary to "nature," or to "natural law," or to God's intention in creation. To the extent that this is internalized, the individual will likely regard her- or himself as freakish and unnatural in this very fundamental way. Frequently, of course, the "unnatural" label is coupled with psychological notions of illness, perversion, and arrested development, or even with religious notions of idolatry.

The religiously-sensitive therapist can assist the client on several levels: for example, the cognitive process of sorting out the natural-law argument. Several points deserve attention. One is the grounding of this argument in a static metaphysical world view that appeared appropriate to the Middle Ages but is quite inappropriate today. There is no fixed human nature which can be read off the structure of human biology. Because human beings are constantly in the process of becoming, the definition of what is "naturally" human is forever being modified and changed. Numerous theologians now recognize this, even within the Roman Catholic Church, which has been most heavily committed to the tradition of natural law. Thus, Father Gregory Baum (1974) argues that what is normative for "normal life" is the human nature toward which we are divinely summoned—the life of mutuality, in terms of which homosexual love is not to be excluded or seen as contradictory.

Related to the above are the biological assertions that procreation is the primary purpose of sex and that, since homosexual intercourse is by definition nonprocreative, it is unnatural and contrary to creation. Mainstream Protestant thought began to move away from the primacy-of-procreation position three centuries ago; more recently much Roman Catholic thought has done likewise. Indeed, the church has always recognized the validity of the marriage in which sterility made procreation impossible, and since 1931 the Catholic Church has officially endorsed love-making without baby-making through approval of the rhythm method. If the primary purpose of sexual expression is communion or love, then it is difficult to exclude any type of love-making, heterosexual or homosexual, which is either intrinsically or deliberately nonprocreative. The central question is thus the inescapable one: What is the fundamental meaning of our sexuality?

Finally, it should be remembered by both counselor and client that most natural-law arguments against homsexuality, whether they articulate it or not, rest upon an assumption of "gender complementarity." It is assumed that men and women are naturally constituted with essentially different personality configurations (e.g., men are cognitive, women are intuitive, etc.), so that one sex is incomplete until finding its complement in the other. But this notion is based upon disproven sex-role stereotypes, covertly supports an unjust dominance-submission relation between the sexes, and allows neither sex to develop its androgynous possibilities. What the arguments misses, in short, is the uniqueness of human personality. We are, indeed, destined for communion with others. We do, indeed, find our loneliness assuaged and our deficiencies met with another's strengths. But such can be the case in the homosexual couple just as fully as in the heterosexual. It is not biologically destined. The gay or lesbian client can be encouraged to tap personal experience to verify this.

Closely related to and overlapping the above natural-law arguments is a position officially subscribed to by several major church bodies today. It holds that while homosexuality as an *orientation* is contrary to God's created intention, the homosexual *person* ought not be adversely judged or rejected by the church. Often this position carries the acknowledgement that sexual orientation is seldom if ever the result of voluntary choice and that constitutional homosexuality appears largely unsusceptible to psychotherapeutic reorientation. While some church people see this as a more tolerant and compassionate view than outright condemnation, it places gay men and lesbians in at least two impossible binds.

One, of course, is the individual's recognition that her or his own sexual orientation is as natural and as fundamental to identity as is the color of the skin. It is both naive and cruel to tell a lesbian or gay man, "Your sexual orientation is still unnatural and a perversion, but this is no judgment upon you as a person." The individual knows otherwise.

The other bind concerns churchly pressure toward celibacy. When the church presumes to be non-judgmental toward orientation but then draws the line against any genital expression, it is difficult to understand how the sense of guilt—even in the celibate—will be significantly alleviated. In most lesbians and gay men it is likely and understandable that anger will increase.

In the face of this, both client and counselor can realize two important things. One is that there are both intellectual and psychological contradictions in any position which is based upon an outmoded version of natural law or which attempts to make sharp distinctions between orientation and genital expression.

The second recognition is equally important: There is a significant and increasing pluralism within organized Christianity with regard to these issues. Theologians and churches, both Protestant and Catholic, simply do not have a unified mind, and the client needs to know this. In spite of the official Vatican position, there are distinguished Catholic theologians who publicly proclaim homosexuality as Christianly valid, and there are creative and affirming Catholic ministries to gay and lesbian communities. Within Protestantism, the spectrum is even greater. Here, too, one can find an increasing number of significant theological voices giving full affirmation to lesbians and gay men— not only among "liberal" theologians but now also among those who identify themselves as "evangelical."

There have been ordinations of publically affirmed gay and lesbian persons in at least two major Protestant churches (the United Church of Christ and the Protestant Episcoal Church) and pressures in other denominations for similar openness. In recent years, several denominations have undertaken major studies of human sexuality, occasioning considerable reassessment of traditional Christian attitudes about homosexuality. Further, since 1968 there have arisen gay-lesbian organizations within virtually every major American denomination (Gearhart & Johnson, 1974). And a new movement, the Metropolitan Community Churches, with ministries and congregations organized primarily by and for gay men and lesbians, has become a rapidly expanding urban religious phenomenon in this country and abroad (Perry, 1972).

The point is this: Particularly within the last dozen years there has been a vigorous ferment about homosexual issues within American church life. In every case except the most conservative and fundamentalist groups, this ferment has produced new openness toward and affirmation of lesbians and gay men. If, as is sadly true, the legacy of rejection is still alive, it is also true that changes are occurring within the churches as never before within recent centuries. It would be a mistake for any therapist or client to assume that the church is a monolithic, condemning entity.

Questions Surrounding Gay-Lesbian Spirituality and Life-Style

It is probable that proportionately fewer lesbians than gay men are still attempting to find their spiritual home in the organized church. After all, in spite of some encouraging progress on feminist issues, the churches are still unquestionably male-dominated. Hence, lesbians have two strikes against them—their sex as well as their sexual orientation—and feeling their power-lessness in the church, a number have voted with their feet. Yet, for those lesbians and gay men who still seek a religious life within organized Christian communions, what are the important resources for their wholeness and mental health?

One resource is the experience of community. It is imperfectly present in some churches, sadly absent in others, but genuinely available in some congregations and in all of the specifically gay-lesbian Christian groups. The internalization of such labels as "sinner," "sick," and "unnatural" inevitably leads to shame and guilt, and thence to social withdrawal. The need for a community of acceptance and affirmation more personally inclusive than can be found in the bars and baths is real. That this enormously important resource does exist for gay men and lesbians—at least in some religious groups—ought not to be overlooked by therapists and clients. When the religious community can assist the coming-out process, help to mitigate its pain, and help the individual to celebrate new openness, the rewards are particularly great, inasmuch as the energy drain and heightened possibility of self-hatred in the closeted person forced to live the double life can take a heavy toll.

Feelings of guilt over homosexuality can be exacerbated to a point of moral scrupulosity by the internalization of negative attitudes toward sexuality itself. A positive, indeed celebrative, religious attitude toward human sexuality, then, is another resource possible within the church. Even though much of the church throughout much of its history has been remiss on this score, the foundations for sexual affirmation are central to Christianity's theological tenets.

Christianity is a religion of incarnation. At the core of its belief system is the affirmation that the Word has become flesh and has dwelt among us, full of grace and truth. This is a radical proposition. It claims that the most decisive experience of God is not in doctrine or creed or other-worldly mystical experience, but *in flesh.* Insofar as this is taken seriously, the embodiment of God is not limited to the critical manifestation in the historical Jesus but continues in our human flesh now. Against any Greek dualism dividing spirit from body, proclaiming the eternal spirit good and the temporal body corrupt, suspect, even evil, an incarnationalist faith sees the body as good. We can be both fully spiritual and fully sexual—indeed, that is our destiny.

Christian faith at its core is not only incarnationalist, it is also a religion of grace. In contemporary terms, grace means radical, unconditional acceptance. This means (even if some elements of the church have little understood it) that we are accepted and affirmed as sexual selves. Our bodies, our sexual feelings and fantasies, our ascetic attempts at self-purification, our hedonistic flights from authentic relationship, our femininity and our masculinity, our homosexuality and our heterosexuality—all are accepted by God.

The dynamics of grace, of God's radical acceptance, afford a whole range of possibilities in sexual growth. One is growth in self-acceptance. Such positive self-love personalizes the body and puts us more in touch with the roots of our emotions. Another possibility is growth in sensuousness, in the self's ability to experience the erotic throughout the entire body (not only in the genitals), and in the self's increased capacity to give and receive pleasure. Still another arena of growth is that of androgyny, for grace aims at the fullest possible development of each unique individual beyond all of the constructions of sex-role or sexual-orientation stereotypes. Perhaps all of these possibilities of growth are summarized in one word—love. For love means the increasing ability to integrate fully our sexuality and our capacity for caring and intimacy.

If the majority of Christians have internalized some sex-negative attitudes from their religion, lesbians and gay men have been susceptible to an even heavier dose than have heterosexual men and women. Forced by a hostile majority to focus more attention and energy upon defending their own sexual orientation, gay people are forced to deal more constantly with their sexuality in general. Hence, the likelihood of internalizing shameful feelings simply because of *being sexual* is all the greater. Given this, I cannot overestimate the importance of the therapist's awareness of the need for positive religious approaches to sexuality. To be sure, our salvation (or "health" or "wholeness"— the words all have the same root) is always incomplete. Because none of us is whole, the unhealed parts of our sexuality will continue to hurt us and others. But the religiously concerned client needs to know that the first and last word of the Christian message is incarnate grace: grace as acceptance and grace as empowerment for new growth and life as a body-self. The Word is made flesh, and our flesh is confirmed.

What does all this mean for a moral life-style for the religiously sensitive gay or lesbian? Celibacy is one option. It is an option to be honored when voluntarily chosen for positive rather than negative reasons. If celibacy is embraced not from a belief that homosexual genital expression is intrinsically wrong, nor out of generalized fear of sex and intimacy, nor because celibacy is believed to be religiously more meritorious, but rather is embraced because celibacy best expresses the person's own sense of integrity or vocational commitments, it is to be celebrated. The celibate is still "a sexual celibate" for whom her or his positively affirmed sexuality, while not genitally expressed with another, is the grounding of emotional richness and interpersonal intimacy (Goergen, 1975; Gustafson, 1978).

But celibacy ought not to be considered the only Christianly valid life-style for the gay man or lesbian. Against the biologism that sex and erotic love are moral only when they are potentially procreative, there is a second major Christian tradition. It might be called "the transcendent approach" to sexuality, for it strives to transcend biological determinations of eroticism and love (Boswell, 1980b). Though it will surprise many, this latter approach has more New Testament grounding and was, in fact, dominant in theology for several centuries in the early Christian era (a time when, significantly, ecclesiastical opposition to homosexuality was very rare). If current secular society is now ahead of the church in its tolerance of "non-biological" love, the church needs to reclaim its earlier tradition and not capitulate to the fears of ultra-conservative Christians who would move us back into an even more stringent biological determinism.

Human sexuality, for all of its similarity to animal sexuality, is different. It is not under the tyranny of biology. Our sexuality is highly symbolic in its meanings and capable of expressing the depths of human self-understanding and desires for relatedness. Our sexuality is capable of expressing and sharing a total personal relationship that contributes immeasurably toward our intended destiny as human beings—that of lovers after the image of the Cosmic Lover.

Hence, the core issue for sexual ethics is not the assessment of certain types of physical acts as right or wrong. Abnormality or deviance ought not to be defined statistically, but rather in reference to the Christian norm—authentic humanity as revealed in Jesus the Christ. Gay men and lesbians desire and need deep, lasting relationships no less than do heterosexual people, and appropriate genital expression should be denied to neither.

Thus, the appropriate ethical question is this: What sexual behavior will serve and enhance, rather than inhibit and damage the fuller realization of our divinely intended humanity? The answer, I believe, is sexual behavior in accordance with love. This means commitment, trust, tenderness, respect for the other, and the desire for responsible communion. On the negative side it means resisting cruelty, utterly impersonal sex, obsession with sexual gratification, and actions that display no willingness to take responsibility for their consequences in human lives. This kind of ethic is equally appropriate to both heterosexual and homosexual Christians.

But this statement deserves a word of qualification. The social and religious oppression experienced by most gay men and lesbians has driven many—especially men—to rely heavily upon the satisfactions of impersonal sex associated with cruising, the baths, and "tea rooms." While such impersonal sex is by no means a homosexual monopoly, it is understandably more of a temptation when the majority society does all in its power to discourage lasting homosexual unions and when most of the church refuses to bless and support the covenants of gay and lesbian couples. Given the realities of social oppression, it is insensitive and unfair to judge gay men and lesbians simply by a heterosexual ideal of the monogomous relationship. What can be said to all persons regardless of orientation is that genital expression can find its greatest fulfillment within a relationship of ongoing commitment and communion. That other sexual encounters and experiences can have elements of genuine good in them even while falling short of the optimum remains an open possibility.

For the gay male or lesbian couple who intend a covenant of indefinite duration, will "fidelity" always mean "genital exclusivity"? Some such couples (as is true of some heterosexual couples) have explored relationships that admit the possibility of sexual intimacy with secondary partners. For these couples, "infidelity" does not have a simple biological meaning (sex with someone other than the permanent partner). Rather, infidelity means the rupture of the bonds of faithfulness, trust, honesty, and commitment between the partners. On the positive side, fidelity is seen as the enduring commitment to the partner's well-being and growth, a commitment to the primacy of this covenant over any other relationship. While there are undoubted risks for such a course of action, and while the weight of Christian tradition is on the side of sexual exclusivity, there are also risks when a couple's relationship becomes marked by possessiveness.

These, then, are guidelines and ideals that can assist the religiously sensitive individual in deciding about appropriate genital expression. They are guidelines, however, and not legalisms. They respect the necessity of personal decision, and they function within a Christian understanding of forgiveness and new beginnings when our sexual expression has become more destructive than creative of our destined humanness (see Nelson, 1978, chaps. 5 and 6).

Homophobia and the Church's Need for Gay and Lesbian Christians

Thus far my emphasis has been upon the resources which gay men and lesbians might find within Christian faith. What remains to be emphasized is the need of other Christians to have homosexual brothers and sisters within the religious community. In a word, churches and society both desperately need release from homophobia, that irrational fear of same-sex orientation and expression.

While some resistance to homosexuality is, to be sure, based upon calm and reasoned religious belief (though my own disagreements with its major arguments have already been indicated), undoubtedly much is based upon unreasoned, ill-understood emotional reactions. Without the presence of homophobia it is difficult to understand the persistence of selective biblical literalism and long-disproven homosexual stereotypes among so many church members.

While homophobia can be accounted for by a variety of psychodynamics, importantly including the projection of fears about homosexual feelings in the self, its deep roots in the twin forms of alienating sexual dualism need also to be recognized. Spiritualistic dualism (spirit over body) is likely to be present. Virtually everyone in our society suffers from the internally divisive effects of spiritualism and longs for (in unconscious as well as conscious ways) the essential reunion of the body-self. And, since stereotypes insist that gay men and lesbians are more sexually defined and simply "more sexual" than heterosexual men and women, they become the targets of subconscious envy. Hence, the stereotype bears its curiously unintended harvest, but one which gives a powerful dynamic to homophobia.

The dynamic of sexist dualism may be even stronger in Western society, as witnessed by the predominance of biblical concern with male homosexuality as compared to lesbianism. Male homosexuality appears to threaten "normal" masculine gender identity. It calls into question the dominance-submission patterns of any patriarchal society as well as the myths of super-masculinism by which that society lives. And, unconsciously, the heterosexual male seems to fear that an acceptance of male homosexuality in others would open him to the risk of being "womanized," losing his power, and becoming the same sort of sex object into which he has made women.

Thus, not only gay men and lesbians, but surely also heterosexual people within the church and in society generally, have enormous benefits to gain by being released from the destructive dynamics of homophobia. Insofar as this occurs there will be release from dehumanizing sex-role stereotypes and liberation from fears about the continuum of sexual feelings within the self. There will be more genuine self-acceptance and self-affirmation, and with this greater relational equality. There will be enriched possibilities for intimate friendships with fewer debilitating sexual fears between the sexes, as well as in same-sex friendship patterns. We can expect a diminution of male-biased social violence in its myriad forms. There will be more permission for each individual to develop her or his own human uniqueness. And the churches will learn more of the heart of the Christian message, including the freedom, inclusiveness, and justice which come from taking incarnate grace seriously. In a word, gay men and lesbians need to know how much everyone in society will benefit from the gains in their own struggle for liberation. While it is grossly unfair to place the burden of liberating the oppressors upon the oppressed, it may be that the latter can find reason for augmented self-assurance in knowing how deeply they are needed by the former. And such knowledge can be therapeutic.

REFERENCES

Baum, G. Catholic homosexuals. *Commonweal*, 1974, *99*(19), 479-482.
Boswell, J. E. *Christianity, social tolerance, and homosexuality*. Chicago: University of Chicago, 1980. (a)
Boswell, J. E. A crucial juncture. *Integrity Forum*, 1980, *6*, (6), 1-6. (b)

Browning, D. S. *The moral context of pastoral care*. Philadelphia: Westminster, 1976.
Gearhart, S., & Johnson, W. *Loving women/Loving men*. San Francisco: Glide, 1974.
Goergen, D. *The sexual celibate*. New York: Seabury Press, 1975.
Gustafson, J. *Celibate passion*. San Francisco: Harper & Row, 1978.
Nelson, J. B. *Embodiment: An approach to sexuality and Christian theology*. Minneapolis: Augsburg, 1978.
Nugent, R. Gay ministry. *Ministries*, November 1980, 6-27.
Perry, T. *The Lord is my shepherd and He knows I'm gay*. Plainview, NY: Nash, 1972.

BIBLIOGRAPHY

Recommended for Biblical and Theological Issues

Bailey, D. S. *Homosexuality and the Western Christian tradition*. London: Longmans, Green, 1955
Boswell, J. E. *Christianity, social tolerance, and homosexuality*. Chicago: University of Chicago, 1980.
Horner, T. *Jonathan loved David*. Philadelphia: Westminster, 1978.
Kosnick, A., Carroll, W., Cunningham, A., Modras, R., & Schulte, J. *Human sexuality: New directions in American Catholic thought*. New York: Paulist, 1977.
McNeill, J. J. *The church and the homosexual*. Kansas City: Sheed, Andrews, and McMeel, 1976.
Pittenger, N. *Time for consent*. London: S.C.M., 1967.
Scanzoni, L., & Mollenkott, V. R. *Is the homosexual my neighbor?* New York: Harper & Row, 1978.
United Church of Christ. *Human sexuality: A preliminary report*. New York: United Church, 1977.
Woods, R. *Another kind of love: Homosexuality and spirituality*. Chicago: Thomas More, 1977.

Recommended for Counseling Issues

Babuscio, J. *We speak for ourselves*. Philadelphia: Fortress, 1977.
Borhek, M. V. *My son Eric*. New York: Pilgrim, 1979.
Clark, D. *Loving someone gay*. Millbrae, CA: Celestial Arts, 1977.
Jones, C. R. *Homosexuality and counseling*. Philadelphia: Fortress, 1974.
Jones, C. R. *Understanding gay relatives and friends*. New York: Seabury Press, 1978.

PSYCHOANALYTIC PSYCHOTHERAPY
FOR HOMOSEXUAL CLIENTS:
NEW CONCEPTS

William G. Herron, PhD
Thomas Kinter, PhD
Irwin Sollinger, PhD
Julius Trubowitz, EdD

ABSTRACT. This article argues that psychoanalytic psychotherapy can be valuable for homosexual patients. The authors examine the psychoanalytic theory of homosexuality, present the evidence for and against homosexual "pathology," and describe their own conceptual schema for therapy: a psychoanalytic approach designed to improve the client's social and sexual functioning. The article is illustrated with clinical examples of clients who learned to understand and express their sexual orientations, which were primarily homosexual.

In the past, psychoanalysis has had a reputation for "helping" homosexual men and women by attempting to change their sexual orientation to heterosexuality. These attempts were based on a theoretical conception of homosexuality as inevitably pathological and therefore in need of change. Many recent developments in psychoanalytic theory and practice, however, cast doubt on the assumption of pathology and question the accompanying goal of sexual reorientation.

The authors view psychoanalysis as a treatment method capable of alleviating numerous problems in living and, in particular, improving a person's sexual functioning. This, of course, can include homosexuality. It is our purpose in this article to show that psychoanalysis is indeed useful to homosexual clients.

Dr. Herron is a Professor in the Department of Psychology, St. John's University, Jamaica, New York 11439 and is in private practice in New Jersey. He is a graduate of Fordham University and the Adelphi University Postdoctoral Program. His books include *Reactive and Process Schizophrenia, Contemporary School Psychology*, and *Issues in Psychotherapy*.

Dr. Kinter is a Clinical Supervisor at Westside Lodge, San Francisco, California 94103.

Dr. Sollinger is a graduate of Columbia University, New York University, and the Adelphi Postdoctoral Program. He maintains a private practice in Fairfield County, Connecticut.

Dr. Trubowitz is in the Department of Educational Psychology, Queens College, City University of New York. He is the author of *Changing Racial Attitudes of Children*.

We will first consider psychoanalytic theory, in terms of what it means to us and what it has generally meant in regard to the treatment of homosexual patients. Next we will evaluate the evidence for the pathology of homosexuality per se. Then we will describe our own conceptual framework for treatment and conclude with illustrations from clinical cases in which the psychoanalytic psychotherapy appeared to help the clients understand and express their sexual preferences, which were predominantly homosexual.

Theoretical Orientation

While all schools or systems of psychotherapy cannot be defined precisely, they do have approximate meanings that are generally understood in the psychotherapeutic field. Within this framework our orientation is psychoanalytic. This raises a number of issues for us when we are working with someone who presents herself or himself as "homosexual."

The first task is to ascertain what homosexuality means to the patient. Does he or she want to change their sexual orientation or does the patient consider it incidental to other problems, such as anxiety and depression? The patient's professed goal may be to become heterosexual, or to feel less guilty about homosexuality, or to leave the sexual orientation as is and focus on other issues experienced as disturbing.

After having found an answer, as far as is possible at this point in the therapeutic process, we then tell patients that our role is to help them explore their lives: past, present, and future. In so doing they will have the potential for developing new understanding of their behavior. We explain that much of their behavior is and has been unconsciously determined, and that through a combination of constitutional predispositions and learning, the development of their personalities over time has produced their current life-styles. Patients must be willing to explore their total life development. In the process, they may realize their goals for therapy are not the same as when they began, or that they cannot achieve fully their original goal. Our basic message is that through the psychoanalytic process patients can discover unconscious material available for insight and behavioral change.

The analytic process can be used to work toward a number of possible changes. One possibility is the change in sexual orientation to heterosexuality, but the evidence indicates this is very unlikely to occur. Although a few psychoanalysts report success in this regard (Bieber, Dain, Dince, Drellich, Grand, Gundlach, Kremer, Rifkin, Wilbur, & Bieber, 1962; Socarides, 1978), their work gives no proof of absolute or eternal absence of all homosexual interests, desires, and thoughts in their "changed" patients. Gonsiorek, who has reviewed most of the psychoanalytic contributions to the treatment of homosexuality (1977), points out the limited data base used in generalizations about the power of psychoanalysis to "cure" homosexuality. Nevertheless, Socarides (1979) asserts that a cure is indeed possible in some instances. Freud (1974) postulates a universal potential for sexual orientation with either sex, though one sex is usually preferred. Changing a person's sexual *behavior* from homosexual to heterosexual might be accomplished by working with a potential already present, but this would not really change the person's *preference*. While it may appear that psychoanalysis can change a person's sexual orientation, in truth this is a limited accomplishment that happens only occasionally and even then is of questionable duration.

Nonetheless, there continues to be a strong trend among psychoanalysts to attempt to "cure" homosexual men and women of their homosexuality. Socarides (1974) exemplifies this position, for although he recognizes the variability in homosexuality, he also views all "homosexualities" as pathological per se. His belief has considerable historical precedent: Religion has often denounced homosexuality as sinful, the law has proscribed it as criminal, and the mental health establishment has insisted it is a mental illness. Freud (1905) regarded homosexuality as a form of arrested development, and much of psychoanalytic thought has continued in that vein, construing homosexuality as a perversion, a form of ego-syntonic pathology that definitely requires treatment.

We agree that homosexuality, as do many other forms of sexual expression, can serve as part of a pattern of disturbance in the patient's personality structure. We disagree with the idea that the homosexual orientation is automatically equivalent to psychopathology. In fact, the more usual treatment goal for our homosexual patients is the integration of their sexual orientation into a viable life-style. We use the analytic process to facilitate self-understanding free of value judgments on a particular sexual orientation. This view is in accord with the positive side of our culture's ambivalence toward homosexuality. Society is beginning to give credence to the possibility that exclusive homosexuality is one of a number of potentially effective sexual life-styles, others being asexuality, bisexuality, and exclusive heterosexuality. None of these is seen as being necessarily pathological. This view was reinforced in 1974 by the exclusion of homosexuality from the list of psychiatric disorders in the *Diagnostic and Statistical Manual* of the American Psychiatric Association (APA).

The majority psychoanalytic position, however, remains at variance with the APA decision. Kwawer (1980), having traced the evaluation of psychoanalytic thinking regarding homosexuality from Freud to the present, concludes that there has been a shift from a focus on a disturbance in the oedipal period, with guilt and castration anxiety as key factors, to a concern with preoedipal factors, such as difficulties in separation-individuation and wishes to merge with a maternal object. Despite this change, the reigning psychoanalytic attitude continues to be that homosexuality is a developmental disturbance to be resolved by conversion to heterosexuality. Hopefully, the increased knowledge about human development will provide greater understanding of the emergence of sexual identities and serve to rebut the notion that homosexuality is pathological.

Until recently, the possibility of offering useful psychotherapeutic services to people who may wish to recognize, explore, and accept a homosexual orientation came mainly from a model other than psychoanalysis (Coleman, 1978). (There were some exceptions, of course. Thompson, 1947, mentioned the possibility of homosexuality as an adaptive solution to certain interpersonal problems. Ovesey, Gaylin, and Hendin, 1963, suggested additional motivations for homosexuality, such as power and dependency. Mitchell, 1978, recommended exploring the psychodynamics of homosexuality but did not necessarily link them to a belief that homosexuality is an illness.) Lately, however, the prospect of psychoanalysis being used to acquire a successful homosexual identity has been suggested by Hencken (in press) and Hencken and O'Dowd (1977). The potential includes the expansion of psychoanalytic developmental theory to accommodate recent social and biological findings; the use of psychoanalytic interpretations to understand meaning-systems; and the employment of psychoanalytic concepts to investigate the interrelationships among gender, sex roles, sexual orientation, personal identity, and sexuality. The present authors have described in detail one example of using a psychoanalytic approach to facilitate sexual- and self-expression in a homosexual client (Herron, Kinter, Sollinger, & Trubowitz, 1980). Lachman (1975) had already moved a bit in the direction of our thinking. In questioning the concept of genital primacy, and noticing how limited for some homosexual persons is the relationship between their sexuality and other aspects of living, he appeared not to ascribe standard psychoanalytic notions to homosexuality.

We view psychoanalysis as a developmental psychology with therapeutic applications that enable the patient to learn to make life choices based upon self-understanding. We believe sexual orientation to be one of these learned decisions, a decision based on constitutional and experiential occurrences. It is often formed with a limited awareness on the part of the individual as to the manner and cause. The psychoanalytic method can help any person to discover the development, purpose, and consequences of any and all sexual orientations.

The psychoanalytic approach emphasizes the meaning of behavior within the context of the person's life development. The therapist's personal value judgments about the pathology or non-pathology of sexual orientations are not inherent to the psychoanalytic method. Neither are the value judgments of the patient: Indeed, the psychoanalytic focus on unconscious motivations can enable homosexual clients to make more informed, less dutiful choices about therapeutic goals.

Sexuality and Pathology

A person can manifest non-sexual conflicts through their sexual expression. This is the belief, for example, of psychoanalysts who consider homosexuality to be motivated by anxiety and to involve a variety of preoedipal and oedipal disturbances, such as the inability to distinguish adequately between the self and others, confused gender identity, and disturbances of thinking and perception. Such a description suggests the average homosexual man or woman ought to "look sicker" on criteria of mental health than their heterosexual counterpart, but the existing research does not support this contention.

The most comprehensive and balanced review of the literature to date is by Gonsiorek (1977), who has shown the complexities involved in research on homosexuality, as well as the conclusions that can be drawn from existing research. Gonsiorek points up the fallacies in the persistent belief that anything but heterosexuality is a sign of psychic disturbance and in the practice of interpreting all individual differences between heterosexual and homosexual persons as indications of pathology. Major studies comparing the two sexual orientations do not support the idea that homosexual men and women are significantly maladjusted (Bell & Weinberg, 1978; Saghir & Robbins, 1973). The most general finding of differences is in the direction of homosexual individuals showing more intrapsychic stress. This is to be expected, however, considering the negative reaction of society to homosexuality. While it is possible to discover some differences between heterosexual and homosexual people apart from their sexual orientations, Gonsiorek concludes: "It does not seem that homosexuals differ from heterosexuals in most important and measurable ways" (1977, p. 37).

Socarides (1974) is apparently unimpressed with this. He admits that some homosexual persons *appear* to function well, but he maintains this is superficial, that the sexual deviation (namely homosexuality) has momentarily neutralized conflicting intrapsychic forces. The sexual behavior allays anxiety and makes the individual look as if he or she were functioning adequately, yet the conflict remains and will continue as long as the individual does not adopt the appropriate human sexual pattern, heterosexuality.

A useful feature of Socarides' work is his concern with patient motivations, a concern shared by behaviorists in their dispute over offering orientation-change programs to homosexual patients (Davison, 1977). We concur that the motivations of homosexual clients require special scrutiny in order to learn what they really want from the therapy. We believe the psychoanalytic method provides a viable way to identify and attain the therapeutic goal, but the therapist must avoid outguessing the patient. Views such as Socarides' and Davison's show a lack of respect for the client's ability to form a sound judgment. Davison is the more ambivalent of the two, yet he states: "Even if we could affect certain changes, there is still the more important question of whether we should. I believe we should not" (1977, p. 203). We disagree, and once we ascertain the client's sexual orientation has really been established, we do what we can to help the client enjoy their sexual orientation.

In its concern with homosexuality as an emotional illness, psychoanalysis often focuses on the dynamics of the homosexual behavior. (We ourselves take a broader view of personal and social functioning as part of a complete developmental approach.) Exemplifying the narrower, more traditional approach, Socarides (1978) describes five major forms of homosexuality, three of which are supposedly derived directly from unconscious conflicts.

The first, the *preoedipal* form, is the result of fixation in the developmental phases between birth and 3 years of age. It arises from anxiety, which tends to persist, and involves disturbances of gender identity and sexual identity. The homosexual behavior is obligatory and ego-syntonic. By identifying with a partner of the same sex, a man achieves masculinity and lessens castration fear. A similar reduction of this fear is found in the female who has a resonance identification with a female partner.

The *oedipal* form also involves castration fears, as well as a failure to resolve the Oedipus complex. The male assumes the role of the female (mother) with other men (the father); the situation is reversed for a female. The homosexuality is ego-syntonic, with guilt arising from conflicts of ego and super-ego whenever the person engages in homosexual acts, dreams, or fantasies.

The other three forms mentioned by Socarides are *schizo-homosexuality*, which is the coexistance of schizophrenia and homosexuality; *situational homosexuality*, which results from inaccessibility to heterosexuality; and *variational homosexuality*. Socarides also mentions *latent homosexuality*, meaning the preoedipal or oedipal psychic structure but without overt sexual activity with a partner of the same sex. Finally, there is *sublimated homosexuality*, which denotes behaviors designed to avoid homosexual conflict, and what Ovesey (1976) calls *pseudohomosexuality*, namely heterosexual persons' anxieties about being homosexual.

These taxa can be useful in describing developmental patterns and discerning key areas of conflict, but we have not found them unique to homosexual clients; nor have we always found the postulated correlations between a dynamic, such as castration fear, and homosexuality. Ross (1970) has pointed out that the sexual functioning of an individual may or may not reflect the sexual adequacy of other psychological functions. Lachman (1975) described four patients whose personality organization included a homosexual orientation. In each case different dynamic formulations appeared as to the origin and role of the sexual orientation. This in turn suggested variations in treatment, which included such goals as "adaptive homosexuality" and exclusive heterosexuality. Lachman remarks that to consider homosexuality either as psychopathology or only as a sexual orientation is simplistic. Instead, he suggests viewing homosexuality as a configuration of drives, defenses, and adaptive processes. Although his treatment goals comprehend therapy with patients who choose sexual orientations other than exclusive heterosexuality, in Lachman's article these other orienttions appear to be "second best," rather than truly equal alternatives. On the other hand, Lachman's emphasis on the personality configuration of the patient and his caution against automatically equating sexual orientation with the levels of interpersonal relations and ego development do represent an important shift from the usual psychoanalytic conceptions of homosexuality. Bell (1974) suggested that in doing therapy with homosexual clients it is more useful not to view them as troubled primarily by sexual concerns, but rather to see them as individuals who have a variety of interpersonal and intrapsychic styles with varying antecedents and consequences. May (1977) affirms this position for anybody, regardless of their sexual orientation.

Our aim, then, is by using psychoanalysis as a developmental framework to understand the patient, and by employing psychoanalytically oriented methods to increase the patient's insight into her or his own choices in order that they may act from greater self-knowledge.

We believe there are reasons for all behaviors, including sexual behaviors, and we explore these possible reasons with the patient through verbalizing associations, fantasies, and dreams. In a number of instances an apparently "symptomatic" behavior (e.g., homosexuality) will develop considerable autonomy from its origins. Behavior that started and even persisted for reasons that could be considered pathological, such as homosexuality born of a fear of the opposite sex, may now exist and ultimately continue for different reasons that could not be labelled pathological. For example, the fear may disappear but the homosexuality may continue because it is enjoyable in itself.

Conceptual Framework for Treatment

Psychoanalytic therapy is concerned with the entire life cycle, from birth through all developmental phases: infancy, early childhood, preadolescence, adolescence, early adulthood, middle age, and old age. Depending on the age of the client, some of these phases will be past, some present, and some— such as death—in the future. In accord with our psychodynamic orientation we are very concerned with the past, particularly the preoedipal (0-3 years) and the oedipal (4-7 years) periods. These ages appear especially important in forming the adult personality, influencing sexual orientation as well as the images, of the self and of others, that are related to any person's sexual preferences and sexual behavior.

For the therapy to be of value, the patient must participate fully in the analytic process and tolerate the anxiety engendered in the procedures of self-disclosure and self-discovery. The emphasis of therapy will be on phases most related to the issues of major concern to the patient, but the entire life cycle is appropriate material for exploration. While we believe that humans are inherently sexual beings, we do not believe that sexual orientation is an automatic indicator of a person's ability to function successfully in life. In particular, it is erroneous to assume that the presence of heterosexuality establishes the presence of good interpersonal relationships, or the absence of symptoms. Conversely; the absence of symptoms and the ability to relate to others do not indicate the presence of heterosexuality.

Our conceptual schema within the psychoanalytic tradition is a mixture of ego psychology (Blanck & Blanck, 1974, 1979) and object-relations theory (Horner, 1979). We start with the idea that the individual has undergone a continuity of development that includes a pattern of progressions and regressions, the major thrust being progressive. The infant begins as a psychophysiological organism and proceeds through the various developmental phases. These involve different processes designed to build upon and complement each other and to eventuate in a mature, capable person.

The first of these phases, often called narcissistic or autistic, has an amorphous quality of total, but simplistic, responsivity. At about 6 months of age this gives way to some patterned organization of responding, seen particularly in an attachment to a mother-person. This period, frequently named symbiosis, probably involves fusion of mental images of the mother and child. Symbiosis serves as a bridge to the development of various aspects of a sense of independence and self-identity.

It is followed by the separation-individuation stage, with its four substages. In the first of these, hatching or differentiation, the child sees itself as separate from the mother, who at the same time operates as a frame of reference for the child. The second stage is practicing, when, through locomotion, perception, and learning, the child experiences separateness, particularly from its mother. This is followed by rapprochement, when the child in its continuing striving for autonomy moves from a certain independence to the security of dependence and support. Finally there is the development of a relatively constant view of others, a beginning sense of identity, and a generally positive perception of significant others in the environment. This tends to be accomplished by the third year of life and results in an autonomous identity complete with sexual feelings and preferences.

At ages 5 and 6 there develop more intense sexual feelings toward the parent figures. Identification with parents and the taking on of various parental characteristics continue through other stages, such as adolescence—stages of greater autonomy and major social and sexual identifications of the self and others, stages that lead more directly to the individual's adult identity.

Sexual orientation evolves from the discovery of sexual sensations and pleasures and from the growth of autonomy, which includes a sense of the self as a sexual being and the desire to put one's sexual interest into action. The etiology of the homosexual orientation is a constitutional predisposition to an erotic preference for a body shape, female or male, activated by environmental factors. Although this does not eliminate the potential for other-sex interactions, a single sexual orientation is reinforced and becomes dominant.

In doing therapy with an individual who considers their sexual orientation to be homosexual, we are interested in the various components of their sexual identity. These include biological sex, gender identity, social sex-role, and sexual orientation (Shively & De Cecco, 1977). The biological sex, usually assigned at birth and confirmable by such criteria as genitalia and hormonal secretions, is something about which most patients are quite certain. Gender identity, or the person's conviction that they are female or male, should correspond to biological identification, but that is not always the case. Gender identity is formed in the course of the preoedipal stage and is usually established by 3 years of age. The relation of confused gender identity to homosexuality needs to be explored further. Our homosexual clients have spoken of transient confusion; constant gender identity confusion, on the other hand, appears to be infrequent. In general, homosexual males have a basic sense of maleness, homosexual females a basic identity of femaleness.

Social sex-role confusion is more common among homosexual clients, who feel conflicted over conforming to the culturally approved, rather stereotyped behaviors marking a person as feminine or masculine in this society. Social sex-roles appear in the oedipal period (ages 4 to 7) and are heavily influenced by adult models, particularly parents. These roles—often categorized in terms of physical attributes, mannerisms, speech, interests, and personality traits (Shively & De Cecco, 1977)—are not inherent to biological sex or to gender identity. Nevertheless, most people do conform to the role expected for members of their sex. Openly to disregard the social sex-roles is to risk being labelled as deviant and can bring the person into conflict with society.

The final component of sexual identity is sexual orientation. Considering that American society actively promotes heterosexuality, it is intriguing to ask how and why anyone would *choose* homosexuality. In attempting to answer the question, one recognizes that homosexuality is not a homogeneous categorization. Nor is there a single reason to explain the orientation of all homosexual men and women. Cass (1979) presents a theory of homosexual identity formation over six stages: identity confusion, identity comparison, identity tolerance, identity acceptance, identity pride, and identity synthesis. Hencken and O'Dowd's (1977) developmental approach to homosexual identity formation includes awareness, behavioral acceptance, and public identification. In both cases the authors concentrate on the experience and its meanings but suggest no probable genesis of the homosexual identity. Psychoanalysis is rather specific about why people become heterosexual, but it too offers little to explain the homosexual identity, other than theories of "developmental disturbance," an inaccurate simplification. Cooper (1974) reviews genetic theories, hormonal theories, social explanations, and psychological theories for the development of homosexuality. He considers none completely acceptable and instead offers "a holistic psychoanalytic approach. . .that homosexuality is acquired by various learning processes in individuals probably sensitised by hormonal and early life experiences" (1974, p. 1).

Our own view is that the sexual orientation of an individual is determined by many agencies, though primarily by psychological factors occurring relatively early in life. If the biological aspects of sexual desire are normal, the key factors will be the person's self-images and self-representations, and the interactions of these with images and representations of other people, especially parents. In the course of physical and psychic development, sexual orientation becomes endowed with a personalized meaning. An imagined model of sexual satisfaction is formed out of fantasized identifications, and at some point this is pursued into action. Later behavior refines and reinforces the sexual orientation deemed most pleasurable.

Clinical Material

The cases of a number of patients whom we have seen in psychoanalytic therapy during the last 10 years serve to illustrate various derivations and uses of homosexuality. All of these people were experiencing problems they regarded as connected to their homosexuality, although not all saw their sexual orientation as the major source of concern. None would be considered in the category "Close-Coupled" as described by Bell and Weinberg (1978).

Four of the people were married. The first, a man, traced the origins of his homosexuality to early childhood indoctrination by his older brother. Certain of the patient's characteristics, such as speech and mannerisms, were noticeably feminine and caused many people to assume he was homosexual. He protested about this, yet tended to flaunt these characteristics whenever possible. His wife apparently knew nothing about his homosexuality, which must have required massive denial on her part. Their sexual relations were infrequent, and the patient considered them unsatisfactory. He viewed heterosexuality as a service to his partner and fretted about his adequacy to perform this duty. In homosexual relations he played a "passive" role and consequently felt served, considering it the most pleasurable kind of sexual experience. The patient felt very guilty about his homosexuality, however, and was constantly vowing to give it up. He identified most strongly with his mother and appeared to feel he was restoring symbiosis through homosexual acts, since then he was being served as was his mother. Both his father and his older brother (whom his father favored) derided the patient and impugned his masculinity. He felt he was searching for the "ultimate cock," which would prove better than, or at least equivalent to, the penises of his father and brother. He liked to talk about his homosexual thoughts, feelings, and activity. He stressed the superiority of the gay world yet kept announcing his desire and intention to forswear it. He had focused on his homosexuality with two previous therapists. One, a woman, had worked on getting him to stop it, while the other, a man, had stressed acceptance. He left both therapists after 2 years, which may symbolize his peak of person-relatedness, namely prior to object-constancy. Thus, he may have been unable to relate consistently because of increasing anxiety as to possible loss of personal identity.

Subsequently, when in therapy with one of us, he appeared to be heavily invested in the symbiotic period, his professed ambivalence about sexuality being primarily a defense against dealing with still more basic issues. He was extremely anxious, intermittently depressed with suicidal ideation, and filled with rage toward the world. He lacked basic trust or a sense of personal identity, and ranged in self-esteem from abasement to grandiosity. The therapist indicated to him that, in his opinion, the patient's concern about homosexuality was the least of his problems. The therapist helped him through a severe depressive episode. There were also a few sessions with the wife, who seemed to be immature, demanding, and so narcissistic as to be oblivious to the true nature of their sexual relationship. The only things she found disturbing were some of his symptoms, particularly flashes of anger directed at her. It was possible for the patient to establish some equilibrium of job and family functioning, which led to greater self-esteem and independence. Unfortunately repeating his flight from relationships, after approximately 2 years the patient again stopped treatment, although the therapy was incomplete from the therapist's point of view. The patient considered himself primarily homosexual at that time, but the therapist described his sexual orientation as "confused." It is probable that if he returns to therapy more could be done for him, but he needs to stay with a therapist and permit a therapeutic alliance to form that would allow a complete investigation of his life.

Another married patient, also male, approached the issue of his homosexuality differently. He told his wife about his homosexual desires, but for years he did not act upon them. He too had an older brother. A younger brother also had homosexual feelings but never acted on them. When the patient was a child, the home atmosphere was always one of conflict; the parents divorced when he was in high school. Both parents were demanding and critical. His mother showed some warmth, however, favoring the patient over both his brothers. The patient's homosexuality appeared to derive from longing to be with and to create a happy family: with his wife as a devoted mother caring for him, with himself as the strong, protective father. He saw a homosexual partner as the reincarnation of the deprived child he had been but who now would both fulfill and be fulfilled. Once he actually had a male lover, the patient experienced more turmoil with his wife than as a result of self-guilt. His wife also entered therapy. Gradually it became apparent that the patient had strongly bisexual interests. This alleviated his wife's fear that he was "really homosexual" and might want to leave her. Both of his sexual relationships, with his wife and with his lover, now appear to be quite permanent, but neither partner likes the concept of being part of a fantasy "family" for the patient. His rather narcissistic orientation interferes with his comprehension of how his wife and lover feel about him and how they feel about his behavior towards them. This narcissism, rather than the homosexuality, has become the focal problem of his therapy.

Another man unearthed his homosexual interests during the course of therapy but is primarily interested in autoerotic sex. He rarely has intercourse with his wife and as an adult has had no sexual experience with anyone else. The idea of a homosexual experience appeals to him, however. He had a domineering mother and sister, with a passive, ineffectual father. The patient had adolescent homosexual experiences, which he recalls favorably, but he really seems very afraid of any sexual experience, particularly if he might have to initiate it. The immaturity of his sexuality in general is an issue that combines with his general passivity and fear of people. His interest in homosexuality seems to be a wistful solution to the more basic fear of people, as well as repressed anger over an emotionally deprived childhood. In homosexuality he would unite with the desired parent.

Another patient was a woman who had been married but separated from her husband after about 5 years. She lived with a number of women after the separation. She describes this as a "safer" solution for herself than trying to live with a man. She had suffered considerable rejection by her father and became a very angry, assertive person, but quite successful in many aspects of her life. Indeed, she became a psychotherapist. She has a deep, ambivalent attachment to her mother, who was very domineering. The patient repeats this pattern with her female lovers, whom she dominates. She has occasional satisfactory sexual experiences with men. She lives with a woman but says the sex is not as good as with a man. She does not appear to experience guilt about the homosexuality and never presented it as a major issue in therapy. What concerned her more was her anger, depression, lack of impulse control, and occasional hallucinatory and delusional experiences. As the issues of the relationships with her parents and with several siblings were worked through in therapy, the depression lifted, her mood was optimistic, and therapy was concluded. Her sexual orientation is primarily homosexual and appears to be working well as a living style.

Among the homosexual people we have seen who have never been married, there is a woman who entered therapy with the belief that her problem was her lesbianism. She had suffered a series of losses, including her mother's death during her adolescence; emotional distance from her father, who had been passively seductive at one time; and, at the time of starting therapy, rejection by a woman to whom she had admitted being sexually attracted. The patient viewed lesbianism as a disturbed life-style yet feared sexual intercourse with men, although she had experienced it and, at times, had enjoyed it. Her homosexual quest appeared to be directed toward regaining at least the image of her lost mother. She currently lives with a woman and finds this a comfortable situation, though she does not consider it permanent. It is her ideal to have a husband and children. The deprivation in her childhood, particularly the cold, austere home atmosphere and the death of her mother, seems to have prompted a search for another family, specifically for a mother. She has that now; sexual demands from her partner are kept at a minimum. At present much of her therapy is concerned with her distrust of herself and of others, and with the possibility of increasing her sensuality and sexuality. She retains some sexual interest in men but prefers women, although all her sexual activity, including masturbation, is quite limited, inhibited, and guilt-laden.

Two patients are priests, both of whom moved when in elementary school into an all-male environment where sexuality was discouraged and the only outlets were with the self or with a person of the same sex. Both men have domineering mothers. One has an outwardly angry father, while the other's father is more passive and frightened. The elder of the two priests is more committed to homosexuality and has no interest in women. His main problems center around excessive oral gratifications, such as alcohol and drugs, as well as a very poor self-image, which he feels can be enhanced only by a sexual encounter with an attractive man. The younger priest feels excessive guilt about his sexual desires. He contemplates leaving the priesthood as a solution because he equates not being a priest with somehow becoming heterosexual. A major obstacle to this plan, however, is that his only sexual experiences have been homosexual. He is sexually inexperienced with women and, in addition, he is afraid of them. Through therapy he has begun to realize that leaving the priesthood would actually allow him to pursue a homosexual life-style more freely, which is both appealing and frightening. Both men feel a conflict between their roles as clergy and their sexuality, since as priests they are supposed to be celibate. Role conflicts have consequently played a large part in their therapies, as has the relationship of their role to their self-image.

Concluding Comments

This paper contains considerable psychoanalytic terminology, which in itself has a reputation for emphasizing pathology and for being a secret language. Hopefully none of that will prevent readers from understanding that psychoanalytic theory, research, and practice can be very helpful to homosexual men and women.

Homosexuality was present in some form in all the patients we described; some were bisexual, others were exclusively homosexual. All had concerns related to their homosexuality, such as guilt and social disapproval. Yet their sexual orientation as such was not what was pathological. In these patients we identified a variety of possible origins and uses of homosexuality—some protective, some enjoyable, some disturbing. We also discovered a variety of problems, with apparent origins and expressions in different developmental phases. Our aim is to consider the patient's total personality organization, not just their sexual orientation, and to focus on the desired development of that organization.

In none of the cases cited did we prompt homosexual patients to convert to heterosexuality. Increasingly we find that people come to us with the hope of learning to enjoy their sexuality, whatever their orientation. They have a relatively good idea of what they would like to do, but they are having trouble doing it. We believe psychoanalytic psychotherapy is quite capable of facilitating sexual enjoyment. Through a non-judgmental working alliance using explanations and interpretations in the context of a developmental psychology, we can help the patient achieve greater self-fulfillment regardless of their sexual orientation.

In viewing the choice of sexual orientation as an open possibility, we are departing from the customary psychoanalytic (and societal) view of identity development, of which a key characteristic is a sexual desire for members of the opposite sex. But we do not see our approach as nonpsychoanalytic. We do see it as a reformulation of the characteristics of a "healthy" feminine and masculine identity. The developing body of work on androgyny (Kaplan & Bean, 1976) requires reconsideration of previous conceptions of sex roles and the characteristics of gender identity. While our own formulations are tentative and limited to a particular area at the moment, more general revisions of psychoanalytic thinking are occurring (Gedo, 1979; Klein, 1976). These support a focus on the intentions and inner states that lead to varied behaviors. In our opinion, they involve a less restrictive view of what it means to be "healthy" in psychoanalytic terms.

Finally, Kwawer (1980) has suggested that how an analyst views homosexuality (that is, as pathology per se, or not) can be a statement of countertransference and can have an effect on interpretations made in the analytic situation. Under the guise of appropriate treatment flowing from accepted theory about homosexuality, the analyst may be operating more from her or his inner needs than the needs of the patient. Analysts should ask themselves about their opinion of homosexuality as such, for only if they view it as a "sickness" will they try to "cure" it by aiming for a change in sexual orientation. Our belief that all sexual behavior can serve a variety of purposes includes the conviction that homosexuality can be a "healthy" sexual orientation.

We realize such an approach is open to debate, but we regard this debate as appealing and helpful. For too long in psychoanalytic circles the estimate of homosexuality had been fixed. We base our own on the evidence, research and clinical. After years of personal analysis for all of us, we do not believe our position is founded on a desire to justify particular sexual orientations. In fact, we think that kind of countertransference is likely to operate more in those who insist all homosexuality is pathological. For ourselves, we like to think that we are returning to the exploratory character of psychoanalysis which was so evident in its founder.

REFERENCES

American Psychiatric Association Committee on Nomenclature and Statistics. *Diagnostic Statistical Manual of Mental Disorders*, 1980.

Bell, A. Homosexualities: Their range and character. In J. K. Cole & R. Dienstbier (Eds.), *Nebraska Symposium on Motivation, 1973*. Lincoln: University of Nebraska Press, 1974.

Bell, A. P., & Weinberg, M. S. *Homosexualities: A study of diversity among men and women.* New York: Simon and Schuster, 1978.

Bieber, I., Dain, H. J., Dince, P. R., Drellich, M. G., Grand, H. G., Gundlach, R. H., Kremer, M. W., Rifkin, A. H., Wilbur, C. B., & Bieber, T. B. *Homosexuality: A psychoanalytic study.* New York: Basic Books, 1962.

Blanck, G., & Blanck, R. *Ego psychology: Theory and practice.* New York: Columbia University Press, 1974.

Blanck, G., & Blanck, R. *Ego psychology II. Psychoanalytic developmental psychology.* New: York: Columbia University Press, 1979.

Cass, V. C. Homosexual identity formation: A theoretical model. *Journal of Homosexuality*, 1979, *4*, 219-235.

Coleman, E. Toward a new model of treatment of homosexuality: A review. *Journal of Homosexuality*, 1978, *3*, 345-359.

Cooper, A. J. Aetiology of homosexuality. In J. A. Loraine (Ed.), *Understanding homosexuality: Its biological and psychological bases.* New York: American Elsevier, 1974.

Davison, G. C. Homosexuality and the ethics of behavioral intervention: Paper 1 - Homosexuality, the ethical challenge. *Journal of Homosexuality*, 1977, *2*, 195-204.

Freud, S. Three essays on the theory of sexuality. *Standard Edition*, 1905, *7*, 125-145.

Freund, K. Male homosexuality: An analysis of the pattern. In J. A. Loraine (Ed.), *Understanding homosexuality: Its biological and psychological bases.* New York: American Elsevier, 1974.

Gedo, J. *Beyond interpretation.* New York: International Universities Press, 1979.

Gonsiorek, J. Psychological adjustment and homosexuality. JSAS *Catalog of Selected Documents in Psychology*, 1977, *7*, 45.

Hencken, J. D. Homosexuality and psychoanalysis: Toward a mutual understanding. *Journal of Social Issues*, in press.

Hencken, J. D., & O'Dowd, W. T. Coming out as an aspect of identity formation. *Gay Academic Union Journal: Gai Saber*, 1977, *1*, 18-22.

Herron, W. G., Kinter, T., Sollinger, I., & Trubowitz, J. New psychoanalytic perspectives on the treatment of a homosexual male. *Journal of Homosexuality*, 1980, *5*, 393-403.

Horner, A. J. *Object relations and the developing ego in therapy.* New York: Aronson, 1979.

Kaplan, A. G., & Bean, J. P. (Eds.). *Beyond sex-role stereotypes: Readings toward a psychology of androgyny.* Boston: Little, Brown, 1976.

Klein, G. *Psychoanalytic theory.* New York: International Universities Press, 1976.

Kwawer, J. S. Transference and countertransference in homosexuality: Changing psychoanalytic views. *American Journal of Psychotherapy*, 1980, *34*, 72-80.

Lachman, F. M. Homosexuality: Some diagnostic perspectives and dynamic considerations. *American Journal of Psychotherapy*, 1975, *29*, 254-260.

May, E. Discussion of: "Recent trends and new developments in the treatment of homosexuality" by James J. Hinrichsen and Martin Katahn. *Psychotherapy: Theory, Research and Practice*, 1977, *14*, 18-20.

Mitchell, S. A. Psychodynamic homosexuality and the question of pathology. *Psychiatry*, 1978, *41*, 254-260.

Ovesey, L. Pseudohomosexuality. *Medical Aspects of Human Sexuality*, 1976, *10*, 147.

Ovesey, L., Gaylin, W., & Hendin, H. Psychotherapy of male homosexuality. *Archives of General Psychiatry*, 1963, *9*, 19-24.

Ross, N. The primacy of genitality in the light of ego psychology: Introductory remarks. *Journal of the American Psychoanalytic Association*, 1970, *18*, 267-275.

Saghir, M. T., & Robins, E. *Male and female homosexuality: A comprehensive investigation.* Baltimore: Williams & Wilkins Co., 1973.

Shively, M. G., & De Cecco, J. P. Components of sexual identity. *Journal of Homosexuality*, 1977, *3*, 41-48.

Socarides, C. W. The sexual deviations and the diagnostic manual. *American Journal of Psychotherapy*, 1974, *32*, 414-426.

Socarides, C. W. *Homosexuality.* New York: Aronson, 1978.

Socarides, C. W. Some problems encountered in the psychoanalytic treatment of overt male homosexuality. *American Journal of Psychotherapy*, 1979, *33*, 506-520.

Thompson, C. Changing concepts of homosexuality in psychoanalysis. *Psychiatry*, 1947, *10*, 183-188.

ORGANIZATIONAL AND STAFF PROBLEMS IN GAY/LESBIAN MENTAL HEALTH AGENCIES

John C. Gonsiorek, PhD

Since late 1973, this writer has worked in a variety of gay/lesbian mental health situations. These have included providing service and case supervision in a gay/lesbian identified mental health setting, consulting locally and nationally to such organizations, providing services and case supervision in non-gay/lesbian identified organizations, and providing training and education for mental health and chemical dependency programs on gay and lesbian issues. In particular, this writer was associated with Gay Community Services of Minneapolis for over seven years, in a variety of roles. The purpose of this article is to discuss a number of problems that are common in gay/lesbian mental health settings and to gay and lesbian therapists. Some of the rewards of working in this area will also be discussed. Many of the points made in this paper may be germane to any number of alternative mental health services, although this paper will focus only on gay/lesbian mental health services.

Organizational Problems in Gay/Lesbian Mental Health Programs

It is crucial to understand the experimental nature of gay/lesbian mental health programs, and the social contexts in which these organizations operate. Primary among these considerations is that, until very recently, no one ever offered gay/lesbian affirmative mental health services in an organized fashion. A central issue, then, is that such organizations start out with no model as to how to accomplish their task. Furthermore, these organizations developed during the 1970s—a decade in which major reconceptualizations and accumulation of new data about homosexuality took place, as well as major changes in community mental health services, diagnosis, the role of mental health in political and social change, etc.

Against this context, the task of gay/lesbian mental health agencies was to provide services that no one really understood how to provide, to communities that no one had ever before attempted to serve, in a theoretical climate where all relevant knowledge was in rapid flux. Further, no one really knew how to organize such a service, whether sufficient integration between gay/lesbian affirmative mental health ideas and traditional mental health practice could actually occur, or what those syntheses might look like. The entire enterprise of gay/lesbian affirmative mental health services has been experimental, and remains so in all areas. The only area to have attained sufficient maturity actually to discuss in detail is the psychotherapeutic endeavor and related theoretical formulations—as the existence of this volume attests. Areas such as organizational issues in gay/lesbian mental health, and the relationship between gay/lesbian mental health organizations and the communities they serve, however, have typically not yet coalesced in the thinking of those who are active in these areas. This chapter, then, will be highly impressionistic and descriptive, and can best be used as a set of observations about what has occurred and some recommendations for change—with a dose of seasoned, but still personal, bias. Nothing in this chapter should be construed as set or final. The purpose of this chapter is to raise questions, not to answer them.

Gay/lesbian mental health programs undertake a new and radical task: the provision of gay and lesbian affirmative mental health services. The manner in which this is to be accomplished is typically very unclear. Often, there exists a belief that the organization should not resemble established heterosexual agencies in its organizational structure and internal processes and workings. At times, it may be clearly stated that the organizations' structure and process should be self-consciously anti-establishment. The reasons given for these beliefs are that the task and the process to accomplish the task should be congruent in terms of their radicalism.

Although these beliefs are not necessarily logical, they are understandable. The staff members involved have knowledge of or have experienced serious malpractice perpetrated upon gay male and lesbian clients, and are attempting to make certain that it does not occur in the new organization. Also, the leadership of these organizations is typically made up of individuals who came out in the late 1960s or early 1970s, a time of considerable political ferment, and who often link the gay liberation movement to other political movements. Although these assumptions may make sense in terms of historical development or personal experience, however, no logical imperative exists that a new and different kind of mental health service requires new and different organizational and staff processes. What is important for this discussion is that predictable kinds of staff problems emerge in many of these organizations.

As with many alternative agencies that provide services to underserved populations, laypersons and paraprofessionals are usually the primary impetus behind the establishment of gay/lesbian mental health services. A non-hierarchical, or perhaps collectivist, leadership style is generally favored or even dictated by the group, who may view hierarchical structure as too "establishment." At this level, many gay/lesbian mental health services disband after a brief existence. Non-hierarchical, collectivist decision-making is probably the most strenuous and time-consuming of all organizational models. Further, these structures tend to work only when the individuals involved can delay their personal agendas for the common good, and can operate with considerable objectivity and clear, dispassionate thinking. This is hardly likely in a group of often politicized, anti-establishment individuals who are trying to provide services for a disenfranchised population, and who have a strong and personal sense of mission.

Those organizations that do survive usually begin to experience a growing tension. There develop increasing pressures to move toward professionalization of services and staff. These come from both internal and external sources. Internally, as the organization attracts more clients, it tends to attract a greater variety of clients. Whereas the initial clients were individuals who appeared to have uncomplicated coming out issues, needs for social support, and issues primarily related to victimization by oppressive social forces; clients usually begin to present other problems in addition: severe depression, schizophrenia, affective disorders, severe neuroses and character disorders, chemical dependency, etc. It may also be the case that early clients had these problems but that they were not recognized.

Some organizations may respond to this change in clientele by becoming more politically dogmatic and cognitively rigid. New client problems are not seen for what they are, but instead as political or victimization issues. Services rendered by such a group often become increasingly incompetent. Its reputation suffers, and the group either disbands or shrinks as dissatisfied staff members leave. Other organizations will respond by remaining paraprofessional, but limiting their scope and referring more difficult clients to other mental health agencies. Such organizations tend to evolve into phone hot-lines or information and referral services, perhaps doing minimal peer counseling or running an occasional support group. Such organizations serve an important but limited mental health function.

Those organizations that simultaneously exist in a favorable political, social and professional climate, and are flexible and clearly committed to quality client care as a primary goal (as opposed to political goals) begin to develop, organizational relationships with other mental health programs, family service agencies, etc., in the traditional mental health system, for the purpose of providing better service for those new clients. Case consultation and referral, and staff training and development begin to occur between organizations. The new alternative organization slowly begins to carve out a place for itself in the traditional mental health system. As the impetus for these liaisons is better care for the newer, more difficult clients, the gay/lesbian mental health organization often wins grudging respect from previously hostile traditional mental health practitioners. If nothing else, they are often relieved that a group exists to take difficult gay and lesbian clients out of their caseload.

Another internal pressure for change may come from some staff of the gay/ lesbian organization who, by virtue of professional training or for other reasons, believe in greater professionalization and overtly or covertly work toward that goal. The primary external pressure for professionalization is usually due to funding. Funding sources, for good reason, are reluctant to deal with organizations having diffuse leadership—such organizations are notoriously unpredictable. To obtain funding, organizations must typically develop a Board of Directors, at least a partial hierarchical structure, and must partially professionalize both services and service providers. It is at this stage that the organization develops true accountability. The staff no longer operates to please itself, but is held accountable by a Board of Directors, the funding source, and other mental health agencies. On occasion, an organization may skip this development of accountability if it obtains funds without demands for accountability, or if it obtains funding prior to the development of the organizational maturity and administrative skill required to handle it. The results of this are typically disastrous, and will be discussed below.

The organization at this point, then, has survived the push toward professionalization, usually has some funding, enjoys increased stature in the mental health community, has a Board of Directors and a staff composed of professionals and paraprofessionals, has developed some degree of external accountability, and serves a diverse clientele. At this point, it may enjoy a honeymoon, particularly if the level of funding and stature continues to increase.

At this level, the organization is vulnerable to internal stress on account of professional-paraprofessional tensions. Usually, the development of that staff mix was tolerated in a spirit of doing whatever is necessary to make a service organization work. Differences tend not to be discussed, or if discussed, are hastily smoothed over. Trouble may erupt on a variety of fronts. Paraprofessionals may resent case supervision and management by professionals due to the power differential (which the paraprofessionals often do not believe ought to exist) or because of genuine disagreements about case management related to philosophical differences about therapy. The paraprofessionals may form the "old guard" of the agency whose power is rapidly being eroded by the newer, professional staff, who may be perceived as, or actually be, somewhat condescending to paraprofessional staff. The realities of legal liabilities and professional ethics, as well as outside accountability, demand that the professional staff assume responsibility for cases, yet the paraprofessional staff (who need to have the professional staff assume those roles to continue funding, etc.,) often want to retain their decision-making authority on case matters. Use of psychological testing, referral for medication, or hospitalization of a client may be precipitating events for a struggle, as these actions are often viewed by paraprofessionals as being too "establishment." On an administrative, as opposed to case management, level a similar struggle for power ensues. Some of the more politically militant groups in the gay and lesbian communities will often develop a growing resentment toward the organization, because not only is it becoming establishment, but is prospering in the process. They will often join the paraprofessional faction, and attempt to exert pressure on the Board of Directors or funding source, either by persuasion, or attempts to embarrass them. Paradoxically, the militants may inadvertently, or even overtly, join the conservative mental health establishment in attempting to undermine the gay/lesbian mental health agency.

Organizations can take a variety of routes at this point: collapse, complete professionalization, de-professionalization, enshrinement of mediocrity, or redefinition of roles in the agency. Unfortunately, collapse is all too common. Usually, this occurs when the professionals, unwilling to endure the increased stress and politicization of the conflict, leave the agency. Since professionals are often accustomed to working in settings where hierarchical structures are taken for granted, and are insulated from political conflict on the community level, many of them find such stresses intolerable. Stature within the mental health community drops, the funding source withdraws, and the organization folds.

Complete professionalization occurs on occasion. The Board of Directors and/or funding source side with the professional faction in a decisive enough manner to convice them to stay. The paraprofessionals leave or are forced out. The organization then becomes essentially a private practice group. While adequate levels of competent service can be maintained in this outcome, programmatic flexibility and creativity are often lost. The organization usually becomes less responsive to the needs of the gay and lesbian communities, and more responsive to the needs of the professionals involved.

In de-professionalization the professionals leave, funding and reputation are diminished, but a small group of paraprofessionals continue the organization. Usually this occurs when the Board of Directors, or part of it, backs the paraprofessionals. Due to the recent conflict, anti-professional sentiment is high and aspects of treatment that are viewed as "establishment" are dropped or even banned by the group. Quality of client care rapidly diminishes, causing further weakening of organizational reputation. Doctrinaire political beliefs are often foisted on clients under the guise of therapy. If the behavior of an organization in this stage is sufficiently incompetent or offensive, the chances for *any* funding of gay or lesbian services in that community may be killed. A more benign possibility is that the new paraprofessional organization will limit its scope and essentially become an information and referral service.

Another possible outcome is the enshrinement of mediocrity. This is characterized by the most vocal proponents of both the professional and paraprofessional view being forced out or silenced by group pressure. The organization is then led by individuals who are just competent enough to maintain the administrative workings of the agency. These individuals are often skilled at fundraising, which keeps them in power, but are often weak managers, poor program developers and lacking in clinical skills. Their function is to enforce the organizational rule that differences must not be acknowledged or discussed; or if they are, only in a superficial manner. Because of their generally weak skill level, they usually abdicate crucial managerial functions leaving the profesional and paraprofessional factions to carve out their turfs, and so give the veneer of conflict resolution and cooperation. Neither faction is threatened by this arrangement, and an uneasy peace can ensue.

If the fundraising skill of such leaders is high, this level of adjustment can persist for some time, as all parties are allowed enough leeway to expand their particular programs within the organization. Staff in this situation often develop a giddy, hysteroid flavor, with considerable diffuse free-floating affect that is labelled warmth, openness and nurturance. Perhaps the most salient characteristic of such an organization is that the most trivial, day-to-day mediocre accomplishments are profusely praised by the leader and by staff in general, while genuinely outstanding and creative accomplishments are ignored, because they pose too great a threat. At times, such systems may even re-define incompetent performance as competent. Staff with poor skills are often kept on, or even promoted. The purpose of this is to reduce threat to the increasing mediocrity of the organization. The pervasive tone is one of denial, and mediocrity is enshrined. To outsiders, such a staff may appear unusually cohesive and dedicated, and this may actually become a selling point in fundraising. However, the organization's structure is becoming increasingly chaotic due to lack of managerial focus, and the staff become increasingly alienated from each other and a realistic appraisal of the agency.

This system usually disintegrates when the ability to raise more funds to cover chaotic program expansion is interfered with, either because of general fiscal belt-tightening in the larger world, or a growing sense of uneasiness about the leaders. Once the general chaos of the organizational structure is laid bare in a fiscal crisis, the bubble bursts. Alternatively, new staff in the organization may see the situation for what it is, and open the eyes of other staff. The professional-paraprofessional dispute re-emerges against a generally chaotic background, and the organization enters a seriously dysfunctional period which is ended when the agency chooses one of the other four resolutions.

It is this writer's observation that the "enshrinement of mediocrity" phenomenon besets a variety of mental health organizations for other disenfranchised groups, as well as gay/lesbian organizations. Its main function seems to be to submerge differences that might potentially divide and immobilize the organization. However, it may serve another temporary function in keeping an organization in a somewhat stable "holding pattern" until resources are found to move on to another outcome.

Another possible outcome to professional-paraprofessional tensions is the redefinition of roles within the agency. What usually occurs is that the provision of clinical service becomes the domain of the professional staff—satisfying the professionals, the funding source, and the external mental health community. At the same time, new and genuinely important roles are created for the paraprofessional staff, usually in the areas of education, community development, advocacy, peer support groups, etc. These roles satisfy the paraprofessionals and their supporters. This outcome may usher in a period of considerable creativity and intellectual fervor; a true renaissance.

Oddly enough, the clients served by the organization may have a very differt view of the organizational problems than either the professionals or the paraprofessionals. What matters to the clients is the quality of service. Therefore, the clients themselves tend to be indifferent to the major philosophical debates about organizational structure, except inasmuch as it affects the quality of care they receive. If anything, clients often seem to favor increased professionalization as it makes sense both in terms of the quality of care and the long-term stability of the agency. As many gay men and lesbians have either directly or vicariously experienced poor mental health care, they will often be very sensitive to changes in quality of care.

Some problems related to Boards of Directors deserve special mention. As the organization obtains funding and more varied clients, and becomes more administratively complex, a Board will rapidly need skilled attorneys, accountants, government and business leaders, mental health professionals, clergy and others to serve as members. However, the tendency of Boards of Directors in gay/lesbian mental health organizations is to load the membership with "community" people. This usually is a buzz word for leaders of other gay and lesbian organizations and gay and lesbian political leaders.

This presents some serious conflict of interest problems. As funding in the organization grows, other gay and lesbian organizations may want a piece of it, and use their representation on the Board to do so. This writer sat on a Board of Directors where a proposal to give away one-third of a mental health organization's budget to an essentially political organization was defeated by a one-vote margin. The representatives from the other organizations had banded together and voted as a block. Also, radical political representation on a Board may alienate it from more middle-of-the-road organization staff, and may also alienate the business, legal and professional communities to the extent that they will avoid such a Board. The Board then has a chronic lack of expertise in these areas, which seriously impairs its functioning.

Such a Board is unable to provide the necessary technical assistance to organizational leaders, and should those leaders become dysfunctional, as in the enshrinement of mediocrity phase, the Board will usually be unable to intervene, if they even are aware that a problem exists. Having both a dysfunctional Board and organizational leadership will place an enormous burden on the front-line clinical staff essentially to administer the agency at the same time that they provide service. This leads to a high level of staff attrition and burn-out.

Once a gay/lesbian mental health service has been in existence for a while, it will frequently be deluged with requests and demands from various segments of the gay and lesbian communities to expand services in both the mental health and non-mental health areas. Provision of non-mental health services may jeopardize funding for mental health services or the ability to deliver effectively mental health services. Any programmatic expansion, mental health or non-mental health, can stretch an agency beyond its resources and abilities. Poorly conceived program expansion is one of the main reasons why many gay/ lesbian mental health agencies do not survive. Yet not acquiescing to requests for program expansion will often result in criticism, resentment, and sometimes outright attack. Part of the victimization that has occurred to segments of the gay and lesbian communities is the belief—or even the demand—that any gay/ lesbian organizations that do exist must immediately meet all the needs of all gay and lesbian individuals. Give the tremendous diversity of the gay and lesbian communities, and the limited resources that do exist, insistence on this position is unrealistic and often highly destructive.

The staff at such agencies, then, must weigh a variety of competing factors when making programmatic decisions. Not the least of these is that staff themselves may feel compelled to be all things to all people. This may lead not only to serious errors in program expansion, but also a chronic sense of failure and frustration even when the right decisions are made. Such decisions may ultimately mean that some segment of the gay and lesbian communities will continue to lack a service that it—and perhaps also the staff—thinks it needs. Such staff in these situations will have to exercise considerable organizational sophistication, mature judgment and personal integrity. Even then, they will not always be right, as there is often little experience with comparable situations to draw upon—or the staff involved may not have the personal resources available at that time to make a good decision.

A problem alluded to earlier occurs when immature organizations are suddenly given substantial funding with little demand for accountability. The funders are typically well-meaning liberals, or the organization may be artificially protected by liberal government officials, traditional agency directors, lawyers, etc. Such organizations rarely develop an effective administrative structure which can function on its own, because they are protected and insulated from their own mistakes. Usually, they limp along and disband after a chaotic and undistinguished existence.

Sometimes, however, a very disturbing development occurs. Such organizations may develop a charismatic, almost cult-like flavor under one leader or a number of leaders. Their salient characteristics are a siege mentality in which any criticism of the organization is viewed and responded to as an attack, the development of organizational incest (which will be discussed below), and the firm belief that they, and only they, know how to help gay men and lesbians. Often these organizations are anti-professional and politicized, but in an idiosyncratic manner, depending on the personal agendas of the leadership rather than on any consistent philosophy.

This writer knows of at least two instances of this. Both occurred some years ago in two different major metropolitan areas. Over time, each program became increasingly cult-like and treatment of clients became bizarre and frankly exploitative. Anyone who criticized the program on the outside was perjoratively labelled (e.g., "homophobic" or "chemically dependent") by the program staff, and social pressure was mobilized by program staff to force their opponents into treatment "for *their* own good" and at their program. Once in the program, clients were told that they were "not together about being gay" and "would destroy themselves" unless they totally accepted the program's philosophy and demands. In both instances, attempts by individuals in the gay and lesbian communities to intervene in the increasingly explosive situation were thwarted by the programs' liberal supporters. Damage both to clients and to those communities' ability to attract funding for services was extensive.

The solution to this is for funding sources and supporters to hold gay and lesbian organizations to the same standards of accountability and administrative sophistication as they would any other organization. The process of developing skilled leadership and organizational expertise is one of the most important for gay and lesbian communities to experience. Liberal supporters can be most helpful by providing appropriate assistance and realistic feedback, not by shortchanging the learning process and infantilizing the organization.

This is often easier said than done, however. If the protecting liberal agency or individuals are organizationally intertwined with the dysfunctional agency, they may have a vested interst in covering up problems. This may be because open examination of problems may reveal mismanagement by the liberal supporters if they are in a supervisory relationship; threaten lucrative referral or administrative relationships; expose liberal Board directors to potential lawsuits; and so on. Further, liberal supporters may know only the dysfunctional leaders in the organization, and may be removed from other staff, clients, or other segments of the gay and lesbian communities. They may then regard the leaders as "victims" and may disregard criticism of them.

The gay/lesbian communities often have a role in these problems. Community organizations are often reluctant to confront one another due to a belief that it is improper or politically incorrect to do so, or because of a fear that criticism will attract opposition from homophobic elements in the larger society. While the latter may be true on occasion, it is often short-sighted, as uncorrected problems may later attract greater opposition, and the gay and lesbian communities may end up stereotyping themselves as monolithic, defensive, rigid and lacking in accountability.

The concept of organizational incest was mentioned earlier. White (1978) developed this concept to describe a staff which over time turns in on itself. Members begin to meet not only work needs within the staff, but also personal, social and sexual needs. The organization becomes a closed system, increasingly dysfunctional, and begins to take on some of the characteristics of incest families. The charismatic organizations described above are extreme examples of this problem.

While any organization can develop organizational incest, it is this writer's experience that those most prone to it are organizations which have a special mission, are different or atypical from the rest of the system because of that mission, and experience isolation or ostracism from other organizations. Therefore, gay/lesbian mental health organizations need to take special care to prevent this kind of organizational dysfunction, as some may have predisposing factors toward it. Interested readers are referred to White's (1978) paper for details.

A few other problems will be briefly mentioned. Gay/lesbian mental health organizations must often take special care to make certain that ethical standards are clearly established and consistently high. Ethical violations which might be forgiven if they occurred in traditional agencies can easily ruin a gay/lesbian mental health program, which is often under intense scrutiny by both friend and foe, especially in its early years.

Gay/lesbian mental health programs must early on come to a resolution about two thorny issues. One is the place of politics in mental health. While this issue gets repeatedly played out indirectly within the paraprofessional-professional conflicts, organizations must set some ground rules initially if they are not to be torn apart from the start. It is this writer's bias that politics and the provision of mental health services should stay as much at arm's length from one another as is realistically feasible given that funding must be lobbied for, and gay/lesbian mental health organizations are often politically attacked by both the right and the left. Gay and lesbian populations are primarily characterized by their diversity. Attempts to constrain that diversity for reasons of political ideology are a disservice, profoundly disrespectful, and corrosive to the concept of civil liberties. It should always be kept in mind that it is the clients who are victimized when political orthodoxy is forced upon them overtly or covertly. and if gay/lesbian mental health organizations do not exist to reduce and eliminate victimization of gay and lesbian clients, then there is no reason for their existence. The mere existence of gay/lesbian affirmative mental health programs of course has political implications. Such implications are as close to political involvement as gay/lesbian mental health programs should get, in this writer's view.

Differences between gay men and lesbians must also be resolved and a workable arrangement implemented. Failure to do so will result in considerable divisiveness. It is this writer's belief that the most productive and creative agencies provide services for, and are staffed by, both men and women. Some clients will have strong feelings about sex and sexual orientation of the therapist; others will be indifferent. Clients' needs, and not therapists' ideology, should take precedence in these situations.

Often, many more clients than can be served will seek services from such agencies. This problem may be exacerbated by traditional agencies that "dump" gay and lesbian clients—particularly their most problematic clients—on gay/lesbian mental health agencies. Decisions about who will be served and who will not are very painful, and require much consideration and planning. The answer is usually a compromise between staff abilities and local needs; this will usually be criticized by some segments of the gay and lesbian communities.

Finding competent staff, especially managerial staff and Board directors, who are willing to be identified with an openly gay/lesbian mental health agency, is often a chronic problem. This difficulty exacerbates a number of the problems mentioned above in that there may not be available replacements for dysfunctional or mediocre staff. While gay and lesbian mental health professionals are often somewhat easier to find, they may be difficult to retain because some of the organizational problems described earlier may be intimidating or alien to mental health professionals.

Finally, in a period of increasing political conservatism, the possibility that gay/lesbian mental health organizations can be targeted for either overt opposition (e.g., attempts to remove funding) or covert sabotage (e.g., attempts to foment dissention in an organization or in the gay and lesbian communities) should be soberly considered without either naiveté or paranoia.

Problems for Gay and Lesbian Therapists

When this writer was orienting a new staff member at Gay Community Services in Minneapolis a while ago, the difficulties of operating as a therapist in a relatively small community were being discussed. The new staff member, who had recently moved to the Twin Cities from a small Midwestern town, stated that it sounded to her as if the writer were describing the job situation she had just left. Even in large metropolitan areas, and certainly in small ones, working as an openly gay or lesbian mental health professional is very much like working in a small town.

People tend to have more detailed knowledge of each other's lives in gay and lesbian communities. This could be especially true if a person is a therapist with some visibility. At times, therapists may experience this as intrusive, especially when it relates to issues of transference and countertransference and confidentiality. The likelihood of complicated dual, and multiple relationships is also higher. Colleagues have reported very disconcerting experiences at discovering persons whom they had been dating were friends or ex-lovers of current or former clients, that current clients were involved with their friends, ex-lovers, etc. Unless one takes a detailed social history of everyone one interacts with in the community, such periodic encounters are unavoidable.

What this means for the openly gay or lesbian mental health professional who works in gay or lesbian communities is that they will regularly be called upon to exercise considered professional and personal judgments in sensitive situations. While all mental health professionals experience similar events from time to time, the increased volume for gay and lesbian practitioners can be fatiguing and stressful. The lack of privacy, in particular, can be trying. For example, after a long day with clients, it can be difficult to relax in an evening social situation when clients are present, and espeically if one or more clients attempts to interact with the therapist as a therapist in that situation.

Gay and lesbian therapists will need to think through especially carefully a number of professional and ethical issues. It may take extra vigilance to maintain client confidentiality in a small-town atmosphere. As Anthony has discussed in her paper in this volume, transference and countertransference issues can become clouded. Using colleagues for regular consultation on such issues is a practical necessity, and small mutual consultation/support groups for gay and lesbian therapists are highly recommended—provided, of course, this can be done without confidentiality or dual relationship entanglements.

Being an actively sexual person in the gay and lesbian communities, particularly if one is single, can produce professional tensions, and may also mobilize any internalized homophobia within the therapist (see Malyon's chapter in this volume for a discussion of this). Clients may have a variety of unrealistic and distorted expectations of their therapists, such as: "My therapist is together about being gay/lesbian, and therefore wouldn't need to go to a bar (a certain organization, the baths, etc.)." Or, "My therapist shouldn't have a lover who is so old (young, attractive, unattractive, swishy, butch, political, apolitical, etc.)." Some gay or lesbian clients will project to a greater extent on gay or lesbian therapists, and, in particular, may act out their internalized homophobia or erotophobia in this manner. Should this elicit residual internalized homophobia or erotophobia in the therapist, the situation can become distorted and highly stressful to the therapist.

Gay and lesbian therapists need to have a clear sense of their own ethics about areas that are not covered by professional ethics codes; for example, in the area of social, business, and sexual relationships with ex-clients. Complete prohibition of these relationships is one way to respond to these situations. Another alternative is to have an extended time period (e.g., one year) after termination during which these other relationships are off-bounds. After that time period, the therapist may engage in such relationships only after consultation with other professionals (with more extensive consultation for possible sexual involvement) and if such consultation determines that transference or countertransference issues are not present, and that the ex-client is in no danger of exploitation. The key to reasonable handling of these situations is for the therapist to have a clear sense of his or her values, obtain outside consultation, and proceed with integrity and caution. These complicated grey areas of ethics are difficult for all therapists, and no therapist should tackle them alone.

Another problem exists when closeted or semi-closeted therapists work with gay or lesbian clients. Their internalized homophobia is usually more considerable than openly gay or lesbian therapists. This may feed into the internalized homophobia of their gay and lesbian clients, and create serious distortions in the therapy. It should not be overlooked, however, that openly gay or lesbian therapists can have serious problems with their own sexuality.

One example of this which this writer has encountered a number of times is the closeted or semi-closeted therapist who is out only to a few colleagues, or who has little or no social support in the gay/lesbian communities. The colleagues to whom the closeted therapist has disclosed send that therapist referrals of gay or lesbian clients, either because the colleagues are well-intentioned and believe this to be appropriate or because the therapist has suggested it. The therapist then acts out in any number of ways his or her own coming out issues with the gay or lesbian clients. The therapist may also use these clients for his or her social support system, because building a gay/lesbian support system in the community is too threatening. This constitutes emotional and financial exploitation of clients, and there is also increased likelihood that such a therapist may exploit gay or lesbian clients sexually. This problem also exists among physicians and other health care providers as well. All therapists have a professional responsibility to avoid any exploitation of clients, and not to accept cases with whom their own personal issues would jeopardize their effectiveness as a therapist.

Openly gay and lesbian therapists working in more traditional, non-gay/ lesbian mental health settings may experience the problem areas mentioned above, but often also have a set of unique stresses. Few agencies will be uniformly accepting of openly gay or lesbian staff members. This may result in certain staff consciously or unconsciously undermining gay/lesbian staff. The latter situation can be the more difficult to respond to, as liberal colleagues who are unaware of their homophobia or unwilling to face it may be, on another level, overt supporters of gay and lesbian staff members. Thus the gay/lesbian staff member's attempts to give feedback to such persons may be hazardous politically. Overtly anti-gay/lesbian staff may raise issues about the credibility and professionalism of gay/lesbian staff. This may take many guises, from informing conservative clergy in the area that the clinic has hired a "pervert," to attributing lack of success with certain clients to the therapist's homosexuality, to undermining programmatic efforts within the gay and lesbian communities, and so on. Especially if such opposition is sophisticated, responding directly may result in the gay or lesbian staff member being termed "hyper-sensitive," "paranoid," etc. While these phenomena are experienced by many professionals with various minority statuses, there is probably no other minority status in which individuals in opposition to the minority status feel as free to question the competence, psychological adjustment, judgment and stability of the professional in question, as with gay and lesbian staff. Further, with prob-ably no other minority status is such questioning tolerated by the mental health community.

All this may be perceived to varying degrees by gay and lesbian clients coming to such an agency, and may contribute to their sense of disenfranchise-ment, as well as contribute further to whatever problems brought them to a mental health agency.

One of the most common effects of these events on gay/lesbian professionals is the development of chronic overachievement. The response of many minority professionals is continually to strive to supercede non-minority staff. This may elicit competition and jealousy from non-minority staff, but more importantly, it may create burn-out in the gay or lesbian staff member. This may create a situation in which questions about a gay or lesbian staff member's judgment or competence become self-fulfilling. In particular, gay/lesbian staff may feel con-strained about discussing countertransference issues with other staff, particu-larly if these involve gay or lesbian clients. This may result in gay/lesbian staff acting out countertransference issues.

The gay/lesbian professionals who do survive and prosper in more traditional agencies have typically mastered a number of skills. First and foremost is re-sistance to the cycle of overachievement and burn-out by setting limits on the amount of time spent on professional activities. Second is learning to choose which battles to fight. Those who are goaded into fighting every battle around gay/lesbian issues will soon collapse exhausted, resentful, and defeated. Those who learn to discriminate crucial issues from trivial and those battles that can be won from those that are hopeless, and who develop a sense of timing will usually survive and effect important changes in their agencies.

This description of problem areas alone may sound pessimistic. In some places, openly gay and lesbian mental health professionals have been received in traditional agencies with genuine open-mindedness, and areas of conflict that have arisen have been settled in a productive manner. However, as detailed in *The Final Report of the Board of Social and Ethical Responsibility for Psy-chology's Task Force on the Status of Lesbian and Gay Male Psychologists* (1979), many gay and lesbian psychologists perceive or have experienced stigma from the mental health community as a result of their homosexuality.

A last problem area is frankly exploitative therapists. Sociopathic therapists of any sexual orientation may offer services to gay/lesbian clients because there is money to be made off of gay and lesbian clients who are seeking gay/

lesbian affirmative services. These therapists may have a sympathetic "affirming" pitch, but no real skill or competence in working with gay and lesbian clients. This is an issue both for therapists, who must hold each other accountable to practice only within areas of demonstrated competency; and for consumers, who should question potential providers carefully about training, credentials, how competencies were developed, etc. But ultimately, gay and lesbian mental health professionals must police their own field. As with all mental health services, if mental health professionals do not police themselves, someone else will.

One final word about gay and lesbian graduate students in professional training programs. These individuals may be under considerable stress for a number of reasons. Chronologically, they may be at an age very close to coming out issues, or be just coming out. If they moved to a new location to go to graduate school, they may have no gay or lesbian social support system in their new community, and little time to develop one, given the demands of graduate training. Within the training program, they may be harassed and undermined directly by homophobic faculty, training staff or other students; or indirectly, by homophobic course content and training experiences. These stresses will probably be greater for graduate students who are not in a committed relationship, as they will not have as easily available the support and reality-testing a relationship can offer. None of these stresses are amenable to easy solutions. Developing supportive systems with each other and with gay and lesbian mental health professionals in the field may be a very crucial survival task for gay and lesbian graduate students.

Rewards in Gay/Lesbian Mental Health

This paper has so far focused on problem areas in the provision of gay/lesbian mental health services, in the hope of preventing some problems, and suggesting solutions to others. It would be overly pessimistic to end without some discussion of the positive aspects and rewards of working in this area. One of the greatest rewards is in building a needed and valuable service delivery system from nothing. Fifteen years ago, gay/lesbian affirmative mental health services did not exist. Now, numerous organizations, at different stages of development, exist all over the country.

Therapists working in such organizations have opportunities to do a variety of tasks, not available to colleagues in traditional agencies: administration, program development; fundraising; grant-writing; community development; advocacy; training and others. Given the rapid transitions of these agencies, and their broader mission to serve a neglected community, individuals who work in gay/lesbian mental health agencies often develop a sophisticated understanding of how mental health systems work, and often emerge as the Renaissance men and women of mental health.

The struggle to develop gay and lesbian affirmative models of clinical practice, and to integrate them with the useful aspects of traditional mental health practice produces the kind of intense intellectual ferment which many professionals expected—and never encountered—in graduate training. This intellectual ferment and the shared sense of mission often produce powerful and rewarding professional relationships with other colleagues. There is often a shared sense of being on the cutting edge of mental health practice, and of actively creating "new knowledge." If the agency is in a position to train graduate students, there can be enormous satisfaction in shaping a new generation of mental health practitioners and influencing their training program.

Conflict resolution skills and tolerance for ambiguity tend to become well-developed in those who remain affiliated with gay/lesbian mental health programs for any length of time. The changing nature of the organizations tend also to develop role flexibility and leadership skills.

REFERENCES

Removing the stigma: final report of the Board of Social and Ethical Responsibility for Psychology's task force on the status of lesbian and gay male psychologists, 1979. Monograph available from the American Psychological Association, 1200 Seventeenth Street, N.W., Washington, DC 20036.

White, W. L. *Incest in the organizational family: The unspoken issue in staff and program burnout.* Monograph available from HCS, Inc., 1370 Piccard Dr., Rockville, MD 20850.

INDEX